# GUIDE TO *Kansas* ARCHITECTURE

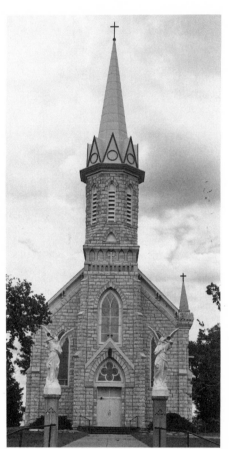

# GUIDE TO *Kansas* ARCHITECTURE

## DAVID H. SACHS & GEORGE EHRLICH

UNIVERSITY PRESS OF KANSAS

© 1996 by the University Press of Kansas

Published by the University Press of Kansas
(Lawrence, Kansas 66049), which was organized
by the Kansas Board of Regents and is operated
and funded by Emporia State University, Fort
Hays State University, Kansas State University,
Pittsburg State University, the University of
Kansas, and Wichita State University

Library of Congress
Cataloging-in-Publication Data
Sachs, David H.
Guide to Kansas architecture /
David H. Sachs & George Ehrlich.
p.   cm.
ISBN 0–7006–0777–3 (cloth : alk. paper). —
ISBN 0–7006–0778–1 (paperback : alk. paper)
1. Architecture—Kansas—Guidebooks.
I. Ehrlich, George, 1925–   .   II. Title.
NA730.K2S23   1996
720'.9781—DC20                            95–49204

2? 2112

British Library Cataloguing in Publication Data
is available.

8—22—96

Printed in Canada

10   9   8   7   6   5   4   3   2   1

The paper used in this publication meets the
minimum requirements of the American
National Standard for Permanence of Paper for
Printed Library Materials z39.48–1984.

# CONTENTS

# Preface

Preparing a guidebook to a state's architecture can be a rather daunting challenge, especially when no previous effort is available to provide a convenient foundation on which to build. We did, of course, have access to a number of sources from which to construct an initial list of possible candidates, such as the Kansas section of the National Register of Historic Places and the Kansas State Register as well as a number of publications specifically focused on localized architecture—and on architects—of the state. From there we moved to other published sources containing potentially useful data. The character of a publication and the rigor used in its preparation influenced our treatment of the information, but all the sources consulted proved helpful in setting the parameters for the field of candidates from which we would draw our final selections. Published materials, however, tended to focus on older buildings or on the earlier periods in a community's history, and we needed to supplement them with other sources in which we could find a good sampling of recent examples of architecture. We perused the lists of awards made by the Kansas and the Kansas City chapters of the American Institute of Architects and also solicited suggestions from a number of architects who could alert us to work located in their cities or regions. Moreover, preservationists and people knowledgeable about state and local history produced some valuable information and suggestions.

The compilation of such data continued fairly steadily throughout the project; yet knowing that we needed to step beyond judgments made by other people or agencies, David Sachs did a systematic field survey through a number of excursions in which he visited the state's 105 counties, some several times, to examine and photograph as many of the listed structures as possible and to record data and his direct observations, which included notes on localized characteristics and regional variations. He also kept himself open to the phenomenon, familiar to all students of architecture, that some buildings or structures make themselves known on their own. The reasons are various and at times might be due more to context or setting than to the architectural or aesthetic quality of the structure itself; nevertheless, such buildings merit evaluation, and a surprising number of these self-nominated structures were added to the list of candidates from which the final selections would be drawn for inclusion in the *Guide*.

While Sachs was assembling lists, doing the field study, and making the initial drafts of the catalog sections, George Ehrlich concentrated on surveying publications likely to have relevance for the preparation of the narrative texts, writing preliminary drafts, and preparing a basic set of maps. A structural outline for the manuscript of the book was developed. We met regularly to exchange materials and discuss our progress, and projects that started out as essentially independent began to meld. As we went through a series of revisions of the manuscript, earlier distinctions of authorship began to fade, and the final draft represents a true joint effort. Along the way, our procedures fused and our criteria for the selection of the entries were refined, as well as the scope of the information to be included in the *Guide*.

We deliberately used a rather broad definition of architecture, namely that it is the humanizing modifications people make to the natural environment. The definition permitted us to include not only obviously important structures designed by trained architects, such as the capitol in Topeka, but also a goodly number of other buildings with sufficient distinction to make them worthy of our attention. It also includes vernacular buildings, some being truly modest structures. Their value lies in their capacity to show the needs, means, and taste of the people who built and used them. Our definition also allowed us to include or refer to such features of the built environment as bridges, dams, power stations, cemeteries, and other designed landscape forms. Thus, since the guidebook had to be both manageable in size and reasonable in cost while also providing a fairly complete and representative overview of a rich and diverse built environment, we had to make some difficult decisions concerning choices, especially in the matter of exclusions.

We made the decisions by using three constellations of criteria: architectural, historical, and cultural; a work had to show significance within at least one of these categories.

> The architectural incorporates all aspects that relate directly to a structure and its physical setting as well as to those people responsible for its design and fabrication. Thus, the use of materials, construction methods, and the quality of craftsmanship are considered, as are a building's stylistic character and its relationship to the site. The quality of the design and the importance of the architect are factors, as is the effectiveness with which a structure serves its purpose or whether it is a truly special or an unusually good example of a general type.
>
> The historical relates to a building's association with special or notable individuals, groups, or events at any time in its history and focuses on how this connection elevates interest in the property, making it noteworthy.
>
> The cultural signifies the ways in which the building or site contributes to a community's special sense of itself, whether past, present, or continuing. Re-

lated to this capacity might be its physical location as well as the degree to which the property has come to symbolize the goals, accomplishments, or both of special groups of people, whether or not they are members of the community in question.

The commentary and criteria indicate what we have tried to do in the preparation of the *Guide,* but we must also stress what this book is not intended to be or do. It is not a list of the "best buildings" in the state, though many very fine structures are included. Nor are the buildings listed necessarily more worthy of preservation than those that are not listed. More to the point, we know that many interesting and important buildings in some locations had to be passed over to make way for entries from other locales that some people might feel are less worthy. Yet one of our goals has been to provide a reasonably balanced and representative coverage for all of Kansas, and thus proper attention must be paid to the less built-up sections of the state, even if at the expense of areas with a much larger stock of candidates.

At the other extreme, in the case of types in vernacular architecture, often only a few or perhaps just one work must serve to represent many similar and certainly equally deserving examples. Other types of architecture are repeatedly represented, however, such as county courthouses, corner bank buildings, and Carnegie libraries, but here one can also illustrate the influence of an architect or the role of changing taste in design. Thus repetition not only indicates the extent of a type's distribution in the state but also how certain building types carry special importance for a community's sense of itself. Finally, preference was given to buildings that could be easily viewed, to those along well-traveled routes or that could be viewed at close range, and (if possible) to those whose interiors are open to the public. We also favored examples that are in a better state of repair.

Despite our best efforts, we know that too many true architectural treasures in the state escaped our notice. We trust that the remedy for that deficiency will come from others who will be stimulated by *Guide to Kansas Architecture* to build upon our efforts and continue the project of making known the built environment of Kansas. The task of encouraging a public to appreciate all aspects of architecture is a shared one, for buildings are not only integral to our daily lives, they are equally important as documents in the history of Kansas and of the nation itself.

# Acknowledgments

In the process of conducting our research we gained not only an appreciation for the architecture of Kansas but also for its people. Our requests for information or access were invariably met with enthusiastic cooperation and genuine kindness. The guidebook is thus a cooperative venture, not only between the coauthors but also with the scholars who came before us and with the many people who assisted us in our work. We can acknowledge only a small fraction of the people who supplied information. To those of you across the state who are not named but who responded generously to the questions of a curious caller, again we thank you for your help. The *Guide* is richer because of your contribution.

We offer our appreciation to the following people who have made significant contributions to our work, especially Eugene Kremer, who helped put us in contact with architects from different parts of the state. The architects who took time to help us find noteworthy buildings in their area included Joe Terrill and the late Jack Bradley in Topeka; Donnie Mars in Emporia; David Irwin in Fort Scott; Jack Jones, Bob Shaefer, Cheryl McAfee, and Scott Enns in Wichita; and Vince Mancini and the late Howard Blanchard in Garden City. Individuals who helped us gain access to key information included Martha Hagedorn Krass of the Kansas State Historical Society, Trudy Aaron of the Kansas Chapter of the American Institute of Architects, and Jerry Ramsey of Southwestern Bell. John Gutowski helped us gain access to a darkroom at the University of Missouri–Kansas City. Scholars, through their research in various areas of the state, were also very helpful, notably Pamela Kingsbury in Wichita and Gene DeGruson in Pittsburg. Mick Charney helped write the initial project proposal. Readers of that proposal, David Gebhard, Sally Woodbridge, Mark Treib, and Richard Longstreth, provided valuable comments and suggestions. The readers selected by the University Press of Kansas to review our submitted manuscript also provided valuable comments, for which we are grateful; their thoughtful suggestions and corrections proved most helpful in the process of making a final revision. Special thanks go to our editor, Fred Woodward, for his patience, his counsel, and his encouragement when it proved most useful. We also appreciate the assistance provided by the production editor, Melinda Wirkus, the copy editor, Claire Sutton, and the designer, Rich Hendel. We are appreciative also for the support of the Kansas State University Foundation, which provided several small grants to support the field survey and photography.

# Guide for Users of this Volume

The *Guide to Kansas Architecture* is divided into seven regions: Metropolitan Kansas City, Northeast, Southeast, Northcentral, Southcentral and Wichita, Northwest, and Southwest. Within each region, architectural works are grouped first according to county and then within the county by city (or proximity thereto).

Each regional section begins with an essay describing the characteristics and demographic factors that have strongly influenced the development of the region and its major cities. A map of the region and a directory follow, which together serve as a guide to the identification and location of the counties and cities specifically mentioned in the catalog of entries. The catalog itself is organized by counties in alphabetical order, and within each county the cities are also ordered alphabetically.

Each catalog entry is identified by a unique alpha-numeric designation, such as **SN 26.12.** This particular binomial (from the Northeast Region) indicates that the building is in Shawnee County (**SN**) and that the city is Topeka (**26**). All coding elements for a region are defined in the region's directory. The numeric extension (**.12**) indicates that this is the twelfth entry in the sequence for Topeka (the structure is Memorial Building, at the southeast corner of the capitol grounds). When there is a map for a particular city, the relevant extension numbers are used to indicate the locations of those buildings. Cities that serve as county seats are indicated in the list with a dagger (†).

The use of catalog numbers ensures not only organizational consistency but provides an easy way to cross-reference catalog entries and illustrations. Another coding element, an asterisk (*) at the end of a building's name in a number of entries, indicates that the structure has been placed on the National Register of Historic Places; a diamond (♦) indicates the Kansas State Register.

In the identification portion of a catalog entry, information about the structure's date(s), architect(s), and address or location—when known—is given in that order. In the commentary portion of an entry, designations of architectural style are capitalized: e.g., Modern or Gothic Revival. When such terms are used as adjectives, they are lowercased: e.g., modern methods, gothic arches.

The maps found in the *Guide* have been prepared by Jackie Johnson under the direction of the authors. The illustrations, unless otherwise indicated, are from photographs taken and prepared by David H. Sachs, during the period 1990–1994.

Population figures cited in the *Guide* are typically rounded off and based on the 1990 census, unless otherwise indicated.

Finally, users of *Guide to Kansas Architecture* are strongly advised to obtain a recent road map of Kansas, such as the official State Transportation Map, to use in conjunction with the maps provided in the book. Likewise, detailed maps of Wichita and of the greater Kansas City area will be useful, especially in the case of the latter to aid in navigating the Metropolitan Kansas City Region.

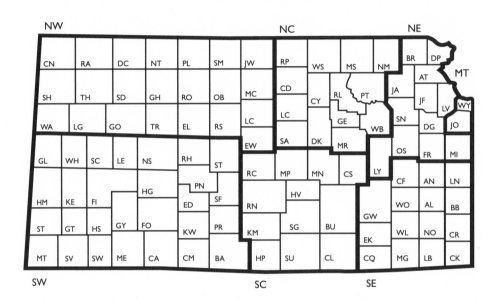

KEY TO COUNTY ABBREVIATIONS AND THEIR REGIONAL LOCATIONS

AL Allen (SE)
AN Anderson (SE)
AT Atchison (NE)
BA Barber (SW)
BT Barton (SW)
BB Bourbon (SE)
BR Brown (NE)
BU Butler (SC)
CS Chase (SC)
CQ Chautauqua (SE)
CK Cherokee (SE)
CN Cheyenne (NW)
CA Clark (SW)
CY Clay (NC)
CD Cloud (NC)
CF Coffey (SE)

CM Comanche (SW)
CL Cowley (SC)
CR Crawford (SE)
DC Decatur (NW)
DK Dickinson (NC)
DP Doniphan (NE)
DG Douglas (NE)
ED Edwards (SW)
EK Elk (SE)
EL Ellis (NW)
EW Ellsworth (NW)
FI Finney (SW)
FO Ford (SW)
FR Franklin (NE)
GE Geary (NC)
GO Gove (NW)

GH Graham (NW)
GT Grant (SW)
GY Gray (SW)
GL Greeley (SW)
GW Greenwood (SE)
HM Hamilton (SW)
HP Harper (SC)
HV Harvey (SC)
HS Haskell (SW)
HG Hodgeman (SW)
JA Jackson (NE)
JF Jefferson (NE)
JW Jewell (NW)
JO Johnson (MT)
KE Kearny (SW)
KM Kingman (SC)

KW Kiowa (SW)
LB Labette (SE)
LE Lane (SW)
LV Leavenworth (NE)
LC Lincoln (NW)
LN Linn (SE)
LG Logan (NW)
LY Lyon (NE)
MN Marion (SC)
MS Marshall (NC)
MP McPherson (SC)
ME Meade (SW)
MI Miami (NE)
MC Mitchell (NW)
MG Montgomery (SE)
MR Morris (NC)
MT Morton (SW)
NM Nemaha (NC)
NO Neosho (SE)

NS Ness (SW)
NT Norton (NW)
OS Osage (NE)
OB Osborne (NW)
OT Ottawa (NC)
PN Pawnee (SW)
PL Phillips (NW)
PT Pottawatomie (NC)
PR Pratt (SW)
RA Rawlins (NW)
RN Reno (SC)
RP Republic (NC)
RC Rice (SC)
RL Riley (NC)
RO Rooks (NW)
RH Rush (SW)
RS Russell (NW)
SA Saline (NC)
SC Scott (SW)

SG Sedgwick (SC)
SW Seward (SW)
SN Shawnee (NE)
SD Sheridan (NW)
SH Sherman (NW)
SM Smith (NW)
SF Stafford (SW)
ST Stanton (SW)
SV Stevens (SW)
SU Sumner (SC)
TH Thomas (NW)
TR Trego (NW)
WB Wabaunsee (NC)
WA Wallace (NW)
WS Washington (NC)
WH Wichita (SW)
WL Wilson (SE)
WO Woodson (SE)
WY Wyandotte (MT)

# GUIDE TO *Kansas* ARCHITECTURE

# Introduction

Kansas is centrally located in the United States, appearing on a map as a rectangular area of some 400-by-200 miles, except for the irregularly clipped-off northeast corner where the Missouri River constitutes the state line. Its east-west dimension the longer one, Kansas reaches from a moderately low-lying, well-watered area of hills and prairie in the east to the semiarid High Plains in the west. Furthermore, the overall terrain of Kansas, which occupies some 82,000 square miles, is far more diverse than commonly assumed. The impression that Kansas is a flat and feature-less place is true only for some portions of the High Plains, which are but one aspect of the various landscapes to be found in the state. Not only is there considerable hill country, but in general the elevations get lower as one heads east and from north to south. The highest point is Mount Sunflower at 4,039 feet, in Wallace County at the western edge of the state. The lowest point, at 680 feet, is within the southeastern corner of the state, in the Verdigris River near Coffeyville, in Montgomery County.

The climate of Kansas varies greatly, not only seasonally and from region to region but also quite rapidly. In common with other states in the nation's heartland, Kansas can be extremely hot in the summer and bitterly cold in the winter, but not always. It is also a very windy place, with the highest velocities in the western third of the state. Kansas is also subject to tornadoes, especially in late spring and early summer. Rainfall can vary considerably from year to year, but on average the annual totals will range from less than twenty inches in the far west to over thirty-five inches in the far east.

Kansas is drained by two major river systems, that of the Kansas River in the northern half of the state, which moves eastward to join the Missouri River at Kansas City, and the Arkansas River. The latter, after entering from Colorado, moves in a great loop across the southwestern quadrant of the state to the Okla-homa border, continuing southeastward until it reaches the Mississippi River. On a number of the lesser rivers in the state, dams have been constructed to create sizable flood-control reservoirs and lakes, which also serve recreational purposes; most are located in the eastern half of the state. The influence of these diverse surface-water features on development has been quite significant. For example, the major rivers and other dependable streams helped determine the paths taken by the early trails that crossed the state. Rivers also influenced the locations chosen for many of the

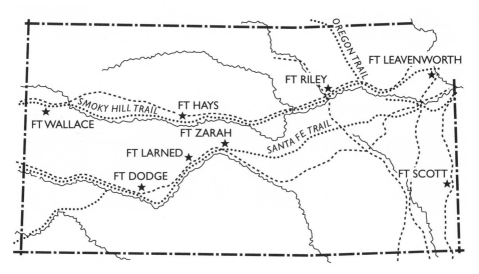

*Early settlement features*

oldest settlements as well as where early railroad lines were laid. And, of course, these streams along with the winds helped shape the landforms of Kansas.

A physiographic map of Kansas reveals considerable variety in the landforms. In the far northeast is a glaciated region of rounded hills and broad valleys; to their south are found the Osage Cuestas, a hill-plain area with plentiful limestone. Immediately to the west are the scenic Flint Hills, stretching south to north across the state. The undulating elevations in this well-watered, bluestem pastureland contain the flint rock or chert that influenced the naming of the region. The Blue Hills and Smoky Hills Uplands are in the north-central section of the state; the south-central portion consists largely of the Great Bend Prairie, a region of irregular hills, sand dunes, and gravel deposits created by the Arkansas River. Near the southern state line are the Red Hills, with buttes, mesas, and areas of rugged hills. The western portion of the state consists of the High Plains.

The availability of water, the climatic conditions, and the local building materials helped influence the size and placement of communities during the early settlement of Kansas as well as the character of the buildings, factors that can still affect development. A number of sectors in Kansas contain good building stone that early on was put to use, such as the Greenhorn limestone formation in the north-central portion of the state. As for locally grown lumber, large stands of oak and hickory trees could be found in the eastern quarter of Kansas, but elsewhere in the state only the flood plains of the rivers nurtured the growth of native trees, mostly cottonwood. This pattern began to change once the settlers started to arrive in Kansas, for they brought traditions and values that led them to introduce additional

*Sod houses on J. B. Porter's ranch, Morton County, 1890s (Kansas State Historical Society)*

varieties of trees, some for their fruit but others for their shade and to act as windbreaks; they also served as leafy mementos of places left behind. Although the variety of trees increased in the state, the amount of area covered did not since much of the original forests in the eastern part of the state were significantly reduced to make way for farmland and settlement, and the western half of the state has remained largely grasslands.

Local stone was used not only for building foundations but also for trim elements on brick buildings as well as for entire structures of diverse sorts. Native oak and hickory timber was used primarily for framing, but most of the finish-lumber consisted of white and yellow pine, which had to be imported. In regions lacking easily quarried stone, or where timber was scarce, sod—topsoil held together by the roots of the local buffalo grass—was used to construct shelters.

The eastern counties with their comparatively abundant water and ready access to building materials understandably attracted early settlement, and they still hold a significant percentage of the state's population, which in 1990 reached 2,477,574. Four of the state's 105 counties collectively contain more than one million of those residents: Johnson, Wyandotte (contiguous and adjacent to the eastern state line), Shawnee, and Sedgwick. Although Kansas is correctly still known as a major farming state, it has also become home to a variety of industries, including manufacturing, mining, oil and gas production, transportation (especially aircraft), and utilities. Today, two-thirds of the state's residents live in cities and towns, of which only a few have populations exceeding 25,000. The largest city in the state is Wichita (Sedgwick County), with a population of 304,000.

The earliest towns established in the state nestled close to rivers and streams. The railroad network that developed between 1865 and 1918 also favored river valleys, and that pairing further encouraged settlements along the rights-of-way. Intersect-

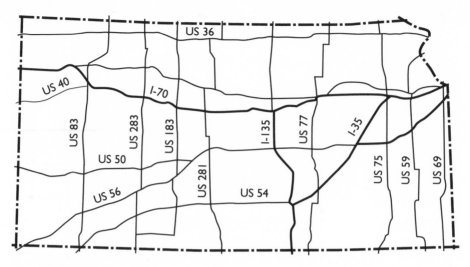

*Principal highways*

ing railroad lines at a town stimulated commerce and encouraged its population growth well into the twentieth century. The network of rail lines, however, is now much reduced in its mileage, and since the 1960s the placement of interstate highways has assumed much of the railroads' earlier role of influencing the rise (or decline) of population centers. An estimated two-thirds of today's population in Kansas live adjacent to the broad corridor containing the Kansas Turnpike, which links Kansas City, Lawrence, Topeka, Emporia, and Wichita. The state is also served by a number of other limited-access highways, of which the longest are Interstate 70 and Interstate 35. Each incorporates a section of the Kansas Turnpike.

The earliest settlers in Kansas were the Native Americans, who arrived long before Europeans began to explore the region. Of those people who lived in villages in the eastern portion of the state, only traces of their structures remain and some descriptions and a few drawings of buildings as they existed in the early nineteenth century. A more durable built environment began with the establishment of Fort Leavenworth in 1827 but more particularly after territorial status was achieved in 1854 and European-Americans began rapidly to settle and build in the easternmost part of the state. Their settlement patterns and the architecture they constructed provide the starting point for the story that became a continuous developmental history in architecture reaching to the present, a history strongly shaped by the inevitable ups and downs of the economy. Yet the economy alone is not sufficient to explain what is built, the use made of it, and how long a structure will stand. Such decisions are made by people who also function within a social and cultural context, which can change not only from place to place but also over time. Therefore, what we call the built environment is more than utilitarian shelter and infrastructure; it also mirrors the status and circumstances of people at a particular place and time, thus informing us about the past even as it serves us in the present. Consequently, the inevitable losses of older architecture act to dim our collective memory of that past, and among those losses are the villages the Native Americans built in Kansas.

Many Indian villages were still in place in the eastern part of the state when Lewis and Clark undertook their expedition up the Missouri River and thence on to the northwest coast in 1804–1806. This first American effort at scientific exploration (with strong political and commercial overtones) grew out of the nation's acquisition of an enormous tract of land reaching from the Rocky Mountains to the Mississippi River, the Louisiana Purchase. A portion became Kansas. Thus it makes sense to start our developmental clock of the state's architectural history with 1804 and to bring the first period in this history to an end when territorial status was achieved in 1854. Subsequent periods are defined by other factors that influenced development in the state, such that the overall history of architecture in Kansas falls into five periods: 1804–1854, 1854–1865, 1865–1890, 1890–1950, and after 1950.

## 1804–1854

The preterritorial period, which included explorations of the new lands acquired by the United States, proved to be a time in which the Native American population experienced major social disruptions. Indian tribes to the east of Kansas were forcibly relocated by the federal government to Kansas and soon thereafter to Oklahoma. Furthermore, two major overland trails were established, to the southwest and to the west, and white settlers began to arrive. Of the architecture produced during this period, very little survives.

Much of our knowledge of the Indians native to Kansas comes from descriptions recorded by early travelers and explorers and through archaeological evidence. Among the several autochthonous tribes of Native Americans who inhabited present-day Kansas, the Kansa and the Osage lived in permanent villages in the eastern portion of the state. They cultivated maize, beans, and squash and supplemented these basic food crops by hunting expeditions. Their housing consisted of fairly large, dome-shaped lodges on a circular plan, made of timber frame covered with earth. This form occurred among other "sedentary tribes" of Indians in the Missouri River valley, such as the Mandan people who once lived farther north along the river and who were documented by the Lewis and Clark Expedition and later depicted by the artist George Catlin in 1832.

The Pawnee had settled in north-central Kansas, but their primary villages were in Nebraska along the Platte River. Farther west, in the High Plains, the Cheyenne, the Arapaho, and the Comanche followed a more nomadic life dependent on the buffalo and so mostly used skin tipis for shelter. The great exception in the High Plains is documented by the ruins of a pueblo (in north-central Scott County), known as El Cuartelejo, that the Taos and Picuric Indians occupied from 1650 to 1720.

The first major incursion into the state by non-Indians, other than explorers and trappers, is connected to the establishment of a trail to Santa Fe. Used for commercial travel to Mexico after it won its independence from Spain, the Santa Fe Trail was inaugurated in 1821, the year that Missouri entered the Union. The trail initially began at the town of Franklin in central Missouri, but within a few years Independence and then Westport (both in Jackson County, Missouri) functioned as the eastern terminus. Westport, near the state line with Kansas, is now part of Kansas City, Missouri. From there, the trail moved southwesterly through Kansas, more or less along the general track of today's U.S. 56 highway. The trail passed through or near such present-day cities as Olathe, Council Grove, McPherson, Lyons, Great Bend, Dodge City, and Cimarron, where the trail then split. The north or mountain branch continued to parallel the Arkansas River into Colorado and thence down to Santa Fe, New Mexico. The south branch moved more directly toward Santa Fe and was known as the Cimarron Cutoff.

Concurrent with the development of traffic along the Santa Fe Trail, starting in the mid-1820s Kansas received nearly thirty Indian tribes, or portions thereof, who were forced to leave a number of states east of the Mississippi River as well as the recently admitted state of Missouri. They were placed on reservations created by reducing the holdings of the tribes native to Kansas. By the time this migration concluded in the mid-1840s new pressures had arisen, this time to remove all the tribes in Kansas to Oklahoma, an action that would ease the way to having Kansas designated as a territory, thus opening the land for white settlers.

The status of Kansas as a sequestered territory for Indian tribes already had been disturbed by the traffic along the Santa Fe Trail, which burgeoned from 1846 to 1848 during the war with Mexico. Moreover, a trail to Oregon had been charted between 1842 and 1844, along which a sizable migration of landseekers moved into the northwest and then into California after the discovery of gold there in 1849. The Oregon (and California) Trail moved northwesterly across Kansas, through or near present-day communities such as Olathe, Lawrence, Topeka, Westmoreland, Blue Rapids, and Hanover.

Traffic on the trails, coupled with the reaction of the Native Americans to increased repression, led to the establishment of army forts in Kansas, the first of which was Fort Leavenworth in 1827, on the Missouri River thirty miles north of the mouth of the Kansas River. Fort Scott was established in 1842, five miles west of the Missouri state line and ninety miles south of the Kansas River. Fort Riley was opened in 1853, on the Kansas River about 125 miles west of Kansas City. Forts Leavenworth and Riley have remained active army posts, but Fort Scott now exists as a restored historic site.

Inevitably, these early army forts attracted white settlers, and soon towns were established nearby: Leavenworth in 1854; Junction City (near Fort Riley) in 1858; and Fort Scott, incorporated in 1860. Farther west, the cities of Hays, Larned, and Dodge City memorialize the locations of forts from the 1860s. In all, nine substantial forts (and four less so) were built in Kansas, along with some military roads to serve them and other forts beyond its boundaries.

Another important influence on early settlement patterns and thus on architecture came from missions established to educate and convert the Native Americans. Serving both the native and emigrant tribes, thirty-two missions were established over a span of thirty-eight years beginning in 1824, the Methodists and Baptists being the most active. Nearly all the missions, some short-lived, were established before Kansas received territorial status in 1854. One-third of the missions were located within an area encompassed by Leavenworth, Wyandotte, Johnson, and Miami counties, a contiguous group along the eastern state line. When the adjacent counties of Franklin, Linn, and Douglas are added to the group, the percentage of missions rises to nearly three-fourths of the total. Most of this seven-county area lies within a sixty-mile radius of Kansas City, Missouri, the riverport that served as a transfer point to the trails. The city's name (initially the City of Kansas), had been selected years before Kansas became a territory, deriving from that of the Kansas River, which joins the Missouri River at a point very close to the original settlement.

## 1854–1865

Kansas as such came into existence during this period, first as a territory and then as a state. Concurrently, the Native American population suffered further forced displacement through land claims made by white settlers, and eventually nearly all the Indians in Kansas were moved south to Oklahoma. The treatment of the Native Americans, especially when directed at the nomadic tribes in the west, made inevitable a series of armed confrontations between the Indians and the settlers (the latter supported by army troops), with the conflict continuing into the early 1870s. Today, only three small reservations remain, in northeastern Kansas.

With the achievement of territorial status for Kansas, large numbers of people began to arrive, and although a great many chose to homestead on individual tracts of farmland, towns also were founded. In addition to those adjacent to army forts, other towns dating to the territorial period include Ottawa in Franklin County, based on a Baptist Mission of 1837; Wyandotte in Wyandotte County, which the Wyandot Indians established in 1843; Atchison in Atchison County, settled primarily by advocates of slavery in 1855; and Lawrence in Douglas County, a town created in 1854 by New Englanders, free-state advocates who then in 1857 also established Emporia, in Lyon County.

Much earlier, European settlers had become well established in Missouri during the eighteenth century, and with them had come the practice of slavery. This situation created a problem when Missouri petitioned for statehood in 1820, a move that threatened the equilibrium existing between the number of slave and free states in the Union. To maintain the political balance among the states, Congress enacted the Missouri Compromise, which in substance proposed the simultaneous admission of Missouri and Maine, the latter a free state to offset Missouri's proslavery position. The compromise also prohibited slavery north of latitude 36° 30′ within the lands of the Louisiana Purchase, except for Missouri. Since the southern boundary of Kansas was drawn along the 37th parallel, ostensibly that territory if admitted as a state would have to be free from slavery. The rule, however, did not suit supporters of slavery, especially those people in neighboring Missouri. Consequently, the issue of granting territorial status for Kansas and Nebraska became quite contentious.

Individuals seeking to expand the range of slavery to newly admitted states, to retain at least parity with the number of free states, argued that Kansas could be slave since Nebraska would be free, thereby continuing the equilibrium among the states. That arrangement, however, would require a repeal of the Missouri Compromise to erase the prohibition of slavery's extension into Kansas, an action taken by Congress concurrently with the creation of the Kansas Territory. Once open to settlement, Kansas attracted large numbers of people from both sides of the issue over the extension of slavery, setting the stage for a tense struggle between the two camps to achieve an indisputable majority in order to control the process of submitting a petition for statehood, a petition that would contain a draft constitution indicating whether Kansas would forbid or allow slavery. Missourians who supported slavery quickly and quite openly (and at times illegally) involved themselves directly in Kansas politics in an effort to influence the outcome. Opponents of slavery were equally energetic, especially the New England Emigrant Aid Company, which had been organized to send large numbers of people to Kansas.

The white population, estimated at no more than 1,500 in spring 1854—of which half were military at the several forts—increased to about 8,600 in 1855 and by 1860 had reached 107,000. As the number of settlers grew so did the potential for confrontations over the issue of controlling the territory, which at first the proslavery group held. By 1856 armed conflict in eastern Kansas began to punctuate the struggle, which also washed over into western Missouri. This bloody rehearsal for a Civil War still five years in the future gave rise to calling the territory Bleeding Kansas. Yet settlers continued to come to Kansas, and during its brief period of territorial status, thirty-four counties were organized. Moreover, the free-state advocates managed to achieve the solid majority they needed to control the framing and then the passage of a constitution affirming that Kansas would indeed be a free state. This political and moral victory, however, did not resolve their problems, for the settlers had to endure periods of drought, one lasting eighteen months during 1859 and 1860, which caused perhaps 30,000 settlers to leave the territory and severely damaged the economy of both Kansas and western Missouri.

The bill admitting Kansas as the thirty-fourth of the United States was signed by the president in January 1861. Several months later the nation—and Kansas—became involved in the Civil War. Missouri, with its citizens sharply divided in their loyalties, managed to remain in the Union. Numerous skirmishes and a number of substantial battles occurred in the southern half of Missouri during the course of the war, which understandably hindered development in both Missouri and Kansas. Though Kansas was strongly Unionist, comparatively little of the armed conflict that beset Missouri washed over the state line, but a damaging guerrilla raid led by William C. Quantrill was directed against Lawrence (Douglas County) in August 1863. A major portion of the town was burned and 150 male residents were killed. Later, in October 1864, a connected series of battles between thousands of regular troops began in Lafayette County, Missouri, then moved into Jackson County where a major engagement occurred south of Westport, and concluded in Linn County, Kansas, at Mine Creek, when the Confederate forces were finally expelled from the area.

With the war concluded in mid-1865, Kansans could again concentrate on the development of their state. Fostering railroad construction was a high priority, but the establishment of schools of higher education and starting work in Topeka on a suitable capitol building also merited special attention. As for the architecture that had been built between 1854 and 1865, enough has survived to provide evidence of the continued importance of the vernacular tradition, which stressed the pragmatic concerns and economical construction techniques favored by the carpenters or masons who designed as well as constructed most of the buildings. Although many such structures, quite plain within and without, are best appreciated as demonstrations of economical ways to enclose various utilitarian interior spaces, other examples do carry features and some embellishments that indicate an awareness of a more

*Massachusetts Avenue, Lawrence, 1867 (Kansas State Historical Society)*

refined architectural taste, probably derived from the illustrations found in the widely used pattern books of the period or directly from the more ambitious buildings beginning to appear in the state. Showing greater complexity of form and ornamental embellishment, the erection of such architecture suggests not only the presence in Kansas of clients interested in work of this type but also the existence of architects knowledgeable in architectural aesthetics. One such architect, John G. Haskell, arrived in Lawrence in 1857. The builder-tradition would continue as an important component in the design of buildings, but trained architects would become an increasingly prominent influence on the architecture produced in Kansas.

## 1865–1890

The population of Kansas, about 150,000 in 1865, grew to nearly 365,000 in 1870, an indication of the great attraction the state held for people, an appeal that would continue for the next two decades to produce a population of more than 1.4 million in 1890. With most of that number electing to become rural dwellers, they became fairly well spread out within the state, soon encroaching on areas that the Indians still in Kansas believed belonged to their people. Another encroachment came from the railroads pushing through the state, a form of improvement that not only assisted in the distribution of the settlers but also led to the organization of counties and the founding of small towns.

As the new homesteaders wrestled with the difficult chore of preparing their lands and making them productive, some of the towns in a number of the new counties engaged in a struggle to win the prize of being named the county seat. Holding that designation presumably would ensure a town's continued existence and perhaps lead to real growth, hence the heated rivalries and often rancorous disputations that managed to lead to some shifts in designation, often through questionable means. In the case of the eighteen counties organized during the 1860s, the "county seat wars" managed to generate hard feelings and corruption as a total of forty-one towns held the title of county seat, though rather briefly for most, before the matter finally was resolved.

Another conflict, but one far more serious and much more sanguine, began in the later 1860s and continued into the first years of the next decade. It involved the Native Americans and the settlers, the latter supported by the army. The nomadic Indian tribes in the central and western portions of the state had seen their traditional hunting grounds invaded by the railroads and the bison herds on which they depended severely reduced and eventually eliminated. In an attempt to preserve their way of life, the Indians struck back against the settlers and the army responded, resulting in a rather bloody war that lasted about ten years and affected a variety of locations in western Kansas. Brutal and cruel, the era of the Indian Wars later became a familiar dramatic element in novels with themes focused on the winning of the West or in films of a similar sort.

Another theme popularized by films and novels grew from the great cattle drives of the last third of the nineteenth century. The cattle were at first driven up from Texas on the Chisholm Trail, which had been extended to Dickinson County in 1867 to meet the Union Pacific Railroad as it progressed westward across the state. The initial railhead where the cattle could be loaded onto railroad cars for shipment to eastern markets spawned Abilene. That city's role as a raucous, western cowtown lasted only a few years, yet that image, now romanticized, managed to become so well known that it is more familiar to most non-Kansans than other cities of consequence that had been established farther west along the railroad, such as Salina, Russell, and Hays. Farther south, where the Chisholm Trail crossed the Arkansas River, a small settlement benefited also for a few years from the cattle drives up the trail. Named for the Wichita Indians who briefly lived in the area before their removal to Oklahoma, the settlement prospered largely through its diligent efforts to become a railroad hub. By the late 1880s Wichita had become one of the principal cities of Kansas.

The importance of having convenient access to railroad service had a strong influence on the shaping of settlement patterns in western Kansas as well as on the de-

*Northern Cheyenne encampment, 1871 (Kansas State Historical Society)*

velopment and growth of urban centers. In the northern half of the state, the Union Pacific reached the Colorado line by 1870; the Santa Fe reached it in the southern half two years later. Among the large numbers of immigrants to the state, a substantial portion came directly from Europe. They included various ethnic or religious groups such as Swedes and German-speaking Mennonites, who not only engaged in agriculture in central Kansas but who also founded towns and colleges. Towns provided an important service role, some serving as the administrative centers for the 105 counties of Kansas but all becoming convenient places where farmers and ranchers could acquire needed supplies and equipment as well as ship out to markets any surplus production they might have. Dimensioned pine lumber represented one category of supplies brought in by railroad, for it had an important role in the efficient and convenient construction of all sorts of buildings. With fairly simple hand tools, structures could be built quickly with nails and such lumber; even a degree of environmental civility could be introduced. Where houses and other buildings were made from locally available stone or from brick, millwork and dimensioned lumber were still necessary for most of them.

Most of the people who came into Kansas during the 1870s sought land of their own and better opportunities. The fairly generous rains during the decade encouraged many settlers to move into the western half of the state by 1880. Among the new arrivals were a large number of Americans escaping oppression: former slaves from the South. Though they were emancipated, their situation had grown

*Pioneer farmstead, later nineteenth century (Kansas State Historical Society)*

ever more precarious as their opportunities in the South were systematically narrowed. Feeling despair over their status, starting in the early 1870s a moderate and steady movement of black people began the difficult trek from Mississippi, Louisiana, Tennessee, Kentucky, and Texas, with the goal of reaching Kansas. There they expected to find not only greater tolerance but also ample lands they could homestead.

Their migration increased dramatically and rather suddenly after the 1878 election led to the termination of martial law in the former Confederate states. As apprehension accelerated among the former slaves, a naive but compelling belief spread rapidly among them that the federal government would provide free transportation to Kansas as well as land there, along with supplies and sustenance for a year. Caught up in what has been called the Kansas Fever Exodus, a surge of literally thousands of the African Americans began a mass movement in 1879 to reach Kansas if they could. Despite being poorly prepared by their history of servitude, their poverty, and the difficulties faced by all immigrants in becoming established and self-sustaining in a new place, a remarkable number of the people made it to Kansas and stayed there. The 1879 migration of the Exodusters added several thousand more to the approximately 25,000 black people who had preceded them to Kansas. African Americans represent only a small portion of the total immigration to Kansas during the later nineteenth century, but a group of them did manage to achieve the goal of homesteading, though more survived by becoming farmhands or by working in the towns and cities as laborers and domestics. Still, a few all-black communities were formed, of which Nicodemus, in Graham County, is best known.

Overall, the migration to Kansas during the 1870s and 1880s brought approximately one million new residents. Though most were rural dwellers, enough had elected city life to encourage the growth of many urban centers, of which a number attracted the attention of real estate speculators during the 1880s. An interesting indication of urban growth is seen in the proliferation of specially designed bank buildings that were located on prime corner lots in the heart of a city's commercial district. In the larger cities, such as Wichita, a considerable and diverse amount of new construction occurred, though a great deal of the speculation focused only on the buying and selling of land. With major buildings being produced by some quite capable architects, Wichita changed measurably in size and appearance during the boom. When the boom collapsed in 1888, the city's population began a rapid decline, but the new buildings remained as a resource to be used for a later renewal. Wichita—and the rest of Kansas—entered the 1890s with reduced energy for new development when compared to the rapid growth and physical development of the previous twenty-five years, but clearly much had been accomplished in a relatively brief period of time.

## 1890–1950

The decade of the 1890s proved difficult for Kansas. The economy had been hurt not only by the rather abrupt end of the real estate boom but also by the additional difficulties resulting from the national depression of 1893 and by the reduced rainfall during much of the decade. Yet Kansas managed to struggle through the problems. Farmers had learned which crops would grow in the newly settled, western half of the state, and thereafter winter wheat reigned as king. Experiments in irrigation helped counter the problems caused by rainfall shortages. The railroad network, though still rather sparse in the west, had evolved to the extent that much of Kansas had a reasonable degree of access to the service on which so many individuals were highly dependent to move people, products, and goods since Kansas lacked a decent road system.

In a number of cities, industrial activities were gaining importance, which over time would grow and help draw population to the cities. The steady increase in the urban component of the state's population after 1910 came at the expense of the rural population, which began a steady decline in absolute numbers. Improvements in the economy of the state were strongly affected by the growth of the urban sector, and the combination stimulated increases in the number and qualifications of the architects working in the state, who were exerting a growing influence on the character of the built environment, which now included large-scale planning. The planning aesthetic associated with the City Beautiful Movement, which flourished in the early years of the twentieth century, attracted the attention of many civic leaders who then supported the construction of new public buildings and the creation of parks and boulevards reflective of this aesthetic; examples can be found in the larger cities of Kansas, such as Topeka, Kansas City, and Wichita. The influence of the movement, when coupled with a surge in development during the 1920s, also produced in many of the smaller communities new civic buildings, such as courthouses and auditoriums.

The national interest in the physical improvement of cities had to compete, however, with the disruptions caused by two world wars and a numbing economic depression that lasted through most of the 1930s. Kansas also had to deal with a prolonged drought that included raging dust storms during 1934 and 1935. With difficulties of this scale, privately funded architectural development essentially halted through much of the 1930s. Despite the problems associated with the Great Depression and the dust storms, Kansas agriculture over the first half of the twentieth century benefited from increased mechanization, enabling fewer workers to manage larger farms. Kansas also grew industrially, assisted by Wichita's becoming an important center for an evolving aviation industry, starting before World War I. The discovery and exploitation of substantial oil and natural gas fields in Kansas contributed to industrial growth, further helping the economy of the state and the development of Wichita as well as some smaller urban centers such as Iola in Allen County and Hugoton in Stevens County.

Even with a larger and more diversified industrial base, the economy of Kansas remained grounded primarily on agriculture and related businesses. During the Great Depression, various federal programs were introduced to ameliorate some of its worst effects; rural electrification, for example, eased work and life in much of Kansas. Other programs concentrated on the construction of new federal buildings such as post offices in a great many cities, a program that provided jobs and increased sales of building materials. The federal government also helped to underwrite a wide range of public works, which left a legacy of some significantly better roads, new bridges, park improvements, and a variety of municipal buildings, many of which are still in service in Kansas.

The federal contribution to highway construction did not solve immediately the road problems in Kansas. Through much of its first century of statehood, Kansas had assigned the building of roads and their maintenance to the counties, who in turn tended to depend primarily on the farmers to carve out the dirt roads that enabled them to get their production to a railroad and to reach town to buy supplies and visit the post office. Many of these roads followed the section lines defined by the mile-square grid system of land division used in the survey of the state, but others were cut to suit individual convenience. With the passage of time, the roads were used to serve other purposes, which by 1900 included rural free delivery of the mail. The roads were also being used more frequently by bicycle riders and automobile drivers, the latter increasing in number despite the poor condition of the roads.

In the quest for better roads, an automobile association had been formed in Kansas by 1912 to exert pressure to improve the roads and their maintenance but had had little effect prior to the 1930s. In or near the larger cities, though, one could find the mileage of paved streets and roads growing. Yet railroad-based passenger and freight service continued to dominate intercity traffic and to have a pervasive influence on the economy of the state. At the end of the 1920s, however, Kansas as well as the federal government began slowly to work toward the creation of a highway system, but the effort concentrated on just a few major roads in Kansas. By 1937 the state finally had two entirely dust-free (but not fully paved) highways crossing the entire state, east to west: U.S. 24 and U.S. 40. Much of the remainder of the highway system consisted of gravel or dirt roads and would remain so until after the end of World War II.

Cities with a significant amount of industry, such as Kansas City and Wichita, required decent roads as well as good railroad service, needs that grew apparent once the nation became involved in the production of equipment, armaments, and the other requirements for the successful prosecution of World War II. The transport of this matériel and the movement of literally millions of people throughout the nation revealed the importance of having not only much improved rail service but also a modern highway system of national scope. A significant program of such improvements would have to wait until the war ended, but by the mid-1950s a major highway program for the nation had been announced. Even earlier, other programs were established to assist the returning veterans, not only in gaining specialized training or a college education but also in the purchase of homes. The latter program indirectly supported the construction of housing and encouraged the growth of suburban communities, such as Prairie Village in Johnson County. These changes would affect many parts of Kansas but chiefly the larger urban centers.

Wichita's population increased substantially during the war years, from 115,000 in 1940 to 192,000 in 1950, displacing Kansas City as the largest city in the state. By 1970 Wichita had a population of 255,000; the 1990 census indicated 304,000, more than double that of Kansas City, the next in size. Development of this scale resulted from various factors, such as the industrial base that grew substantially during World War II. Physical improvements made in and around the city also encouraged growth, for example, the bypasses constructed to move highway traffic away from a city's center, not only in Wichita but also in many smaller communities. Better intercity highways were still needed, but they demanded a level of funding beyond those normal for Kansas.

One solution to the money problem could be found in the example provided by the Pennsylvania Turnpike, a toll road completed in 1940. Funds for it had come from the issuance of revenue bonds to be retired by the tolls collected. Using this model, the Kansas legislature in 1953 created the Kansas Turnpike Authority, who in turn would issue the revenue bonds and then see to the construction of a toll road. Such roads have to be closely monitored in order to assess and collect fees, and thus entry and exit points were limited and controlled. If carefully engineered, a limited-access road with dual lanes would permit safe travel at much higher speeds than those permitted on traditional highways, features that would attract users despite the tolls if the route proved convenient for the drivers. Clearly the Kansas Turnpike met that test, for it connected the state's two largest cities, Kansas City and Wichita, via Lawrence, Topeka, and Emporia, before extending to the Oklahoma line (where it connects to a public freeway that reaches into Texas). Completed in just under two years, in late October 1956, the 240-mile Kansas Turnpike helped not only Wichita to grow but also the other cities it served. The turnpike made vividly apparent the advantages of truly modern highways in a state like Kansas. Though such roads are viewed principally as large-scale engineering projects, when carefully landscaped and fitted with well-designed features they also can be understood as a form of architecture, though one far more linear and certainly more gargantuan than is typical for the term.

Two additional major highways with limited access and dual lanes were constructed through Kansas as part of a federally funded program to create a national system of superhighways. The Kansas portion of Interstate 70, from Kansas City to the Colorado line, was fully completed in mid-1970. Much of Interstate 35, which went southwest from Kansas City to the Oklahoma border via Wichita, was built during the 1960s, with the final Kansas section completed in mid-1977. Both roads have incorporated portions of the Kansas Turnpike, with Interstate 70 leaving it at Topeka and Interstate 35 joining it at Emporia. These and other new or vastly improved highways encouraged more commuting as well as long-distance travel by automobile and a growing use by ever larger trucks for transporting goods and products. The expanding network of better engineered roads also exerted a strong influence on urban and suburban planning and on decisions governing where developers would introduce new subdivisions or industrial parks. By adding in the growing role of air travel and transport during the second half of the twentieth century as another influence on planning, we can appreciate why the character of cities and suburbs began to change, along with the architecture produced for them, architecture that also reflected the increased costs of construction and the introduction of new technologies and materials.

During this period of dramatic transportation changes, the population of Kansas continued to grow slowly but steadily. In 1950 Kansas had somewhat more than 1.9 million people; the 1990 census revealed an increase to 2.5 million. With the number of rural residents declining through those years, the increase in overall numbers meant more people were going to the cities and their suburbs. Yet only a few cities sustained truly sizable growth, such as Wichita and Topeka; most of the others that grew would not be considered especially populous when compared to medium-sized cities nationally. But the matter of a given city's population size assumes a different role when that city is part of a suburban cluster, as is the case in northeast Johnson County. As late as 1950 the county remained essentially rural in character except in the far northeast corner where a few towns existed, primarily as suburban satellites of Kansas City, Missouri. The towns were important contributors to the county's 1950 population of 63,000. Within the next forty years, Johnson County's population would explode, reaching 350,000 by 1990.

Johnson County grew rapidly for numerous reasons, but one important factor was the completion of Interstate 35 through the area and later additions of several other limited-access highways. These roads have facilitated access to and through the sixteen municipalities found in the northeast quadrant of the county. Though the municipalities have remained administratively independent, the opportunity for several to annex large tracts of land has made the group contiguous in their territories, creating a multipart, urban place. Collectively they have attracted not only newcomers to the region but also residents from the two Kansas Cities who found an ever-increasing number of jobs in Johnson County, even as the two core Kansas Cities suffered losses among traditional employers. The population in the core cities also began to drop after the mid-1960s because they had been forced to exert efforts to fully desegregate their schools, while the well-reputed and essentially suburban school districts in Johnson County did not need to face this rather intractable task, thus enhancing their attractiveness.

Of the several Johnson County municipalities that had been able to expand their areas through annexations, Overland Park not only grew substantially in physical size but also in population, reaching 112,000 in 1990. With this growth came the construction of additional apartment complexes, townhouses, and single-family dwellings, but more important has been Overland Park's ever-increasing number of commercial and office buildings intended for the mostly white-collar operations moving in, often at the expense of the core cities. Similar development, though not on the scale of Overland Park, extended into several other cities of the group. Of the sixteen municipalities, many had been established in the nineteenth century and remained separate and small for many years, such as Olathe and Shawnee. Others, such as Prairie Village and Overland Park, were created in the twentieth century as essentially bedroom suburbs for Kansas City, Missouri. The transformation of this mixed group of towns and cities into a formidable urban conglomerate occurred largely after 1970 and apparently is becoming more so. Also continuing is the nearly total dependence of the residents and workers on the automobile, not only to travel in and out of the complex but within it as well. This collective city is, in shape and appearance, clearly influenced by the pervasive role of the automobile in daily life.

Johnson County is now a powerful rival, in size and economy, to the two core cities, a situation that has affected the population mix and the economies of the two Kansas Cities. It also has exerted an ever-increasing influence on the economy and politics of Kansas. In brief, the history of change is represented by the developmental histories of the adjacent Kansas counties of Johnson and Wyandotte, where the former in recent years has been transformed into an economic powerhouse and the latter, for many years the largest city in the state with a formidable industrial base, has since the end of World War II faced a decline in jobs and population. Together they provide a dramatic contrast that illustrates how much Kansas has changed since 1950. Another mirror of those changes and of the many others throughout Kansas in the course of its history exists in the architecture found in the state.

## An Overview of the Architects and Stylistic Trends

The architecture of the state, while reflective of specific material, social, and economic forces, is also subject to aesthetic and intellectual forces; buildings reveal the tastes of their clients as well as the skills of their designers. The evolution of architecture in Kansas is representative of developments in architecture across the country. Kansas' early vernacular architecture, though tempered by the constraints of material availability, often employs forms tested by pragmatic builders in previously settled regions. The emergence of the more deliberately expressive building tradition in the state was dependent upon both imported materials and designers. The first recognized architectural training program in the state was established in 1903; before that time most architects practicing in Kansas had received their training elsewhere.

The earliest examples of high style architecture are concentrated, as would be expected, in the older communities along the eastern edge of the state. Houses from the 1860s and 1870s in Leavenworth and Lawrence follow nationally popular Victorian stylistic norms and in many cases may have been copied from well-circulated pattern books of the time. Authorship of these buildings is often difficult to trace, and relatively little is known about the state's earliest architects. John G. Haskell (1832–1907), one consequential early architect who has been the subject of substantial research, used his training from the Wesleyan Academy in Wilbraham, Massachusetts, and Brown University in Providence, Rhode Island, to make a significant impact on his adopted hometown of Lawrence. Haskell was influential in 1886 in organizing the Kansas Architects Association, the first professional association of architects in the state.

The prosperity of the 1880s resulted in a substantial building boom in Kansas and attracted a number of trained architects. Among them was Seymour Davis (1869–1923), who came to Topeka in 1883 after studying at the Philadelphia Academy of Fine Arts to join Haskell's office. James C. Holland (1853–1919), the influential designer of courthouses, settled in Topeka two years later after receiving training at Cornell University. Both men later served terms as state architect. George P. Washburn (1846–1922), who also designed a number of Kansas courthouses, established his influential practice in Ottawa in 1882 after interning in the office of the Kansas City, Missouri, architect Asa Beebe Cross. The highly original Charles W. Squires (1851–1934) began his practice in Emporia in 1881 after studying architecture in Columbus, Ohio. Although they remained in Kansas only from 1885 to 1891, William T. Proudfoot (1860–1928) and George W. Bird (1854–1953) made a significant impact on the development of Wichita architecture. Bird, the firm's designer, was trained in Philadelphia architectural offices as a member of the T-Square Club. After the end of the boom in Kansas the firm relocated to Utah and later to Iowa. The others continued their practices in Kansas into the twentieth century.

Although much of the architectural work in the state was done by Kansas residents, key commissions also went to architects from outside the state. The Kansas City, Missouri-based firm of Van Brunt and Howe was responsible for a number of buildings, including several stations for the Union Pacific Railroad. Cobb and Frost of Chicago designed several buildings in the state. H. C. Koch of Milwaukee and Charles Sedgewick of Minneapolis also contributed to Kansas' early architectural heritage.

The dominant style for public buildings of the 1880s and early 1890s in Kansas and throughout the country was Richardsonian Romanesque, a term indicating the broad influence of the Boston-based architectural practice of Henry Hobson Richardson. His interpretation of the Romanesque was popular in part because of its easy applicability to a range of new building types. In Kansas the style was often adapted to three key building types demanded by the rapidly expanding population: courthouses, railroad stations, and banks. Residential architecture of the time exhibited considerable variety. The Eclectic tradition allowed architects to base their designs on one of a number of popular styles, including Gothic Revival, Italianate, Eastlake, Queen Anne, and the Shingle Style, all of which are represented in Kansas.

After the turn of the century, architects trained elsewhere began to be joined by those from Kansas architecture schools. The architecture program at Kansas State University evolved gradually, beginning in 1877 when J. D. Walters, a Swiss-trained civil engineer, began offering instruction in architectural drawing. By 1903 a sufficient number of architectural courses were being offered to allow the authorization of a recognized curriculum of study within the College of Engineering. The architectural program at the University of Kansas, which began ten years later, was organized by Goldwin Goldsmith, a graduate of Cornell University and former secretary to Stanford White, of the New York–based firm of McKim, Mead & White. Goldsmith was pivotal in the 1921 organization of a Kansas Chapter of the American Institute of Architects. The two schools were similarly organized, offering programs in both architecture and architectural engineering. The program of Kansas State was larger and developed a strong reputation for the practical aspects of its curriculum, and the program at the University of Kansas was seen to emphasize the artistic aspects of its curriculum. Both schools produced capable graduates who contributed significantly to the architecture of Kansas.

By the turn of the century national architectural tastes had begun to favor more conservative classical approaches to design. Always cautious, Kansas clients followed the trend. This direction can be seen in the changing nature of the work of older architects as well as in the work of early graduates of the Kansas architecture schools, such as Henry W. Brinkman (1882–1949) of Emporia, a 1907 graduate of Kansas State University, who designed traditionally inspired churches for Catholic parishes across the state, and in that of Charles Shaver (1899–1970) of Salina, a 1915 graduate of Kansas State University, who designed churches and community buildings across a five-state region. The practices established by these two architects have similarities that reveal something of the nature of architectural practice in Kansas in the early twentieth century. The core of each of the practices was rooted in the architect's home city, where he designed a variety of building types. Each man supplemented that practice with work focused on a specific building type done across a wider geographic area. It is not coincidental therefore that the two practices thrived in cities with effective rail connections. Each of the practices was a small family business, which was successfully transferred to a younger generation.

The profession continued to be enriched by architects trained out of state. Thomas W. Williamson (1887–1974), a graduate of the University of Pennsylvania who established a practice in Topeka in 1912, and Lorentz Schmidt (1885–1952), a 1913 graduate of the University of Illinois who established a practice in Wichita in 1919, contributed significantly to the architecture of Kansas throughout their long and distinguished careers. As with the locally trained architects already cited, commonalities in the careers of Williamson and Schmidt reveal a glimpse of the evolving nature of the profession. The circumstances of each of their practices changed over time in terms of the nature of their business and the type of work produced. Schmidt practiced both alone and with a series of different partners; Williamson had a series of talented associates. Both men helped to train architects who would later play leadership roles in the profession. For example, Glen H. Thomas (1889–1962), another graduate of the University of Illinois, served his internship under Schmidt, and Theodore R. Greist (1898–1974), a graduate of Kansas State and Harvard University, served his internship under Williamson. Both Schmidt and Williamson began their careers creating rather traditional designs but allowed their work to evolve in concert with the emergence of Modernist sensibilities.

The rather modest amount of progressive work done in Kansas in the early years of the twentieth century was produced largely by practitioners from outside the state. Chicago architects, Frank Lloyd Wright and Patton & Miller, provided effective demonstrations of the Prairie Style. Unfortunately, some interesting examples of innovative work of this period have been demolished; these include the Capitol Building and Loan Association Building in Topeka, designed by Louis Sullivan's former assistant, George Grant Elmslie, and several Santa Fe Railroad depots designed by Louis Curtiss, an intriguingly talented architect from Kansas City, Missouri.

With the prosperity of the late 1920s, Kansas seemed finally ready to accept a modest and evolutionary form of Modernism. Art Deco ornament graced commercial buildings springing up across the state and even began to replace the stylized

*Capitol Building and Loan Building, Topeka, 1924 (Kansas State Historical Society)*

Neoclassical detail most typical of institutional structures. Despite the slowdown in construction that resulted from the depression of the 1930s, Kansas continued to reflect nationally changing stylistic preferences. Projects done under federal relief programs introduced the state to a simplified form of ornament that evolved into the Streamlined Moderne.

The acceptance of Modernism in Kansas was due in part to attitudes fostered at the University of Kansas, where the architecture program was among the first in the country to embrace the new aesthetic tenets evolving in Europe through the 1920s. Clarence Kivett (b. 1905), a 1928 graduate whose firm Kivett & Myers was located in Kansas City, Missouri, was a leader in introducing Modernist sensibilities to the Midwest. Robert E. Mann (b. 1909), a 1932 graduate who joined his father's Hutchinson-based practice, also helped to spread these ideas by the examples of courthouses and schools he designed throughout the western part of Kansas.

In the building boom that followed the construction hiatus surrounding World War II, Kansas clients seemed fully to embrace Modern architecture. Economic factors surely influenced their attitudes, for the new forms proved to be less expensive. The postwar period also saw the emergence of a number of new architectural firms whose members were trained according to Modernist principles and who actively promoted the new forms. The role was played most assertively in Topeka by the firm established in 1952 by William Kiene (1923–1979) and Jack R. Bradley (1925–1991) and in Wichita by that established in 1957 by Robert J. Shaefer (b. 1925) and Henry W. Schirmer. This firm and subsequent ones headed by Shaefer, a 1949 graduate of the University of Illinois, gave particularly poignant expression to the new aesthetic. It was also during this period (in 1949) that Kansas adopted legislation requiring the licensure of architects.

The postwar period brought changes to the practice of architecture nationally and also in Kansas. As building commissions grew larger and more complex, so did the organizations that designed them. Although many Kansas architects maintained small, locally based diverse practices, others began to concentrate on particular building types and to sell their services over a wider geographic area. For example, Kansas State graduate John Shaver (b. 1918) of Salina built a nationally based practice focusing on school design. As a result of such shifts, an increasing number of well-known, large, specialized firms from outside the state, notably Skidmore Owings and Merrill of Chicago and Caudill Rowlett and Scott of Houston, received commissions in Kansas. Kansas architects, particularly those in the northeastern part of the state, faced increasing competition from firms located in Kansas City, Missouri. As might be expected, the changes integrated architectural production within Kansas more fully with national stylistic trends. As elsewhere, recent architecture in Kansas has exhibited greater diversity of expression, and in architecture Kansas remains very much an American place.

We have touched only the high points of the development of the architectural profession in Kansas. There are many other architects who made significant contributions to the life of their communities, but unfortunately too little is known of these important men and women. The catalog of selected examples of the architecture of Kansas will introduce them, and our hope is that it will stimulate research into their lives and work.

# Metropolitan Kansas City Region

The two counties that constitute the Metro Region—Wyandotte and Johnson—are also integral units of the greater Kansas City Metropolitan Area, which incorporates six (some would say eight or even ten) counties spread across the state line between Kansas and Missouri. Of this group, three counties—Wyandotte, Johnson, and Jackson County, Missouri—contain the highly urbanized environment that forms the core of the Metropolitan Area. The nucleus is graphically illustrated by interconnected street grids, most noticeable on a map where the county line between Wyandotte and Johnson abuts the state line.

The proximity and consequent relationships among the three counties have affected their developmental histories. For example, Johnson County's rapid increase in population since 1960 and attendant growth in economic strength are facts that cannot be fully explained without examining the circumstances of its two neighbor counties. Or, reaching back in time, consider the fact that the two most populous cities in the greater Kansas City Metropolitan Area are both named Kansas City. The one in Missouri is the larger and older, having been organized as the Town of Kansas in 1839, fifteen years before the establishment of Kansas Territory. The choice of name (derived from that of an Indian tribe) came from its proximity to the place where the Kansas River (also called the Kaw) joins the Missouri River. The Kansas City in Wyandotte County, however, represents an 1886 consolidation of four communities: Wyandotte, Armstrong, Armourdale, and a sliver of land across the Kaw River and adjacent to Kansas City, Missouri, which also carried the name of Kansas City (Kansas). The decision to designate this consolidated group as Kansas City instead of as Wyandotte, after the oldest and biggest town, was deliberate in order to confuse potential buyers of the newer city's bonds, since the far larger Kansas City, Missouri, had established a good record of attracting outside investors. In 1909 and 1923 two more communities across the Kaw River were added to Kansas City, Kansas: Argentine and Rosedale.

The Kansas side of the greater Metropolitan Area thus evolved in ways closely connected to developments on the Missouri side, and in recent years the reverse is equally true, though state laws differ significantly in how municipalities and other jurisdictions can levy taxes and operate. Furthermore, many residents within the Metropolitan Area can pursue lives without much concern for occurrences beyond their individual communities or even neighborhoods; however, more of the citizenry regularly traverse sizable sections of the two-state area as they commute to work, transact business, seek goods or services, and enjoy entertainments and cultural activities. For them, the sprawling area functions as if it were a single, complex city, except when it comes to a choice of domicile or of location for a business operation. Consequently, within the greater Metropolitan Area, resources and facilities are unevenly dispersed, reflecting not only such choices but also the circumstances of a community's age, size, and degree of wealth.

As a case in point, the early presence of railroad yards and shops, the stockyards and packinghouses, and other industries in the Kaw Valley drew European and Mexican immigrants to Wyandotte County, resulting in a number of ethnic neighborhoods anchored by a church to serve them, such as St. Joseph's Catholic Church built for Polish immigrants (WY 14.21) and the Church of the Holy Family for the Slovenian community (WY 14.22). More recently, the national trend of shifting away from heavy industry and manufacturing, though favoring professional and service jobs, has tended to affect severely the prosperity of various neighborhoods and even their stability. For example, Wyandotte County was once home to a considerable meat industry of packinghouses and stockyards; that industry is now gone and with it a great number of jobs for people from both sides of the state line, resulting in significant social and physical changes, especially in Kansas City, Kansas.

Other changes, such as those that placed an ever greater reliance on trucking for the transportation of freight, have tended to shift warehousing away from compact, older industrial districts in both Kansas Cities, with their multistory structures nestled next to railroad spurs. The new facilities are typically one-story structures dispersed to locations where ample land permits a spread-out footprint while also being conveniently placed for easy access to one or more major highways and even an airport or railroad, as is the case of the North Supply Company near Gardner (JO 03.01), or the PPG Offices and distribution facilities in Lenexa (JO 05.03). As the existing jobs migrated, or newly formed industries chose outlying areas, older neighborhoods were negatively affected.

Another indication of the changing times is found in the development of office buildings and supporting facilities along several miles of two major streets that intersect in Overland Park in Johnson County. Representative of these are the Executive Hills South Building (JO 10.09), the Renaissance/Van Eyck Building (JO 10.10), and the Corporate Woods Office Park (JO 10.12). The success of these buildings in attracting tenants derives largely from their design and placement to accommodate a population—both employees and visitors—who must of necessity (but also from preference) depend on the automobile for their transportation. To succeed, such buildings need to be easily accessible from major roadways, including freeways, and to be well provided with ample acreages of adjacent surface parking. Most of these buildings and their car parks have been erected since 1970, and together the assemblage constitutes a new form of central business district, in this case one for the entire county.

Wyandotte and Johnson counties, despite their proximity and their role as key components in the greater Kansas City Metropolitan Area, have strikingly different developmental histories. A clue to the disparity is found in a comparison of the street grid pattern of the older Kansas City in eastern Wyandotte (dominated by a straight-line, right-angle pattern), and that in northeast Johnson County (with its numerous curvilinear streets), reflecting when these respective areas were platted. Yet both counties started out on similar paths, being within a much larger tract that had been designated by the federal government as Indian Territory, a place in which to relocate some of the Indian tribes being forced to emigrate from the east. The Delawares were placed north of the Kansas River, the Shawnees to the south.

When the Wyandot Indians (formerly of Ohio) arrived in 1843, many of them were already assimilated into the Euro-American culture. They purchased land from the Delaware and created the town of Wyandotte in what is now downtown Kansas City, a location overlooking both the Missouri and the Kaw rivers. When Wyandotte County was carved out of the slightly older Leavenworth County in 1859, it was named for the town. In contrast, the Shawnee Indians were already in residence when Johnson County was organized in 1855, and the location of their reservation's headquarters became the city of Shawnee. The county, however, was named for the Methodist minister who created a Shawnee Indian Mission and school in 1839 (JO 02.01).

Members of both tribes split over the issue of slavery as had their white neighbors, a situation in which the proslavery group was in the majority at first. Thus, while the town of Wyandotte on the wooded bluffs overlooking the two rivers was a logical entry port for white settlers after 1854, the Free-Soilers coming to Kansas were loath to confront possible opposition from the locals who supported slavery. Indeed, violent conflict over the issue of slavery increasingly wracked the territory. Consequently, opponents of slavery decided in 1857 to establish the town of Quindaro, a few miles up the Missouri River and away from the town of Wyandotte. As the only antislavery town on the river, Quindaro prospered from the traffic of like-minded folk who came to settle in various Kansas locations. Tradition has it that Quindaro also served as a station on the underground railroad for slaves escaping from Missouri. By 1859 the Free-Soilers finally achieved preponderance in the territory, which made the city of Wyandotte safe for them; accordingly, the less conveniently located Quindaro declined rapidly. For all practical purposes it ceased to exist by 1861, though a revival of sorts occurred when the Exodusters arrived in 1879 and a considerable number chose to settle in the vicinity of old Quindaro. They were former slaves who participated in a mass exodus soon after the end of the Reconstruction Era in the South, adding to the many thousands who earlier had come to Kansas seeking a better life.

Of the several small towns that amalgamated in 1886 to become Kansas City, Kansas, those south of the city of Wyandotte were younger, created during the 1860s and early 1870s in direct response to the establishment of industries in the Kaw Valley. Thus, this new Kansas City, with a population of less than 18,000, held a special advantage deriving from a strong industrial base, which gave the city the potential of substantial growth, and grow it did. In short order, Kansas City became the state's largest city, and in keeping with that status it initiated various public improvements, especially between 1910 and 1930, including a civic auditorium (WY 14.01), a county courthouse (WY 14.02), and a city hall (WY 14.07). The momentum disappeared, however, when the nation's economy faltered and then became mired in the Great Depression of the 1930s.

Of course similar circumstances occurred in other cities, and with the advent of the war years in the early 1940s they had to grapple with the implications of an improved but war-driven economy with numerous built-in restrictions. By the time those controls were finally lifted in 1947, circumstances had so changed from those of the 1920s that Kansas City, Kansas, had difficulty recapturing its earlier energy. In contrast, Wichita had been able to capitalize on its wartime growth as a major aircraft manufacturing center, and it soon overtook Kansas City in population (and remains the state's most populous city).

Meanwhile, across the state line, Kansas City, Missouri, had reformed its government during the war years and instituted professional planning, which soon led to a program of public improvements beginning in 1947. The planning also generated a series of annexations undertaken between 1950 and 1963, which quintupled the size of the city. Concurrently, the far northeastern sector of Johnson County was being transformed into the preferred bedroom suburb of Kansas City, Missouri.

Until World War II, Johnson County's economy had depended on agriculture. Several towns had been formed in the later 1850s, in addition to Shawnee, but none was adjacent to the state line that defined the western city limit of Kansas City, Missouri. Olathe, the seat of Johnson County, was centrally located. Other early towns came into existence with the construction of railroad lines after the Civil War, such as Merriam and Lenexa, but were some distance from the state line, and none attracted a sizable population. Indeed, at the start of the twentieth century less than 20,000 people resided in the county. In the next forty years the population increased only to 33,000. By then, however, the seed had been planted from which Johnson County's present, sizable population would grow.

The first stage of that growth was the platting of a number of small subdivisions by several developers in the northeast corner of the county, thereby creating a bedroom suburb for Kansas City, Missouri. Mission Hills (1913–1914) became an early and the most fashionable component of that suburb, and residences from the 1920s, such as the Mary Zook Hibbard House (JO 08.04) and the Ruth White Lowry House (JO 08.06), are representative of the essential character achieved and still maintained by that city. The J. C. Nichols Company developed Mission Hills as an adjunct of their Country Club District, the latter (announced in 1907) occupying about 1,000 acres in southwest Kansas City, Missouri. Concurrently, William Strang built an interurban railway between Kansas City and Olathe, and at its midpoint he launched a subdivision called Overland Park. In time, that subdivision— anchored initially by the Strang Line Car Barn (JO 10.03)—evolved into the city of Overland Park, now large both in area and population.

Major development in Johnson County, however, had to wait until after World War II, when federal programs helped underwrite home mortgages. Not only did the subdivisions already established, such as Fairway, begin to fill but also new ones, such as Prairie Village, were platted (1951). Almost all the immediate postwar development remained concentrated in the far northeastern corner of the county, near the state line. To that area came families, a great many of whom depended on Kansas City, Missouri, for jobs, services, shopping, and entertainment. By 1960 Johnson County had 144,000 residents, most still located within easy reach of the Missouri Kansas City's downtown. Although a good deal of the home construction consisted of largely undifferentiated tract houses, several groupings in Prairie Village contained some truly innovative designs, such as those by David Runnels (JO 11.05) and Donald Drummond (JO 11.07), and a number of quite distinctive residences were erected, such as the Hyde House, designed by Bruce Goff (JO 11.02).

By 1990, however, Johnson County contained a population of 355,000, and much more growth was confidently expected. Though most of the residents are still located somewhere in the county's northeast quadrant, inevitably more and more live at a considerable distance from the old commercial core of Kansas City, Missouri. Furthermore, of Johnson County's twenty-one municipalities, sixteen are in the northeast quadrant and are essentially contiguous. Though some of the larger cities are not yet fully platted, eventually they may be. The result is an evolving urban place that is in the process of becoming a new form of city, despite its sixteen municipalities, which range in population from less than 200 to over 110,000.

In dramatic contrast, Wyandotte County today has a population of 162,000, of which 150,000 reside in its Kansas City. The city expanded in area during the 1960s and 1970s so that it now occupies almost the entire county, which today has only three cities. The expansion of Kansas City into western Wyandotte County could not fully compensate for the reduction or actual loss of some of its older industries, some dating back to the late nineteenth century, such as the meatpacking plants and adjacent stockyards. Not only did many jobs vanish, but like other older cities its core contained aging structures that faced the competition of newer developments, more modern buildings, and the increasing job opportunities found in Johnson County.

Johnson County's dramatic growth in population after 1960 came in part from people who previously lived in Wyandotte and Jackson counties. Early among the influences contributing to this shift were the carefully planned subdivisions located adjacent to the state line, continuing the bedroom suburb phase begun years before. The developments were served by the Unified School District no. 512 (better known as the Shawnee Mission District), whose schools held a reputation for excellence and were essentially unaffected by the need to desegregate because virtually no minority students then lived in the area. Furthermore, schools built by the district incorporated influences from the most up-to-date ideas in educational philosophy, with the Merriam Elementary School (JO 06.02), the Antioch Middle School (JO 10.01), the Indian Hills Junior High School (JO 11.01), and the Shawnee Mission Northwest High School (JO 12.04) being representative examples. On the other hand, the federal mandate to desegregate proved difficult to implement for the school districts that served the older sections in both Kansas Cities, especially the one in Missouri. White flight, which began in earnest in the 1960s, not only helped populate Johnson County but also towns in eastern Jackson County and north of the Missouri River in Clay and Platte counties.

Moreover, the urban renewal efforts of the 1960s and the construction of freeways in the urban core that began about the same time ravaged portions of the two Kansas Cities, seriously disrupting older neighborhoods and displacing many people. The new highways also facilitated the migration of residents into the outlying areas on both sides of the state line. As the population of northeast Johnson County grew, where possible its cities expanded through annexations, notably Shawnee, Overland Park, Lenexa, Leawood, and Olathe. And Kansas City, Kansas, also annexed land to the west of its older core, whose limits had been at Thirty-fourth Street.

In Johnson County, the improvement of existing highways and the construction of freeways beyond the northeast corner attracted both commercial and residential development in their immediate vicinity. After 1970 the architecture included substantial office buildings, hotels, warehouses, and the like. Many of the larger office buildings were placed in Overland Park, located chiefly in an area anchored by the highway interchange between U.S. 169 and Interstate 435. Substantial development of this sort gave Johnson County not only a significant employment base and many new residents, but it also made it wealthy. Indeed, the county has become the provider of a substantial portion of the state's annual tax revenues.

Despite the distinct differences between Johnson and Wyandotte counties, and for that matter also with Jackson County in Missouri, the residents in the three-county core of the Kansas City Metropolitan Area treat the many municipal, county, and state lines as completely permeable and move back and forth to pursue numerous activities. That freedom, however, does not change the significant and powerful demographic and political distinctions that remain and that continue to affect development, survival of the older architecture, and the portions that benefit from careful maintenance. Thus, the two Kansas counties—Wyandotte and Johnson—together provide a textbook case of the progress of urban development from the mid-nineteenth century to the present as well as its evolution in many other places in the nation.

Orientation to the architecture that documents the history within the Metropolitan Kansas City Region is provided by the following regional map and directory. The map locates the core portion of the several cities listed in the catalog of entries, and the directory provides an outline for their sequence.

# METROPOLITAN KANSAS CITY REGION

Alpha-Numeric Directory

**JOHNSON (JO)**

**01** Edgerton

**02** Fairway

**03** Gardner

**04** Leawood

**05** Lenexa

**06** Merriam

**07** Mission

**08** Mission Hills

**09** Olathe†

**10** Overland Park

**11** Prairie Village

**12** Shawnee

**13** Westwood

**WYANDOTTE (WY)**

**14** Kansas City†

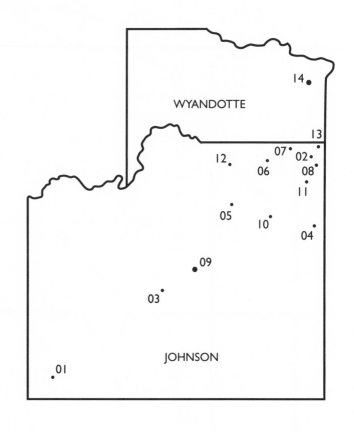

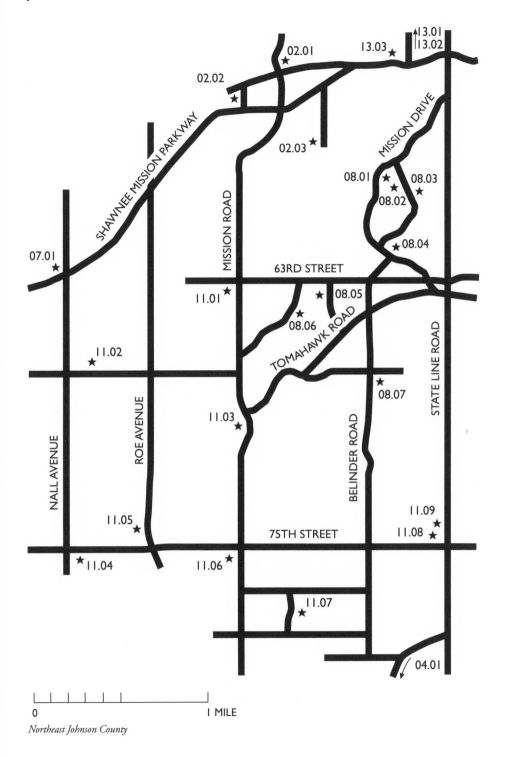

*Northeast Johnson County*

# JOHNSON COUNTY

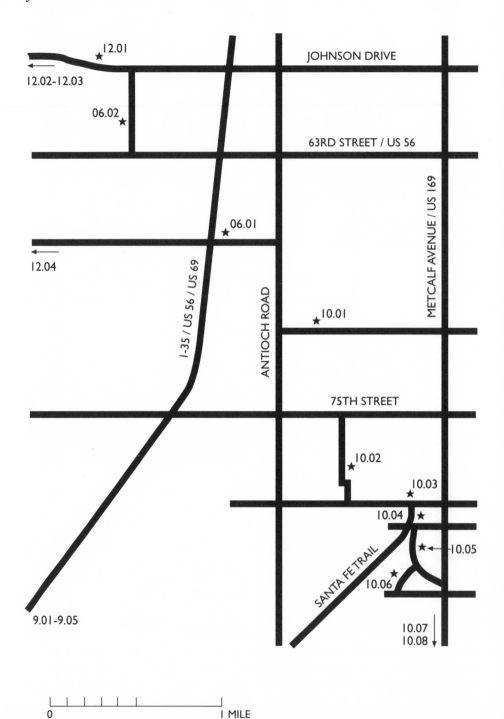

*Northwest Johnson County*

# Edgerton

## JO 01.01
## Lanesfield School
*ca. 1869–1870*
*18745 South Dillie Road*

Carefully restored as a museum, the simple shingle-roofed stone structure provides a clear picture of what a school day must have been like for children in rural areas in the late nineteenth century.

...................................

# Fairway

## JO 02.01
## Shawnee Methodist Mission*
*1839–1845*
*3403 West Fifty-third Street*

Three buildings remain from the sixteen that made up the Indian mission school established by the Reverend Thomas Johnson in 1838. Now a National Historic Landmark, the simple red-brick structures are representative of the sturdy, unselfconscious con-

struction used in the frontier period. The North Building is pictured. It was used as a girls' dormitory and for classes in the domestic arts; the far end originally mirrored the nearer portion but was altered in later years. The West Building, which was the headmaster's residence and the dining facility, now houses the caretaker. The East Building, which originally housed a chapel, a classroom, and a dormitory for boys, now contains exhibits. The mission has been restored as an interpretive museum and is administered by the Kansas State Historical Society.

## JO 02.02
## Residence
*1937. Neal O. Reyburn*
*5352 Neosho Lane*

This white stucco Streamline Moderne house, although an anomaly among its more traditional neighbors, reflects the period's newest trends in design. The circular screened porch attached to a rear corner of the house is of particular interest.

## JO 02.03
## L. R. Freeberg House
*1940. Edward Tanner*
*5622 Chadwick*

Occupying a corner lot overlooking the Kansas City Country Club, this house demonstrates the evolution of modern architecture. It combines the hipped roof and hori-

zontal emphasis of the Prairie Style, the streamlined curvilinear elements and nautical imagery of the Moderne Style, and the cubistic forms and spatial interpenetration of the International Style. Edward Tanner was the principal designer for the J. C. Nichols Company from 1919 until his retirement in 1964. He designed more than 2,000 homes in a variety of styles as well as many commercial and institutional buildings throughout Nichols's developments, which eventually encompassed over 4,000 acres on both sides of the state line.

. . . . . . . . . . . . . . . . . . . . . . . . . . . . . .

## Gardner

**JO 03.01**
### North Supply Company
*1985. Howard Needles Tammen & Bergendorf*
*10951 Lakeview Avenue*

This Modern corporate headquarters building sits on a sixty-acre site between U.S. 56 and the Johnson County Industrial Airport. The building's front facade looks to-

ward the airport and is marked by a series of highly articulated masonry elements; the long graceful curve of the building's all-glass rear facade follows the line of the distant highway. Built to accommodate the addition of several ten-story office towers, this handsome building with its significantly different facades is a clear reflection of its time.

. . . . . . . . . . . . . . . . . . . . . . . . . . . . . .

## Leawood

**JO 04.01**
### J. Findlay Reed House
*1953. David B. Runnels*
*8550 High Drive*

The site of this comparatively early house, in the then recently incorporated city, is located at the end of a cul-de-sac, reflecting a popular aspect in suburban planning of the period. The major living areas face the wooded rear of the property. Runnels, along with a partner, Jim Clark, was responsible for several notable buildings in Kansas City, Missouri, including the Commercial Design Building at the Kansas City Art Institute.

. . . . . . . . . . . . . . . . . . . . . . . . . . . . . .

## Lenexa

**JO 05.01**
### Rising Star School
*1990. Hansen, Midgely & Niemackl*
*8600 Candelight Road*

This building makes skillful use of inexpensive materials. Brick patterning on the exterior adds interest, and decorative blockwork enlivens the interior corridors. The curving entry canopy is innovatively supported by a tension cable running on its perimeter.

## JO 05.02
### Fire Station no. 4
*1991. Shaugnessy Fickel & Scott*
*10855 Eicher Road*

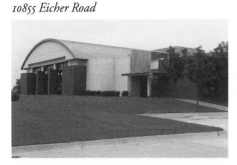

This boldly shaped Modern building occupies a site on a newly opened road. The fire trucks are housed beneath a dramatic arched roof; the remaining portions of the building (occupied by the fire fighters) are more humanly scaled and detailed. The building won a design award from the Kansas City Chapter of the American Institute of Architects. The architects have shown consistent ability, through the skillful application of materials and manipulation of form, in transforming typically mundane building types into structures of considerable interest. Another example of their skill is to be found in the white metal-paneled office/warehouse complex at the corner of 110th and Lackman Road, built in 1980.

## JO 05.03
### PPG Offices
*1989. Patty Berkebile Nelson Immenschuh*
*16505 West 113th Street*

Part of the new Southlake office campus development, this long two-story building

houses both biomedical offices and distribution facilities. The two portions of the building are connected by an entry pavilion, which centers on a circular atrium. The exterior is clad in a carefully refined combination of green glass and silver metal panels. The complex is a good example of the trend late in the century to disperse such buildings to newly developed sites quite distant from the core city and to locate them conveniently to one or more freeways.

. . . . . . . . . . . . . . . . . . . . . . . . . . . . . . .

# Merriam

## JO 06.01
### Seaboard Building
*1980. Theodore Seligson*
*9000 West Sixty-seventh Street*

This three-story brick office building is representative of suburban office buildings of the time. The ground floor is fully glazed, and the upper floors feature continuous bands of windows. The building is notable for its carefully detailed diagonal entry and atrium, which features a graceful cantilevered stair.

## JO 06.02
### Merriam Elementary School
*1969. Marshall & Brown*
*6100 Mastin*

Classroom pods are grouped around the shared central spaces in this brick elemen-

*Seaboard Building*

expressive stained-glass window that fills the east wall of the entry foyer. The church is representative of the ideals, then current, in the architectural community. It won awards from both the Kansas and the Kansas City chapters of the American Institute of Architects.

. . . . . . . . . . . . . . . . . . . . . . . . . . . . . .

tary school. The fragmented massing and hipped roofs help the building blend with its residential surroundings. The windows in the classroom are cleverly placed at a diagonal in the corners of the rooms, permitting windows in adjacent classrooms to share a single exterior opening. The building won an honor award from the Kansas City Chapter of the American Institute of Architects.

. . . . . . . . . . . . . . . . . . . . . . . . . . . . . .

## Mission

**JO 07.01**
### Trinity Lutheran Church
*1952. Mackie & Roark*
*Shawnee Mission Parkway and Nall Road*

This low-roofed geometric Modern brick church sits on a knoll overlooking a busy intersection. On both the exterior and interior it is well ordered but rather Spartan. The building's most distinctive feature is an

## Mission Hills

**JO 08.01**
### A. R. Jones House
*1926. Archer & Gloyd*
*5701 Mission Drive*

Although somewhat larger, this rambling Tudor mansion is representative of the many palatial houses in the area. It spreads along the crest of a hill overlooking a spacious lawn. Restrictive deed covenants have been effective in preserving the character of this most exclusive subdivision developed by J. C. Nichols. He permitted a variety of architectural styles but exhibited a preference for English country styles.

## JO 08.02
### Crosby Kemper House
*1969. I. W. Colburn*
*5700 Oakwood Road*

The house occupies a prominent hillside site at the intersection of Oakwood and Mission Drive, overlooking the Mission Hills Country Club. Its modular repetitive vertical geometric forms give the house a castlelike feeling, despite its obviously recent vintage.

## JO 08.03
### (Second) Donald Hall House
*1991. Taft Architects*
*5801 Oakwood Road*

The offset repeating-gable forms provide a clever Post-Modern parody of the surrounding traditional houses. The architects have developed a national reputation for skillful and playful reinterpretation of regional vernacular forms.

## JO 08.04
### Mary Zook Hibbard House
*1925. Edward Buehler Delk*
*6101 Mission Road*

This restrained Colonial house features a two-story colonnaded porch that covers the front of the building. The architect came to Kansas City in 1919 at the request of J. C. Nichols and was instrumental in setting the tone for Nichols's Country Club Plaza shopping district. The house, which is at the intersection of several curving streets, faces a

small but impressive formal park featuring a fountain and a row of freestanding marble columns. The park, like others that grace Nichols's developments, was designed by the landscape architects, Hare & Hare; they were responsible for the layout of Mission Hills and for many of his other developments.

## JO 08.05
### (First) Donald Hall House
*1950. Kivett & Myers*
*6320 Aberdeen*

Stylistically distinguished from most of its more traditional neighbors, this Modern house is an expanded version of the popular postwar split-level suburban house. Noteworthy for its clarity of form and effective use of materials, it occupies a shaded rise along a curving street in the area's most affluent residential area.

## JO 08.06
### Ruth White Lowry House
*1923*
*Mary Rockwell Hook and Mac Remington*
*6435 Indian Lane*

The house sits in a secluded meadow atop a steep bluff. This romantic stone villa reveals the architect's European training at the Ecole des Beaux-Arts; it also displays an affinity to the Arts and Crafts tradition. The mass of the house is punctuated by humanizing elements that display the skills of the craftsmen and the sensitivities of the architect.

**JO 08.07**
## Residence
*1957. Marcel Breuer*
*Sixty-seventh Street and Belinder Street*

Turned at a diagonal to the adjacent intersection, the house seems to float free of its surroundings. Breuer adapted the principles of the Bauhaus (a German school of design where he was both a student and then a teacher) to the problem of the American suburban house. Breuer is noted for the bent tubular steel furniture he designed early in his career and for the later monumental institutional structures of concrete as well as for his houses. As both a teacher at Harvard University and a practitioner, Breuer was inspirational to a generation of architects.

. . . . . . . . . . . . . . . . . . . . . . . . . . . . . . .

# Olathe

**JO 09.01**
## J. B. Mahaffie House*
*1857*
*1100 Old Kansas City Road*

This rectangular gable-roofed two-story vernacular stone house is symmetrically arranged around a central hallway. The house as well as an adjacent wood-peg barn and stone ice house have been restored as a museum. The buildings (on the largest farm in

the area) were located along the Santa Fe Trail and between 1865 and 1869 became the first stop on the stagecoach line between Westport and western destinations.

**JO 09.02**
## Johnson County Courthouse
*1952/1972. Hollis & Miller*
*Santa Fe Drive and Cherry Street*

The courthouse reflects the dramatic growth of Johnson County and the changing nature of county government. The building pictured is a major addition, made in 1972, to a courthouse constructed in 1952. The earlier building, in turn, had replaced one that had served the county for sixty years. The 1972 portion is more like an office building than a traditional courthouse, for it serves the county's increasingly complex administrative role, the 1952 portion contains most of the judicial operations. The distinctive interpenetrating limestone, brick, and glass elements suggest the multiplicity of governmental functions.

**JO 09.03**
## Isaac O. Pickering House*
*1870*
*507 West Park*

Characteristics of several popular late-nineteenth-century styles are displayed in this house. Its basic form and the articulation of its main block are of Italianate inspiration; the ornate carving on the porches

ments, such as the decorative trusses in the gables, are combined with turned porch spindles popular in the Queen Anne Style and with ornamental cresting along the roof line more reminiscent of Italianate designs. The overall form is suggestive of the designs of the English architect, Charles Locke Eastlake. It looks as if a tall hipped-roofed central portion of the house has been imposed over a long gable-roofed form.

reflects Queen Anne tastes. The house had several additions, including the porches.

. . . . . . . . . . . . . . . . . . . . . . . . . . . . . .

## JO 09.04
### Frank R. Lanter House✦

*1901. George P. Washburn & Son*
*562 West Park Street*

Reflecting the influence of the Neoclassical Revival, this formal symmetrical house features a two-level, columned, half-round entry porch with a conical roof, flanked by octagonal tower bays that intersect the corners of the main body of the house. The architect is better known for the thirteen courthouses he designed around the state than for his residential work.

## JO 09.05
### Martin Van Buren Parker House*

*ca. 1869–1880*
*631 West Park*

This house provides an example of the creative possibilities of the eclectic application of Victorian design motifs. Stick Style ele-

# Overland Park

## JO 10.01
### Antioch Middle School (Milburn Junior High School)

*1956. Marshall & Brown with Perkins & Will*
*8200 West Seventy-first Street*

Located in the midst of a residential area, this low, sprawling Modern school is similar to the many schools built in the county in the 1950s to accommodate the area's growing suburban population. Clearly articulated, special-use areas cluster around the entry, and classroom wings spread across the site. The elements frame a pleasantly scaled entry courtyard. The building won a design award from the Kansas City Chapter of the American Institute of Architects.

## JO 10.02
### Seaton House
*1948. I. L. Roark*
*7715 Hardy*

Although this low-roofed one-story brick and wood building appears modest by current standards, it holds interest as an early example of the modern suburban house. It won an honor award from the Kansas City Chapter of the American Institute of Architects.

## JO 10.03
### Strang Line Car Barn
*1906*
*Seventy-seventh Street and Santa Fe Drive*

This large utilitarian stone shed terminates the north vista of Santa Fe Drive, in the center of Overland Park's original downtown district. The building was erected to service the interurban rail line, built by William B. Strang, to connect Kansas City, Missouri, with Olathe. The restored structure now houses a furniture store.

## JO 10.04
### Overland Park Campanile
*1989. Richard C. Coleman*
*7900 block of Santa Fe Drive*

The tower and pergola were constructed as part of an effort by the city of Overland Park to rejuvenate the original downtown portion of the city. The tower is intended to become a memorable focal point and catalyst for future development. The city has recently added an open pavilion adjacent to the tower to accommodate a farmers' market. The architect was a planner for the city of Overland Park.

## JO 10.05
### Overland Park Presbyterian Church
*1930. Ernest O. Brostrom*
*Eightieth Street and Overland Park Drive*

This English Gothic Revival Style church building, both picturesque and convincing, occupies a shaded site facing a park near the town's original commercial district. The architect designed a series of small churches in a variety of traditional styles as well as a number of significant, progressively styled commercial structures through the first half of the twentieth century.

## JO 10.06
### Robert D. Campbell House
*1966. Robert D. Campbell*
*8126 Hamilton*

A large steel-framed dome covers much of the structure, making it a house within a house. The area between the shell of the dome and the house within contains a swimming pool and a lush, semitropical garden. The house opens to this space by means of a glazed wall that can be lowered into the basement. Robert Campbell is a structural engineer who, beginning in the mid-1950s, worked as consultant to a number of Kansas architects, notably John Shaver of Salina.

## JO 10.07
### King Louie West Bowling Alley
*1948/1965. Manuel Morris & Associates*
*Eighty-eighth and Metcalf*

Stretching along a major strip, this stone-faced building is a distinctive example of a usually nondescript building type. Repetitive piers and a low-ribbed folded-metal

roof disguise the building's bulk. The side entry is marked by a heavy timber-supported porte cochere and by a pointed stone and metal tower. It is vaguely reminiscent of Frank Lloyd Wright's Taliesin West complex. The portion of the building visible from the street contains an ice rink, which was added to the original thirty-two-lane bowling alley.

## JO 10.08
### Glenwood Theaters
*1963. Donald Philo*
*9100 Metcalf*

This Modern commercial building occupies a corner site along a busy commercial strip.

The street has undergone continuous redevelopment over the past thirty years, and the building is emblematic of the early phases. It also represents an interesting phase in the evolution of the building type, from the Main Street movie house to the multiplex cinema. Although several additional theaters have been added over the years, the grandeur of the concrete vaulted entry lobby with its oversize chandelier has been retained.

### JO 10.09
### Executive Hills South Building
*1989. Patty Berkebile Nelson & Immenschuh*
*Metcalf and College Boulevard*

Located at the intersection of the area's most prominent commercial streets, this fifteen-story building sits in a landscaped parking lot. The alternating ribbons of dark precast concrete and tinted glass that cover the building's curving mass reveal little of its interior or inhabitants. It is representative of the many elegant yet generic speculative office buildings constructed in the economic boom of the early 1980s.

### JO 10.10
### Renaissance/Van Eyck Building
*1984. Howard Needles Tammen & Bergendorf*
*7707 College Boulevard*

This structure is one of three loosely related speculative office buildings that occupy a hillside site overlooking the busy street. The L-shape of the six-story building allows it to address both the street and the rear-facing entry. The building's shape as well its well-appointed lobby rotunda, the curving glazed conference areas, and the open balconies help to distinguish it.

### JO 10.11
### Mast Advertising
*1984. Patty Berkebile Nelson Associates*
*7500 West 110th Street*

This five-story suburban office building is distinguished from other similar structures in its vicinity by the type, depth, and interest of its exterior articulation. The horizontal overhangs and protruding corner windows, which lend relief and shadow to the exterior walls, seem to have been inspired by the Prairie Style. The novelty of the wall treatment is most apparent in the rear facade, which is fully visible from Interstate 435. The building received a design award

from the Kansas City Chapter of the American Institute of Architects.

## JO 10.12
### Corporate Woods Office Park
*1974–1979*
*Marshall & Brown with Sasaki Walker Associates (landscape architects)*
*Antioch Road to Overland Parkway and Interstate 435 to College Boulevard*

This office complex initiated the development of a satellite business district or edge city in the metropolitan area. Intended to serve as an attractive alternative to the traditional downtown setting, the location away from the older core city was chosen in the recognition that abundant parking and a heavily landscaped parklike environment would be pleasant and convenient for individuals who were moving into the upscale residential districts being developed within easy commuting distance. The original twelve buildings represent adaptations of structures built earlier in other places.

## JO 10.13
### Johnson County Community College/Cultural Education Center
*1990. Peckham Guyton Albers & Viets*
*12345 College Boulevard*

The Cultural Education Center is part of the Johnson County Community College, yet it stands apart for aesthetic as well as for functional reasons. Although using the basic palette of the campus, it is rendered in a more ornate Post-Modern vocabulary. Yardley Hall, the auditorium, is among the most highly rated in the region for its acoustics. Productions presented there serve both the campus and the general community. The skylit foyer, with its brick relief murals, is of considerable interest.

## JO 10.14
### Johnson County Community College
*1974/1982. Marshall & Brown*
*12345 College Boulevard*

The original buildings of this open hilltop campus were planned around a large central-pedestrian courtyard. The campus has undergone a number of additions through the years as the student population of the college has continued to grow. Most of the additions, including a major expansion designed by the Hollis and Miller Group and completed in 1982, have followed the stylistic lead of the original architects. The buildings are characterized by their crisp geometric shapes, dark brown brick exteriors, black steel windows, exposed concrete structure, and spare detailing. Subsequent additions have given the scheme an increasing complexity, but the common palette of materials and forms gives the campus a pleasing sense of unity.

. . . . . . . . . . . . . . . . . . . . . . . . . . . . . . .

# Prairie Village

## JO 11.01
### Indian Hills Junior High School
*1966*
*Kivett & Meyers & McCallum with*
*Perkins & Will*
*6400 Mission Road*

The layout of this flat-roofed brick and glass Modern school is straightforward, and the construction is economical. It achieves a measure of distinction through skillful placement to take advantage of the slope of the site, careful detailing, and effective use of a limited palette of materials. The building received a design award from the Kansas City Chapter of the American Institute of Architects. The architects were a dominant force in Kansas City architectural community following World War II, winning thirty of the seventy-five design awards given by the local chapter of the American Institute of Architects in a thirty-year period.

## JO 11.02
### Hyde House
*1966. Bruce Goff*
*2020 West Sixty-seventh Street*

At a glance, the exterior of this house is not too different from its neighbors since it is of similar scale and is clad in modest materials. Yet on closer inspection the idiosyncratic character of the house and its designer become apparent. It is governed by a pervasive geometric logic that creates interesting juxtapositions between the masses of the house and curious junctures between the building's materials; the influence of the geometric logic touches even the smallest details. In the interior, all the major living spaces of the house open onto a tall central skylit space focused on a hearth with a freestanding flue.

The only enclosed spaces on the main floor are the bathrooms, and even these are configured to permit an uninterrupted flow of space to all parts of the house. The architect was internationally recognized for his innovative free-spirited designs. Born in Alton, Kansas, he practiced briefly in Kansas City in the mid-1960s. Another house designed by Goff is at 7821 Fontana Street.

### JO 11.03
### Prairie Village Shopping Center
*1948. Edward Tanner*
*Sixty-ninth Street and Mission Road*

A consistent Colonial motif and effective landscaping unite the elements of this early shopping center. The series of drives and courtyards that traverse the groupings of shops enable pedestrian and vehicular traffic to mingle successfully. The J. C. Nichols Company developed the center and much of the surrounding residential area as well as the Country Club Plaza district in Kansas City, Missouri. The architect and developer worked together for nearly fifty years, beginning in 1919.

### JO 11.04
### Congregation Ohev Sholom
*1968. Manuel Morris & Robert Sixta*
*Seventy-fifth Street and Nall Road*

The plan for the synagogue was derived from the six-pointed star. A dramatic and expressive tentlike roof covers the major worship space and determines the character of the building on both the exterior and interior. The worship space is linked to a more rectilinear, straightforward two-story administration-classroom wing.

### JO 11.05
### Houses
*1949. David B. Runnels*
*7334–7356 Roe Circle*

This grouping of similar, modest houses surrounds a shaded park (the one pictured is located at 7342 Roe Circle). Although the houses share a common vocabulary of forms, including low-pitched roofs and semidetached flat-roofed garages, and a common palette of materials, notably vertical wood siding, brick trim, and horizontal sliding windows, each is distinctive. The elements of the houses are arranged to take full advantage of the small lots and to provide usable outdoor space for each homeowner. The developer, Donald Drummond, used many of the features of this group of houses in his subsequent designs.

### JO 11.06
### Shawnee Mission East High School
*1958*
*Neville Sharp & Simon with Perkins & Will*
*Seventy-fifth Street and Mission Road*

The school, like the many others built by the Shawnee Mission School District in the 1950s and 1960s, displays a straightforward

use of their sites through the inclusion of patio walls, pergolas, covered walkways, and picture windows. They make generous provision for the automobile and represent an ideal, affordable suburban house.

## JO 11.08
## Capitol Federal Savings and Loan
*1975–1976. Kiene & Bradley*
*Seventy-fifth and State Line*

The heavily landscaped bermed site is used to set off this simple yet elegant rectangular Modern two-story building. The upper story is sheathed in exposed aggregate concrete panels; the south-facing windows are deeply recessed. The top portion appears to float above a lower story that is sheathed in glazed brick and glass panels. A drive-through passes underneath the building. The architects were also responsible for a number of the newer courthouses across the state.

almost industrial image of alternating sections of unadorned brick panels and repetitive glass curtainwall. It employs the typical strategy of separating the classroom wing, which here consists of a single long three-story block, from the specialized functions, which in this case are located across a landscaped courtyard. Many of these schools were designed, in collaboration with various local associates, by the Chicago architects Perkins and Will, who were seen as experts in school planning.

## JO 11.07
## Residential District
*1950–1951*
*Donald Drummond (builder/developer)*
*Seventy-seventh Street to Seventy-ninth Street and Canterbury to Chadwick*

The residences exhibit a number of carefully thought-out common features, including low, sloping roofs and sensitively detailed wood siding (3111 West Seventy-seventh Street is pictured). The houses make good

## JO 11.09
## Locton Companies
*1986–1987. Nearing Staats Prelogar & Jones*
*7400 State Line*

This L-shaped two-story brick-clad Modern corporate headquarters displays a sensitivity to the building's relationship to a largely residential setting, for its configuration is used to shield the parking area. Vehicular entry to the complex passes under the building and adjacent to the two-story glazed lobby,

which breaks free at the intersection of the two wings. The building's interiors were designed by Calcara Duffendack Foss and Manlove.

. . . . . . . . . . . . . . . . . . . . . . . . . . . . .

# Shawnee

## JO 12.01
### Hocker Grove Junior High School
*1956. Voscamp & Slezak with Perkins & Will*
*10400 Johnson Drive*

Representative of progressive attitudes in school design of the period, this school consists of one-story classroom wings spread across the landscape. The end walls are brick, but the long sides are formed with a glass curtainwall system. A notable aspect is the pleasantly scaled entry courtyard, which is framed by the building on three sides and a covered drop-off area on the fourth. The building is reminiscent of the revolutionary Crow Island School, designed by the Perkins and Will firm in association with Eliel Saarinen.

## JO 12.02
### St. Joseph's Catholic Church
*1969. Brinkman & Hagan*
*Johnson and Flint Drive*

This round barnlike structure stands apart from its rather cluttered surroundings. Radial-curving laminated wood beams support its low conical roof. The building won an award for its lighting. It is the last of the many churches across the state designed by the architects. Henry W. Brinkman opened the office in 1908; his son, Jerome Brinkman, closed it after the death of their common partner, Stanley Hagan.

## JO 12.03
### Broken Arrow Elementary School
*1990. Abend Singleton Associates*
*5901 Alden Road*

The building makes good use of its steep hillside site; entry is from the upper level. The geometric classroom pods are decorated with colorful, patterned brickwork. The central facilities are housed in a child-scaled village set within a large, glazed volume in the center of the classroom elements. The building received a design award from the Kansas City Chapter of the American Institute of Architects. This acclaimed firm has earned a reputation for design innovation.

## JO 12.04
## Shawnee Mission Northwest High School

*1968. Marshall & Brown*
*12701 West Sixty-seventh Street*

The school relies on the contrast of form and material to give scale to a massive building. The forms of the classroom elements and specialized functions clearly express the nature of the interior volumes, and the concrete structure of the building is clearly distinguished from the brick-faced infill walls. The school is organized around a central sky-lighted interior street, which passes through the building. The classroom wings are located on one side, the common facilities on the other.

. . . . . . . . . . . . . . . . . . . . . . . . . . . . . . . . .

# Westwood

## JO 13.01
## Westwood City Hall

*1991. Patty Berkebile Nelson Immenschuh*
*Forty-seventh Street and Rainbow Boulevard*

This L-shaped building is hinged by a circular council chamber, which protrudes

toward the adjacent intersection. Parking and entry are from the opposite side. The dramatic, carefully detailed wood-paneled council chamber is open through an arcade to the foyer. One wing contains a large meeting room; the other houses city offices. The fragmented massing and patterning in the brickwork reveal the building's Post-Modern spirit.

## JO 13.02
## Hudson Oil Company Building

*1955. John Lawrence Daw*
*4720 Rainbow Boulevard*

Classically composed, this single-story glass box is an excellent example of Miesian modernism. The roof is supported from exterior beams, which rest on columns set outside the exterior wall; the beams appear to span the entire building. Interest is added to the building by the exterior white-painted vertical sunscreen fins, which contrast sharply to the dark glass and black mullions.

## United Telecommunications Garage and Office Building

*1981. Howard Needles Tammen & Bergendorf*
*2330 Shawnee Mission Parkway*

This Modern precast-concrete 450-car garage and 125,000 square-foot office addition nestle behind extensive landscaping along the side of a busy highway. The building takes advantage of its southern orientation; deep recesses shade the windows from the sun, and solar collectors provide hot water to the building. Its strong sculptural form is modulated to minimize its apparent bulk and impact on the surrounding residential neighborhood.

*Kansas City*

# Kansas City

## WY 14.01
## Soldiers and Sailors Memorial Building*

*1924. Rose & Peterson*
*600 North Seventh Street*

Six giant Ionic columns frame the five entry doors to the auditorium building. The Beaux-Arts detail of the exterior is amplified in an exuberant two-story lobby space. The building was built with moneys from a special bond issue to commemorate the service of the men of Wyandotte County in World War I.

## WY 14.02
## Wyandotte County Courthouse

*1922–1927. Wight & Wight*
*Seventh and Barnett*

This grand Neoclassical limestone building features an arcade of six four-story Doric columns and in the interior a two-story barrel-vaulted upper hallway. The commission for the courthouse came as the result of a competition won by Kansas City's premier civic architects of the 1920s and 1930s. Thomas Wight and his younger brother William were natives of Canada. Before coming to Kansas City, each had worked for ten years in the prominent New York architectural firm McKim, Mead & White. Other notable buildings by their firm are found in Kansas City, Missouri, and include the City Hall, the Jackson County Courthouse, the Nelson-Atkins Museum of Art, and the Kansas City Life Insurance Company.

## WY 14.03
## Scottish Rite Temple*

*1909. William W. Rose*
*803 North Seventh Street*

The three-story Tudor Revival building has an entry story of rough stone supporting the vertically articulated brick upper stories that are trimmed with stone and capped by vigorously executed crenellation. The building features stained-glass windows, leaded-glass entry doors, and rich interior woodwork. Pictured to the side of the temple is the 1973 Municipal Office Building, designed by Charles E. Mullin with Meyn and Fennel.

## WY 14.04
## Huron Cemetery (Wyandotte National Cemetery)*

*1843–1844*
*Minnesota Avenue, between Sixth Street and Seventh Street*

Containing approximately 400 graves, the cemetery occupies a wooded hilltop in the center of the downtown commercial district. Its strategic location has made it subject to repeated but unsuccessful attempts at commercial encroachment. Its presence reminds us of the forced migration in the nineteenth century of the Wyandott Indians to the Kansas City area and then again with other tribes to present-day Oklahoma to make way for white settlement in Kansas Territory.

## WY 14.05
### New Brotherhood Building
*1949. John Maultsby*
*735 State Avenue*

Via a through-block arcade, this office building connects to the smaller Old Brotherhood building, which faces Minnesota Avenue. It is an early and relatively pure demonstration of the principles of the International Style; the alternating broad bands of steel sash windows and equally sized brick spandrel panels reveal the building's function, and the regular interruption of the window bands marks the building's structure. The architect was still in his twenties when the building was erected.

## WY 14.06
### Kansas City Public Library
*1965. Radotinsky Meyer Deardorff Architects*
*625 Minnesota Avenue*

The library is representative of the understated Modern aesthetic of the time, which is characterized by the clear expression of efficient construction systems. The functions contained within—the main library on the lower two floors and the school system's administrative offices on the top level—are expressed clearly on the building's main facade: the fully glazed lower floor indicates the public portion of the building, the mostly closed second level conceals the stack areas, and the strip window of the third floor reveals the series of smaller offices located on that level. In contrast to surrounding buildings, the library is set back from the street, thereby indicating its civic nature.

## WY 14.07
### Old Kansas City Hall and Fire Headquarters*
*1910–1911. Rose & Peterson*
*805–815 North Sixth Street*

The southern portion of this three-story stone-trimmed brick Renaissance Revival block is the oldest public building in the downtown area. The northern half and the adjacent stripped Classical fire station were added in 1929–1930. The architect for the addition was Charles E. Keyser.

## WY 14.08
### Sumner Academy
*1937–1939. Joseph W. Radotinsky*
*1610 North Oak Street*

The building features an articulated two-tone-patterned brickwork with limestone trim. The decorative motifs are characteristic of the streamlined Art Deco ornament popular in the federally sponsored public works projects of the depression years. The massing is indicative of the emerging influence of European modernism, notably that of the Dutch architect, Willem Dudok. The school was built during the era of racially segregated facilities to accommodate black students.

**WY 14.09**

### Charles E. Abraham House

*1908. J. G. Braecklein*
*2800 Parkwood Boulevard*

The house is part of the Parkwood subdivision developed by Henry McGrew, near the old city of Quindaro. The layout of the subdivision reflects the planning principles of the English Garden Cities movement and features curving streets and underground utilities. The house is typical of many others in the area; the plan is straightforward and compact. Formal features, including the broad hipped roof, articulated base, and horizontally aligned windows, are reminiscent of the then popular Chicago-based Prairie Style.

**WY 14.10**

### St. Augustine Hall (Mather Hall)*

*1896/1904*
*Martin Vrydagh and Thomas B. Wolfe*
*3301 Parallel Avenue*

St. Augustine Hall sits atop a broad hill in a shaded campus setting. Its distinctive tower, added in 1904, is visible from some distance. The contrast between the main building and the tower is illustrative of the shift in stylistic influence, from Richardsonian Romanesque to more Classical referents. The building was intended to be the first of five designed to house Kansas City University. After the university failed in 1933 due to financial difficulties, the campus was purchased in 1935 by the Recollect Augustinian Fathers, who preserved the buildings as the Monastery of St. Augustine. It now is used as a conference center. Martin Vrydagh had practiced in Kansas City, Missouri, through the boom years of the 1880s but returned to the east after the economy flattened.

**WY 14.11**

### Chelsea Elementary School

*1914. Rose & Peterson*
*1834 North Twenty-fifth Street*

The four-room schoolhouse presents an interesting mix of stylistic influences. The gables, chimneys, and some of the decorative elements are reminiscent of the Jacobethan Revival; other elements of the massing and ornamentation suggest the influence of the Prairie Style. This building and an adjacent school designed in 1923 by the same architects were part of a major building program continued through the 1920s by the board of education.

## WY 14.12
### Westheight Manor Historic District*
*1915*
*Wood Avenue to State Avenue and Twenty-fifth Street to Eighteenth Street*

Developed by Jesse Hoel with the support of J. O. Fife and Hanford Kerr, this subdivision is notable for its quality of planning and for the architecture it contains. The design of the gently curving streets and periodic landscape amenities was completed by Hare & Hare. The houses are set on generous lots and are typical of the best of eclectic interwar tastes. The district contains houses designed by some of Kansas City's more notable architects, including Victor J. Defoe, John C. Braecklein, Charles A. Smith, Charles E. Keyser, Edward Buehler Delk, Courtland Van Brunt, Cecil E. Cooper, Joseph W. Radotinsky, and Louis S. Curtiss.

## WY 14.13
### Jesse Hoel Residence (Westheight Manor Historic District)
*1916. Louis S. Curtiss*
*2106 Washington Boulevard*

The house is a clear demonstration of the compositional prowess of one of Kansas City's most distinctive early-twentieth-century architects. It consists of a series of tightly interwoven, low, tile-roofed single-story stone pavilions with expansive wood-framed windows and sprawls in a rooted fashion across its prominent corner site. Influences from local vernacular traditions as well as from the Prairie Style, the Beaux-Arts, and Japanese traditions can be seen in the fragments of the complex yet highly integrated composition.

## WY 14.14
### Henry G. Miller House (Westheight Manor Historic District)
*1920–1921. Louis S. Curtiss*
*2404 Washington Boulevard*

This idiosyncratic one-story tile-roofed stucco residence sits atop a knoll overlooking a small triangular park. It was the final house designed by the increasingly hermetic architect, who spent his final years preoccupied by esoteric concerns, notably the relationship between geometry and structure. The house is composed as a pastiche of varied and highly decorative elements. The equally expressive interior remains largely intact.

## WY 14.15
### Thomas Torson House (Westheight Manor Historic District)
*1922–1923. Victor J. Defoe*
*2300 Washington Boulevard*

A variety of influences are combined in this tile-roofed stone residence: the low, hipped roofs are reminiscent of the Prairie Style; the details reveal an Arts and Crafts influence; and the overall massing, consisting of a two-story central volume flanked symmetrically by one-story wings, is almost Neoclassical. The influence of the nearby houses designed by Louis Curtiss is also evident in the boldness of the composition. The architect designed a smaller but similarly massed and detailed residence across the street, the Fred Robertson house at 2210 Washington Boulevard.

## WY 14.16
### William C. Rickel House (Westheight Manor Historic District)
*1919. Louis S. Curtiss*
*2000 Washington Boulevard*

The one-story tile-roofed stucco residence displays many stylistic features characteristic of the architect's later residential work, including geometric screens and broad eaves supported on decorative brackets. The building is carefully adapted to its site, and the open porch commands a panoramic view from its position at the crest of a hill above an irregular street intersection.

## WY 14.17
### Westheight Court (Westheight Manor Historic District)
*1924. Edward Buehler Delk*
*Twenty-fourth Street and Nebraska Avenue*

This group of nine houses surrounds a central common pedestrian mews at the ter-mination of Nebraska Avenue; automobile access is from a ring road behind the houses. Each of the modest two-story stucco houses is unique although they share a similar character. The project seems to have been inspired by the work of English architects involved with the Garden Cities Movement, such as Barry Parker and Raymond Unwin.

## WY 14.18
### Wyandotte High School*
*1934–1937*
*Hamilton, Fellows & Nedved, and Joseph W. Radotinsky*
*2500 Minnesota*

This large high school is organized along two parallel classroom wings, connected at the center and at the ends by an auditorium and a gymnasium. The pale stone trim on the red brick facades is carefully detailed in a modified Gothic/Moorish mode. The sculptor Emil Robert Zettler collaborated on the ornamentation. The building, which sits diagonally to the facing intersection, is integrated into a comprehensive site design prepared by the landscape architects Hare & Hare.

## WY 14.19
### Old Fire Station no. 9*
*1910. William E. Harris*
*2 South Fourteenth Street*

Exhibiting a curious display of ornament, this playful building combines Classical,

Tudor, and Prairie Style motifs. The result is comparable to the work of the Scandinavian National Romantic movement. The fireman gargoyles recall those of Geselius Lundgren and Saarinen's Pohjola Insurance building in Helsinki. The structure was reworked to become a neighborhood center and the renovation praised in the November 1979 issue of *Progressive Architecture*.

WY 14.20
## St. Peter's Catholic Church
*1924–1927. Henry W. Brinkman*
*414 North Grandview Boulevard*

This large Gothic Revival stone church sits atop a hill in a small-scaled residential neighborhood. It is distinguished by a skillfully articulated and vertically oriented semi-attached bell tower capped by a tall, roofed lantern. The church became the cathedral of the Archdiocese of Kansas City in 1948.

WY 14.21
## St. Joseph's Catholic Church
*1916/1921. Henry W. Brinkman*
*811 Vermont Avenue*

The church, occupying a corner of a steeply sloping site, is an inventive and skillful adaptation of Renaissance and Classical Revival styles. A pair of tiled hipped-roofed towers flanks a grand arched portal set in the gable end of the nave. The elements of the dark brick building are bound together by a bold stone entablature set at the eave line.

The church was built to serve the area's community of Polish immigrants.

WY 14.22
## Church of the Holy Family
*1925–1927. Henry W. Brinkman*
*Sixth Street and Ohio Avenue*

A triangular park forms an effective fore-court to the church, whose design recalls the Romanesque Revival tradition through its massing and details: a triple-arched door-way, a large rose window, and an arched cor-beled brick cornice. The square tower, which is capped by an octagonal lantern, continues the feeling. The building's care-fully developed proportions and skillfully wrought details give it a pleasing sense of repose. It was built to serve the area's com-munity of Slovenian immigrants.

## WY 14.23
### Wellborn Villa
*1974. Robert Edward Sixta*
*5122 Leavenworth Road*

A housing project for elderly residents, Wellborn Villa consists of five similar circu-lar buildings placed stair-fashion on a ter-raced hillside. Each building consists of six-teen small pie-shaped apartments arranged around a central, common garden. The buildings represent a thoughtful approach to the problem of communal housing; they create a hierarchical series of spaces that pro-vide residents with a sense of both privacy and identity while supporting social inter-action.

## WY 14.24
### Memorial White Church✦
*1904. William W. Rose*
*2200 North Eighty-fifth Street*

This modest gabled stone church is entered on the long side through a squat hipped-roofed tower. It contains striking stained-glass windows. The church is the third built on the site of a Methodist mission to the Delaware Indians established in 1832. The architect was the most prominent and pro-lific in the city from the late nineteenth through the early twentieth century. He be-gan his practice in 1886 with James O. Hogg and then worked on his own from 1893 to 1907, when he joined with David B. Peter-son for the final twenty years of his career.

## WY 14.25
### West Wyandotte Branch Library
*1986. Buchanan Architects & Associates*
*1731 North Eighty-second Street*

The exuberance of the building reflects a renewed acceptance of an expressive and ex-perimental approach to architecture. It is composed of a complex series of forms deco-rated with an eclectic mix of shapes and tex-tures. Rounded forms intersect with angular elements, arched windows contrast with voids formed between parallel protruding walls, and horizontal rounded raised-brick banding is interrupted by metal fascia pan-els. The interior spaces are equally frag-mented.

## WY 14.26
### Grinter Place*
*1857*
*1420 South Seventy-eighth Street*

The house (in the Muncie area of the city), built of brick from clay on the site, lime from the surrounding hills for the mortar, and wood hauled from Leavenworth, sits high on a hill above the site of the first ferry across the Kansas River, which was established by Moses Grinter in 1831. The house follows the Georgian I-plan of vernacular tradition and consists of a pair of rooms on each of the two levels arranged symmetrically about a central stair hall. Grinter is credited as being the first permanent white settler in Kansas, and the house is the oldest unaltered one in the county. It is maintained as a museum by the Kansas State Historical Society.

## WY 14.27
## Anthony Sauer Castle*
*1871*
*945 Shawnee Drive*

This tall Italianate villa sits amid generous but untended grounds on a bluff overlooking the Kansas River valley; its isolated and decrepit appearance would seem to invite visitors from the hereafter. The house was

built by a German immigrant who established a tannery in Kansas City. Materials for the house were brought from St. Louis, and many of the interior furnishings were imported from Europe. It stands as a monument to the affluence of the trading community. A traditional attribution to the pioneer architect of Kansas City, Missouri, Asa Beebe Cross, lacks documentation.

## WY 14.28
## Shawnee Street Overpass*
*1932–1934*
*Over the Seventh Street Trafficway, at Shawnee Street*

This bridge supports Shawnee Street as it runs along the crest of a high knoll overlooking the Kansas River from the south, where the Seventh Street Trafficway cuts through to cross the river. It is supported on a pair of graceful steel arches that spring from the exposed rock cliffs on either side of the cut.

## WY 14.29
## George Rushton Baking Company♦
*1919. Ernest O. Brostrom*
*814 Southwest Boulevard*

The building is a good example of the commercial application of the Prairie Style; unfortunately, key features have been altered. Sculpture by the Kansas City artist Jorgen C. Dryer has been removed, and a curious wood-shingled mansard roof has been added at the entry. The architect continued to do progressive work into the mid-century. A similar but better preserved example of his interpretation of the Prairie Style is the 1918 Jensen-Salsbery Laboratories in Kansas City, Missouri.

## WY 14.30
### Rosedale World War I Memorial Arch*

*1923. John Leroy Marshall*
*Mt. Marty Park (near Booth and Drexel)*

This Classic stone triumphal arch sits atop a north-facing outcropping, high above the south banks of the Kansas River. The plaza surrounding the base of the arch was completed in 1974 and provides an excellent vista down the river valley to downtown Kansas City, Missouri. Lighting around the base makes the monument highly visible in the evening.

## WY 14.31
### Judge Louis Gates Residence*

*1922. Clarence E. Shepard*
*4246 Cambridge*

The house represents an interesting interpretation of the Prairie Style initiated by Frank Lloyd Wright in suburban Chicago during the first decade of the twentieth century. Although the composition and detail of the residence are derivative of this style, the formal massing is more vertical and compact. By the time the house was constructed, interest in the Prairie Style had begun to wane. The architect worked comfortably in a variety of styles, and he designed more than 600 houses for the J. C. Nichols Company.

## WY 14.32
### J. C. Harmon High School

*1974. Marshall & Brown*
*2400 Steele Road*

The building is representative of the Brutalist aesthetic, which is characterized by the domestication of the industrial vernacular. Black-painted steel-framed window elements, delicate and carefully detailed, contrast sharply to more massive forms enclosed in eight-inch-by-eight-inch dark brown block walls. The contrasting elements articulate a clearly ordered plan in which the L-shaped two-story classroom block wraps around the larger common spaces: the gymnasium and the cafeteria. The steel-framed elements mark the circulation corridors that link the other units. The building is similar in character to others by the same architects, including the Shawnee Mission Northwest High School (JO 12.04), the Johnson County Community College (JO 10.14), and the Penn Valley Community College in Kansas City, Missouri.

# Northeast Region

The Northeast Region contains two different landforms divided almost equally by the valley of the Kansas River. The northern half consists of round hills and broad valleys formed by glacial action; the southern half is part of the terrain known as the Osage Cuestas, a physiography consisting of hills or ridges whose eastern slopes are steeper than the western and in which ample limestone is found. Originally, the area of the Northeast Region carried a patchwork cover consisting of bluestem prairie and an oak-hickory forest. Near the Missouri River, however, where it defines the far northeastern corner of the state, the forest predominated, as the prairie did in the region's northwestern quadrant. Well watered by rains and with numerous streams, the area encompassed by the Northeast Region early on proved attractive and accessible to both farmers and town builders.

In the early years of the nineteenth century the principal occupants of the region were the Kansa Indians, but beginning in 1825 the federal government negotiated treaties requiring them (and the Osage farther south) to cede land, which then was divided into reservations to accommodate the eastern tribes who were being forced to leave their homelands. On the new reservations various Christian denominations soon established missions, an activity confined almost entirely to the Northeast Region and with sites located fairly close to the Missouri line. Although some of the missions were short-lived, others existed for several decades, and a few became the rootstock from which towns later grew, such as Ottawa and Highland in Franklin and Doniphan counties.

With the establishment of Kansas Territory in 1854, new treaties were negotiated with the Indians that further constricted their landholdings. As white settlement increased, the Native Americans were slowly but steadily forced once again to emigrate, this time to the south on land that eventually became Oklahoma. Today, only three small reservations remain in Kansas; all are in the Northeast Region, in Brown and Jackson counties. Though most of the new settlers tended to locate on farms, others were interested in organizing towns, and Atchison, Leavenworth, Topeka, and Lawrence were established. Meanwhile, counties were being organized in the eastern third of Kansas Territory. The earlier status as Indian Territory influenced the selection of many place names in Kansas, which in the Northeast

Region include Shawnee, Miami, and Osage (counties) and Topeka, Ottawa, and Osawatomie (cities).

Today the twelve counties of the region contain approximately 465,000 people, of whom 66 percent reside in but three (Shawnee, Douglas, and Leavenworth) and then primarily in the largest cities of the region: Topeka (120,000), Lawrence (67,500), and Leavenworth (38,500). The next three in rank are Emporia (25,500), Ottawa (10,700), and Atchison (10,700). The six cities contribute significantly to the diversified economy of the region, which also includes a considerable agricultural component.

A special characteristic of the region, relative to the rest of the state, is the comparatively large number of institutions of higher education: three public universities, four private universities/colleges, a public junior college, and the federally funded Haskell Indian Nations University (formerly Haskell Indian Institute). Another regional asset is Topeka's status as the state's capital city. In addition, Fort Leavenworth and the two penitentiaries in Leavenworth County—one federal, the other state—are important to the area's economy, as is the role of Shawnee and Douglas counties as important centers of manufacturing within the state.

Five of the six largest cities in the region are also among the oldest in the state; thus, their early histories were strongly affected by the intense controversy generated by the issue of whether Kansas would be admitted to the Union as a free or slave state. Proponents of slavery had established the towns of Atchison and Leavenworth, but free staters organized Lawrence, Topeka, and Emporia. Opponents of slavery eventually became dominant in the territory, ensuring the approval of a constitution that made Kansas a free state when it entered the Union in 1861. By that time, however, bitter conflict over the slavery issue had generated much bloodshed. Lawrence was besieged in 1856 and then attacked by proslavery forces. Both factions engaged in other acts of violence, which spread into Missouri where the citizenry was deeply split, especially through the years of the Civil War. Inevitably the war affected Kansas, and many men joined the Union army. The most memorable episode associated with the war, however, is the attack on Lawrence in April 1863 by Quantrill's guerrillas, when 150 male citizens were killed and much of the town burned.

Lawrence (Douglas County), founded in 1854 by the New England Emigrant Aid Company, quickly became the center for free-state activities in Kansas, a factor that made it an attractive target for Quantrill. Located on the south side of the Kansas River and about forty miles west of Kansas City, Lawrence managed to recover from the raid, helped by the arrival of railroad service in 1864, and then by being selected as the seat for the state university, where enrollment started in 1866. The university is located on and around Mt. Oread, a prominent hill approximately two miles southwest of the historic core of Lawrence.

The campus grew steadily over the years and thus contains good examples of the various architectural styles that were popular in the state, such as the Richardsonian Romanesque (DG 08.06). The area between the central business district and the campus contains one of the city's oldest residential neighborhoods, where one will find many fine and well-preserved examples of late-nineteenth-century houses. Among them are several of the few surviving residences designed by the prolific pioneer Kansas architect, John Haskell, including his own house (DG 08.01). He came to Lawrence in 1857 and practiced there and in Topeka until his death in 1907.

The University of Kansas has been an extremely important stimulus in the growth and overall development of Lawrence, whose economy has become increasingly diversified, especially since 1960. Another contributing influence to that growth came from the construction of the Kansas Turnpike (1954–1956) and the later reconstruction of Kansas 10 as a limited-access freeway (1980s). The former brought Lawrence closer (in time) to Topeka as well as to the expanding Kansas City Metropolitan Area, growth assisted by the K 10 freeway. The increase in the ease of travel has encouraged more people to commute to and from Lawrence since only thirty to sixty minutes are needed to reach most destinations, undoubtedly a convenience that contributed to Lawrence's becoming the fifth largest city in the state.

Like other communities that have grown significantly in recent decades, Lawrence has experienced strip development, notably to the south and west along Twenty-third and Iowa streets. The city, however, has resisted the development of a major suburban shopping mall, and thus its traditional central business district along Massachusetts Street has remained viable while also preserving much of its historic character (e.g. DG 08.18).

Leavenworth's developmental history is quite different. The fort on the west bank of the Missouri River came first. Established in 1827 to provide protection to traders from Indian raids, Fort Leavenworth's responsibilities grew to include protecting the growing numbers of people emigrating westward. It then played important roles in the war with Mexico and during the Civil War. An active army base, the fort has been the home of the Army Command and General Staff College since 1881. Various buildings at the fort, including a portion of the U.S. Disciplinary Barracks, are historically significant (see LV 16.01).

Immediately south of the fort is the city of Leavenworth (Leavenworth County), organized and platted in 1854. The city's early years were marred by fraudulent voting and political violence generated by the free or slave controversy, in which the proslavery faction predominated, including Missourians who openly participated. The free staters finally became a majority in 1861, by which time the town had a population of nearly 8,000, making it the largest in the state.

A major boost for the town's economy came from the decision of the Russell, Majors and Waddell transportation company to make Leavenworth its headquarters in 1856. Their overland freighting and stage operation was the nation's largest, and it carried people, supplies, and mail for both the army and the general public while serving as the principal link to the west until the completion of telegraph and railroad lines displaced the company. Even so, Leavenworth's prosperity and growth continued well into the 1880s. By then, however, Missouri's Kansas City had become the region's largest commercial center and thus drew merchants away from Leavenworth and other locales.

By 1900 Leavenworth had dropped to sixth place among the cities of Kansas and by 1990 was eighth, a decline that partially reflects forces affecting the status of all units in the collective that constitutes the Kansas City Metropolitan Area (see pp. 27–33). Nevertheless, Leavenworth has maintained a distinctive character, for it retains many aspects of its storied past, including a substantial inventory of nineteenth-century buildings (e.g., LV 17.08, 17.13, and 17.15). The downtown district is on lower terrain near the Missouri River, having followed the course of Three Mile Creek to the river. Overlooking downtown and the river and its lowlands to the east are the city's suburbs on the high bluffs that reach to the north and south.

Though the development of both Leavenworth and Lawrence in recent years reflect influences stemming from their proximity to the multinodal Kansas City metroplex, Atchison and Ottawa are much less affected, being some twenty-five miles further removed—Atchison north of Leavenworth and Ottawa south of Lawrence.

Atchison (Atchison County), like Leavenworth, is centered on a tributary to the Missouri River, in this case White Clay Creek; similarly, portions of the city stretch north and south along high bluffs overlooking the Missouri River. Atchison became incorporated in 1855 though settlers began arriving as early as 1850. The town secured an important developmental asset when the Atchison Topeka and Santa Fe Railroad finished the track between Topeka and Atchison in 1872, making the latter the line's eastern terminus. That achievement provided an industrial base for the small city and helped its continued growth into the 1880s, after which it settled into comfortable stability. A number of older mansions still grace the community and document the city's late-nineteenth-century prosperity, such as a group on North Fourth Street (AT 01.11, 01.12, and 01.13). Though well known for its Victorian architecture, later developments merit notice, such as a church by Barry Byrne

(AT 01.15) on the campus of Benedictine College (established in 1858). A rather different example is the (mid-1960s) conversion of three blocks of downtown's Commercial Street into a pedestrian mall (AT 01.05). Representative of a once popular planning concept, shopping malls of that type have tended not to flourish in our increasingly automobile-dependent society.

Ottawa (Franklin County) is another case of a city that retains a strong historical presence while incorporating the inevitable changes and additions more modern needs require. The city's origin and subsequent development, however, are quite different from Atchison's. In Ottawa's case we begin with the arrival in 1832 of the Ottawa Indians, who were forced to leave Ohio, and the Baptist mission established five years later to serve them. In 1860 some lay persons chartered a university to serve the population, a project that became feasible only after the Ottawa gave the trustees a sizable gift of land to ensure the education of the tribe's children. Instruction began in 1866, but the following year the Ottawa once again were forced to exchange what remained of their lands in Kansas for holdings elsewhere, this time in Oklahoma. That treaty effectively opened the entire area to white settlement.

Not until the arrival of railroad service in 1868 did the town site (surveyed in 1864) undergo development. Located on the Marais des Cygnes River, Ottawa's growth is documented in the commercial architecture along several blocks of Main Street, which runs south from the river crossing. Many of the buildings are now listed on the National Register (e.g., FR 10.08). An important influence on the architectural character of the city came from the prominent pioneer Kansas architect, George P. Washburn, who after the Civil War settled in Ottawa. A number of the firm's buildings still serve the city, such as the county courthouse (FR 10.06). His practice extended into the twentieth century and then was continued by his son and son-in-law. Another important but quite different influence has come from the continued presence of the Baptist-affiliated Ottawa University, whose original building, Tuay Jones Hall, dates to 1866–1869 (FR 10.01).

Emporia (Lyon County), another university community, was founded in 1857 by Free Staters. The city's development came after railroad service began in 1869. By 1878 Emporia, whose location is close to midway between Topeka and Wichita, had become an important crossroads city, a status it retained after World War II by becoming the interchange point between the Kansas Turnpike and Interstate 35, which skirts the city to the north. A conjunction of major freeways today represents an important economic asset for any city, analogous to becoming an important railroad center in the nineteenth century. Another asset of consequence for the city is Emporia State University (a Regents Institution), which grew out of the Kansas State Normal School founded in 1873. The university anchors the north end of

Commercial Street, the city's main street that runs south to the Cottonwood River, ending in Soden's Grove Park. Other important contributions to Emporia's economy come from manufacturing and agriculturally related industry.

Though less richly endowed with choice examples of nineteenth-century architecture than either Lawrence or Atchison, Emporia contains several notable buildings by the gifted architect Charles W. Squires, such as the Soden House (LY 18.02) and the Anderson Memorial Library (LY 18.15). Squires practiced in the city from 1879 until his death in 1934. Another active architect who made his home in Emporia, Henry Brinkman, began his practice in 1907. The firm continued into the 1970s, led by his partner Stanley Hagan and Brinkman's son, Jerome. Although best known for their ecclesiastical structures throughout the state, especially Catholic churches, they did produce other types of buildings, such as the Lyon County Courthouse (LY 18.05). Another aspect of Emporia's architectural heritage has been recognized through the 1991 selection of the city for participation in the National Trust's Main Street Program.

Although each of the major cities of the region has individual and distinctive qualities, Topeka (Shawnee County) stands out as a truly special case, for it is the capital of Kansas. Its population of 120,000 makes Topeka the state's third largest city, after Wichita and Kansas City. Located thirty miles west of Lawrence, the site of Topeka received its first settlers in 1842, when two French-Canadians established a ferry on the Kansas River at the place where the Oregon Trail crossed. The city, however, was not founded until 1855, when some New Englanders chose the location as being suitable for a railroad center. The city's core runs south from the Kansas River and consists of a street grid oriented to the cardinal points. Topeka's future, however, became certain only when it was chosen by election to be the young state's capital city, an action taken in November 1861.

Topeka grew fairly rapidly after the conclusion of the Civil War, and like many other cities it experienced a major real estate boom of several years during the 1880s. In Topeka's case the boom ended in 1889, but by then construction on the capitol was approaching completion. Work on it had begun in 1866 and had progressed one wing at a time, with the domed rotunda to connect them bringing the project to completion in 1903. The capitol (SN 26.13), which is situated on spacious grounds immediately west of downtown Topeka, is a handsomely detailed traditional building. Among the many decorations, the best known are the murals by John Steuart Curry. Titled *Tragic Prelude,* which refers to the bloody controversy over whether Kansas would enter the Union as a free or slave state, the panel featuring a gigantic figure of John Brown is a dramatic focal point.

In addition to the capitol, a number of historically significant buildings from the nineteenth century still stand in Topeka, notably a group dating to 1888: the Thatcher Building (SN 26.15), the Davies Building (SN 26.17), the Columbian Block (SN 26.22), and the Crawford Block (SN 26.23). Most of the city's fabric is of a later date, however. Though Topeka's economy is significantly fueled by its role as the capital city, other resources contribute, such as the shops and facilities maintained by the Santa Fe Railroad. Furthermore, Topeka is home to the nationally known Menninger Clinic as well as to several interesting museums and historic sites, such as the Kansas State Historical Museum (SN 26.35) and the Ward-Meade House and Park (SN 26.29). Another important asset is Washburn University, which had its origin in a denominational college established in 1865; later it became nonsectarian and eventually a municipally supported institution.

Topeka's growth has been directed primarily west and south, filling the area between Interstate 70, which follows the Kansas River on the north, and Interstate 470/U.S. 75 that provides a link within the city between the western exit of Interstate 70 and the southern exit of the Kansas Turnpike. The area contains a number of significant landscape developments, including the 146-acre Gage Park and Zoo, the Potwin Place Historic District (SN 26.30), the State Fairgrounds (SN 26.03), the State Hospital (SN 26.31), Washburn University (SN 26.02), the Menninger Foundation Campus (SN 26.32), and the grounds of Cedar Crest, the governor's mansion (SN 26.33).

Although much of the region's most significant architecture will be found in its six largest cities, other sites are important. The regional map and directory locate the counties, cities, and towns and provide an outline for the sequence of the catalog entries for the region.

# NORTHEAST REGION

Alpha-Numeric Directory

**ATCHISON (AT)**

  **01** Atchison†

**BROWN (BR)**

  **02** Hiawatha†

**DONIPHAN (DP)**

  **03** Highland

  **04** Troy†

  **05** White Cloud

**DOUGLAS (DG)**

  **06** Baldwin City

  **07** Eudora

  **08** Lawrence†

  **09** Lecompton

**FRANKLIN (FR)**

  **10** Ottawa†

**JACKSON (JA)**

  **11** Holton†

  **12** Whiting

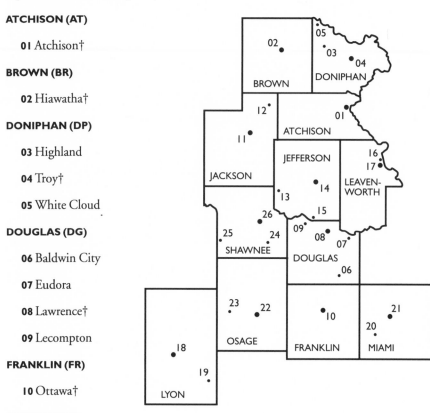

**JEFFERSON (JF)**

  **13** Meriden

  **14** Oskaloosa†

  **15** Williamstown

**LEAVENWORTH (LV)**

  **16** Fort Leavenworth

  **17** Leavenworth†

**LYON (LY)**

  **18** Emporia†

  **19** Hartford

**MIAMI (MI)**

  **20** Osawatomie

  **21** Paola†

**OSAGE (OS)**

  **22** Lyndon†

  **23** Osage City

**SHAWNEE (SN)**

  **24** Berryton

  **25** Dover

  **26** Topeka†

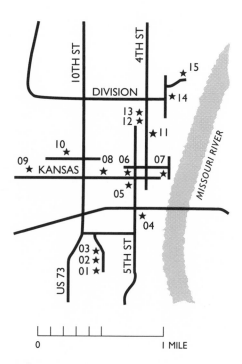

Atchison

# Atchison

## AT 01.01
### Mount St. Scholastica Convent*
*1901*
*801 South Eighth Street*

This U-shaped three-story simplified Romanesque Revival structure of red brick provides an anchor to the connected series of buildings that form the south campus of Benedictine College. The building accommodates dormitory facilities for the Benedictine Sisters and a small chapel. Its most distinctive feature is a robustly ornamented bell tower at an inside corner of the entry courtyard.

## AT 01.02
### Mount St. Scholastica Chapel
*1938. Brielmaier & Son*
*801 South Eighth Street*

The chapel, a rather understated limestone church, sits between the Mount St. Scholas-

tica Convent on one side and the Price Villa on the other. It is more impressive on the interior. The grandly scaled nave is covered by a round arched vault and is flanked by side aisles separated from the nave by a series of arches supported on massive marble columns. The focus of the space is a domed baldachino above the altar. The overall impression is one of solemn grandeur.

## AT 01.03
### Price Villa*
*1872. Thomas Wise*
*801 South Eight Street*

This three-story Victorian house provides a striking juxtaposition of scale to its two near neighbors, the Mount St. Scholastica Chapel and a four-story Neoclassical classroom building. The later buildings considerably diminish the villa's once commanding hilltop presence. Erected by a local attorney, the building was sold five years later to the convent; it now houses the music department of Benedictine College.

## AT 01.04

### Trinity Episcopal Church*

*1867*

*300 South Fifth Street*

One of the oldest buildings in Atchison, this simple Gothic stone church faces the south bank of White Clay Creek, a Missouri River tributary that bisects the city. Built from locally available materials, the building was modeled after a church designed by the noted New York ecclesiastical architect, Richard Upjohn. A number of his churches are illustrated in *Upjohn's Rural Architecture* (1852).

## AT 01.05

### The Mall

*1963–1964. Louis J. Krueger*

*Commercial Street between Fourth and Sixth streets*

A mixture of buildings, including one-story Modern commercial structures, line what was once the principal retail street in the city but reconformed for pedestrian use by converting the roadway to an irregular, grassy, tree-filled median between the sidewalks. Built in the wake of the flooding that occurred in the downtown area in 1958, the scheme remains an interesting example of a brief period when the creation of such malls became popular in the nation in an attempt to help merchants in traditional downtown districts to compete more effectively with the strip shopping centers being erected on

the periphery of towns. Unfortunately, here and elsewhere the strategy did not succeed very well. Another example is located in Parsons, in Labette County.

## AT 01.06

### Atchison County Courthouse*

*1896–1897. George P. Washburn*

*Fifth and Parallel*

Four corner towers anchor this sturdy three-story ashlar limestone Romanesque building to its sloping site on the northern edge of the downtown district. The interior has been remodeled, but a number of interesting details remain.

## AT 01.07

### Earhart House*

*1861*

*223 North Terrace*

This two-story Carpenter Gothic structure sits atop a steep bluff overlooking a great bend in the Missouri River. It is of interest as an example of the houses designed with the aid of pattern books popular in the mid-nineteenth century, such as Andrew Jackson Downing's *Cottage Residences* (1842). More significantly, the house is the birthplace of the pioneer aviator, Amelia Earhart. The Frank Howard house* (1890) at 305 North Terrace also merits attention.

## AT 01.08
### Atchison Post Office*

*1892–1894*
*Willoughby J. Edbrooke and George H. Evans*
*621 Kansas*

A two-story Romanesque building of cottonwood limestone, the post office occupies a prominent position in the downtown district. The structure's central block is surrounded by a one-story element, anchored at the southern corners by round towers with conical roofs. The building's prominence reflects the importance of Atchison as a distribution terminus for trade with the western portion of the country in the latter half of the nineteenth century. Renovations have compromised much of the building's interior architectural character.

## AT 01.09
### McInteer Villa*

*1889–1890*
*1301 Kansas*

This fantastic brick Victorian house occupies a commanding position on a hill to

the west of the downtown district. The roofscape of the house is of particular note, featuring an intersecting array of distinctive turrets and gables. The home was built by John McInteer, an Irish immigrant who made his fortune supplying harnesses to the lucrative overland trading companies, which operated out of Atchison between the opening of the West and the coming of the railroads.

## AT 01.10
### Harwi House*

*1882–1886*
*1103 Atchison*

The two-story brick Victorian home looks down on the central portion of the city to the southeast. Its exterior stone trim and interior cherry woodwork displays a variety of popular decorative motifs. Its most distinctive feature, however, is an octagonal tower roof capped by a tall lantern that springs from its front bay. It was built by A. J. Harwi, a wholesale hardware merchant. Despite its relatively poor condition and the removal of its wraparound front porch, the building is of interest as a demonstration of the ingenuity of late-nineteenth-century builders.

## AT 01.11
### H. E. Muchnic House*
*1887–1888. W. F. Wood*
*704 North Fourth Street*

Part of a district filled with large, fashionable homes of the late nineteenth century, this two-story brick house borrows from a variety of Victorian decorative traditions. Its most distinctive exterior feature is a corner turret, which springs from a lower-level porch framed in elaborately carved woodwork, capped by a tall, conical roof above another open porch that extends from the roof. The interior also features a number of interesting details, such as the parquet floors, carved woodwork, cast-bronze hardware, and stained-glass windows. The building now houses a gallery. Other houses worthy of note in this district include the

(1864–1894) Glancy-Pennell House* at 519 North Fifth Street, which now houses a restaurant, and the (1882) W. W. Hetherington House,* designed by Alfred Meier and John Peterson, with a tower added later; it is now a museum.

## AT 01.12
### J. Patrick Brown House*
*1880*
*805 North Fourth Street*

This picturesque two-story brick home illustrates the flexibility of the Victorian approach to design. A porch with Queen Anne influences is combined with a window and wall treatment reflective of Gothic influences and with an eave and roof treatment suggesting Italianate influences.

## AT 01.13
### B. P. Waggener House*
*1886. H. R. Prudden*
*819 North Fourth Street*

A striking two-story brick house, the residence is a work of apparently deliberate originality. Typical Victorian decorative motifs are distorted in scale and proportion and are juxtaposed in jarring fashion. The disturbing and arresting quality of the house culminates in the dragonlike finials that watch over the composition from their rooftop perches. A similar architectural treatment is extended to a large carriage house at the rear of the site.

B. P. Waggener house

AT 01.14
## St. Benedict's Parish Church*

*1865–1871 (towers added in 1891 and 1905)*
*Francis Himpler*
*Second and Division streets*

This Romanesque brick church is the south-western element of Benedictine College North Campus Historic Complex* and is preserved in its original state. A pair of substantial towers flank the main entry, and inside the tall, arched nave is separated from the side aisles by a row of arches set on distinctive columns. The church is reminiscent of those found in western Germany. The well-landscaped grounds of the campus occupy a bluff overlooking the Missouri River to the east.

AT 01.15
## St. Benedict's Abbey Church (Benedictine College North Campus)

*1957. Barry Byrne*

The modern limestone church is located in the heart of the campus. A guest house, also designed by the same architect and completed a year later, connects the building to the monastery, which was built between 1926 and 1929 and designed by Brielmaier & Son (Milwaukee). The strong geometric shapes of the church complex complement the forms of the Gothic monastery. The interior is noteworthy for its surprising sense of spaciousness. Barry Byrne is best known for his work done early in the century in the office of Frank Lloyd Wright. He later designed a number of Catholic churches, including St. Francis Xavier in Kansas City, Missouri.

# Hiawatha

**BR 02.01**
## Yost Block
*1905*
*805 West Oregon*

This two-story brick commercial structure is an interesting variant on a common building type. It is distinguished by a central cast-iron bay that protrudes well out over the sidewalk and supports a hipped-roofed tower.

**BR 02.02**
## Brown County Courthouse
*1925–1926. W. E. Hulse*
*Courthouse Square*

The courthouse, a three-story Neoclassical building of variegated limestone, occupies the center of a square in the midst of the business district. It reflects the prevailing

taste in civic architecture during the early 1920s. With minor exceptions, the building remains much as it was at the time of construction.

**BR 02.03**
## Davis Memorial*
*1932–1947*
*Mount Hope Cemetery*

Arranged inside a half-wall and beneath a stone-slab roof, this curious monument consists of eleven life-sized figures depicting a local farmer, John W. Davis, and his wife Sarah, at various stages of their lives. Ten of the figures are of marble and were made in Italy; the remaining statue, of granite, was made in Vermont. The memorial was constructed by Davis in honor of his wife, who died in 1930. The final statue depicts Davis's devotion to his spouse; he is shown late in life seated adjacent to an empty chair.

# Highland

### DP 03.01
## Iowa, Sac, and Fox Presbyterian Mission*

*1846*

*K 136 (1.5 miles east of Highland)*

This rectangular gable-roofed three-story building is the eastern portion of the original 106-foot-long mission building. The lower story was built of local stone, the upper stories from brick fired on site; other materials were imported from the East. The mission operated from 1837 until the mid-1860s but was never fully successful in its effort to educate the Indians in the ways of white society or to convert them to Christianity. The building now houses a state-operated museum.

### DP 03.02
## Irvin Hall (Highland Community Junior College)*

*1858*

*On U.S. 36*

The two-story red-brick building was erected as part of the earliest institution of higher learning in the state, Highland University (chartered in 1857). The simple rectangular building is distinguished by raised

pilasters and a small cupola near one end. It is being renovated by the Highland Community Junior College.

### DP 03.03
## Highland Christian Church

*1904*

*Kansas and Main streets*

A single-story L-shaped building, the church is accented by an entry tower that intersects one corner of the main body of the building. The church displays an interesting mix of stylistic features, including light-colored brick quoins that contrast strongly with the dark brick of the adjacent wall, a variety of arched openings, and shingled end-gables, one of which contains a round rose window.

. . . . . . . . . . . . . . . . . . . . . . . . . . . . . . .

# Troy

### DP 04.01
## Doniphan County Courthouse*

*1905–1906. George P. Washburn & Son*

*Walnut and Main streets*

The three-story courthouse of red brick with limestone trim occupies a full block in the center of the business district. Like many of the nine courthouses in the state designed by the architect in the late nineteenth and early twentieth centuries, the building features turrets at each corner and a taller central cupola. Anderson County Courthouse, built four years earlier, is similar.

. . . . . . . . . . . . . . . . . . . . . . . . . . . . . . . .

# White Cloud

**DP 05.01**
## Poulet House*
*1878*
*Poplar Street (between First and Second streets)*

The two-story Italianate brick residence perches precariously on a bluff above this small town on the Missouri River. Built by Alexis Poulet, a banker, the building is a reminder of the profitability of the river trade before the rise of the railroads.

**DP 05.02**
## White Cloud School*
*1872–1873*
*Fifth and Main streets*

The school, a two-story Italianate red-brick building, overlooks the remnants of a once thriving commercial district. It features stone-segmented arched lintels above its windows, doubled brackets supporting a wide eave, a projected pedimented central entry bay, and a bell tower atop the center of its hipped roof. The building now houses a museum.

# Baldwin City

### DG 06.01
### Dilges Barn
*1906*
*U.S. 56 (six miles west of Baldwin City)*

Copied from an earlier barn in Nebraska, this gambrel-roofed wooden barn is typical of many in the region. It was built using hand-hewn eight-by-eight-inch beams and wooden-peg connections.

### DG 06.02
### Santa Fe Depot*
*1907*
*Office of the Architect, Atchison and Santa Fe Railroad. 1601 High Street*

This hipped-roofed brick train depot is the only remaining station along the Leavenworth, Lawrence and Ft. Gibson Line, which was laid down in 1867. The building is now used as a community center.

### DG 06.03
### Parmenter Hall (Baker University)*
*1866–1881*
*Eighth and Dearborn*

The four-story Second Empire classroom building is the earliest of a series of stone buildings that surround a grove of mature trees in the center of the campus. Parmenter Hall was constructed slowly, as funding allowed. The initial phase of construction took six years, and the tower was added ten years later. Until it opened, classes for the state's oldest four-year college were held in the Old Castle, which was built in 1858. The latter has served a variety of uses and now houses a museum.

. . . . . . . . . . . . . . . . . . . . . . . . . . . . . . . .

# Eudora

### DG 07.01
### Kaw Valley State Bank
*1899*
*Seventh and Main streets*

The bank, a two-story red-brick building, anchors the town's most prominent intersection. The patterned relief in the brickwork and the classical portico at the corner entry are of particular interest.

. . . . . . . . . . . . . . . . . . . . . . . . . . . . . . . . .

# Lawrence

### DG 08.01
### John G. Haskell House
*1866–1867 (remodeled 1892). John G. Haskell*
*1340 Haskell Avenue*

John Haskell, a native of New England and a graduate of Wesleyan Academy, became one of Kansas' premier early architects. He designed this house for his own use, and it is representative of his rather eclectic preferences in design. He came to Kansas and established his architectural firm in 1857. For the next fifty years he designed governmental, commercial, religious, and residential structures in many parts of the state, particularly around Lawrence and Topeka. The state capitol, the hospital in Topeka, and the Industrial Reformatory in Hutchinson were among his largest commissions.

### DG 08.02
### Hiawatha Hall (Haskell Indian Nations University)*
*1898. John G. Haskell*
*Twenty-third and Barker Avenue*

Twin towers of differing heights and a grandly scaled arched window give a sense of presence to this simply detailed gabled stone building. It is the oldest remaining building among the loose assemblage of structures that form the campus (a National Historic Landmark originally known as Haskell Institute). The other distinctive structure on the campus is a 17,000-seat football stadium. The institute was established in 1884 to educate Native Americans in "the white man's ways," but as student needs changed so did the school's mission. Hiawatha Hall has proven to be an adaptable structure and has housed a variety of functions.

### DG 08.03
### Reuben Luddington House (Maupin-McCaskey Residence)*
*1870. John G. Haskell (attrib.)*
*1613 Tennessee*

This grand two-story L-plan Italianate brick mansion is among the most elegant of the nineteenth-century homes in Lawrence. Built by a local businessman, it symbolizes the early prosperity of the community, revealed by the fine craftsmanship on both the exterior and interior. The image of the house is dominated by a three-story entry tower featuring arched openings supported on stone lintels, stone quoins at the corners, and a wide overhanging eave supported on carved doubled brackets. The tower is set at the intersection of the L, creating an irregularly balanced silhouette. A large addition from the mid-1880s features a round domed corner turret and an elaborate wooden porte cochere. The interior contains carefully crafted cherry woodwork and gilded moldings.

# LAWRENCE

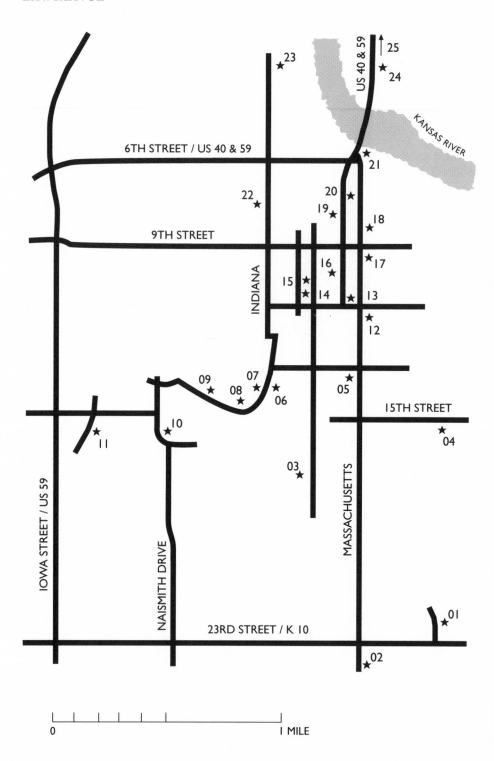

6TH STREET / US 40 & 59

9TH STREET

15TH STREET

23RD STREET / K 10

IOWA STREET / US 59

NAISMITH DRIVE

MASSACHUSETTS

INDIANA

US 40 & 59

KANSAS RIVER

0                1 MILE

## DG 08.04
## Samuel Riggs House*
*1863–1864*
*1501 Pennsylvania*

The three-story entry tower of this Italianate brick villa provides a visual terminus to the wooded southern end of Pennsylvania Street. The main block of the house consists of a single gabled mass, punctuated by window openings set beneath stone lintels of varying shapes. While under construction, the building was burned by Quantrill's raiders and had to be rebuilt.

## DG 08.05
## John N. Roberts House (the Castle)*
*1894. John G. Haskell*
*1307 Massachusetts*

The dominant feature of this massive stone home is a bulky three-story tower, which anchors the building firmly to its prominent corner site. Inside, each of the fifteen rooms is finished in a different type of wood, and each of the five fireplaces is distinctively de-

tailed in brick and marble. The building now houses a restaurant.

## DG 08.06
## Spooner Hall (University of Kansas)*
*1893–1894. Van Brunt & Howe*
*On Jayhawk Boulevard*

The Richardsonian Romanesque library building of red sandstone and limestone is the oldest remaining building on the University of Kansas campus. It is located, as are most of the other early buildings on campus, along a curving street that runs along the ridge of Mt. Oread. When it was completed, the library housed the largest collection of books in the state. The building contains a variety of spaces, including a grand reading room that occupies much of the main floor and extends into a curved space at the rear. It has proven to be adaptable: the building was later used as an art museum and now houses offices of the Department of Anthropology and its museum. The architects, who had opened their office in Kansas City, Missouri, in the mid-1880s, were a major force in architecture of the late nineteenth century. Henry Van Brunt had been trained in the New York office of Richard Morris Hunt and first received acclaim for his work in Boston with his former partner, William Ware.

## DG 08.07
## Dyche Hall (University of Kansas)*
*1901–1902. Root & Siemens*
*On Jayhawk Boulevard*

This limestone building has been identified as Venetian Romanesque, yet the arched portal entry was modeled after that of St. Trophîme in southern France. The building features elaborate carved stonework by the sculptor, Joseph Roblado Frazee, and a visually distinctive and memorable tower. It was built to house the collection of Prof. Lewis Lindsay Dyche, a leading naturalist. The design commission came as the result of a competition entered by many of the region's more notable architects. The winning architect, Walter C. Root, was the brother of the better known Chicago architect, John Wellborn Root.

### DG 08.08
### Lippincott Hall (formerly Green Hall, University of Kansas)*
*1904–1905. John F. Stanton*
*On Jayhawk Boulevard*

The three-story buff brick Neoclassical building originally housed the law school, and the monumental entry portico symbol-

izes the power and tradition of the law. The sculpture at the front of the entry depicts Dean (Uncle Jimmy) Green with one of his students and is by Daniel Chester French, who was one of the most notable sculptors in the United States at the time; among his many works is the seated Lincoln in the Lincoln Memorial in Washington, D.C.

### DG 08.09
### Strong Hall (University of Kansas)
*1904/1918/1924*
*H. P. McArdle / W. Griffith / Gamble &*
*Chandler*
*On Jayhawk Boulevard*

This grandly scaled yellow terracotta Beaux-Arts administration building anchors the center of the campus. Though a highly formal and symmetrical structure, it was built in three phases; the eastern pavilion was begun in 1904, the central section was completed in 1918, and finally the western pavilion was added in 1924. The sequence of architects reflects changes in the state architect's office.

## DG 08.10
## Murphy Hall (University of Kansas)
*1955. Brinkman & Hagan*
*Naismith Drive and Fifteenth Street*

Sprawling and informal, Murphy Hall and a group of other campus buildings of similar character were developed after World War II and extend to the south and southwest of the central portion of campus on Mt. Oread. The building's plan effectively reconciles complex site influences. Its street façade provides an appropriate zone of public entry, and its south-facing courtyard provides a focus for informal activities. The building is also representative of stylistic changes in the latter half of the twentieth century. Rather than being organized within some predetermined envelope, the various elements of the building, including a large auditorium and a smaller recital hall, are clearly and directly articulated in the building's exterior massing. Yet, despite the variety of elements and the number of materials—which include limestone, buff brick, green metal panels, and aluminum windows—the building possesses a sense of unity born of a consistent formal attitude and thus provides an illuminating example of postwar Modernism.

## DG 08.11
## Irene Nunemaker College (University of Kansas)
*1969. Kivett & Myers*
*Engel Road and Fifteenth Street*

Though this small building, with its revealed concrete structure and metal infill-panels, is dwarfed by the series of broad multistory dormitory buildings in the area, it is worthy of attention for its display of many favored motifs of the era, such as its exposed structure, diagonal entries, two-story space, and outwardly expressed stair as well as for its skillful proportions and well-resolved detailing. The building won an honor award from the Kansas City Chapter of the American Institute of Architects.

## DG 08.12
## Douglas County Courthouse*
*1903–1904*
*John G. Haskell and Frederick C. Gunn*
*Massachusetts and Eleventh Street*

This three-story limestone structure demonstrates the compositional flexibility available within the Romanesque Revival tradition. Entries through arched portals on the north and west facades lead to a central glass-covered stair hall, which in turn leads to the second-floor courtroom. The complex plan is easily accommodated within the building's sprawling irregular mass, which is accented by a six-story tower adjacent to the west entry. The design resulted from a competition organized by the county commissioners, who then suggested a collaboration between the two architects submitting the favored designs. The interior was extensively remodeled in the late 1970s and continues to serve its original function.

## DG 08.13
### Watkins National Bank*
*1887. Cobb & Frost*
*1047 Massachusetts*

The bank, a two-and-one-half-story red-brick Romanesque building, was erected by the prominent businessman Jabez B. Watkins. The lower floor housed the bank and the upper floor his primary enterprise, the J. B. Watkins Land Mortgage Company. The building's large windows, tall ceilings, and open plan have made it easily adaptable to other uses. From 1929 until 1970 the building served as the Lawrence City Hall; it now houses the Elizabeth M. Watkins Community Museum.

## DG 08.14
### Colonel James Blood House*
*1870*
*1015 Tennessee*

The most distinctive feature of this two-story Italianate residence is the elaborately detailed wood verandah, which wraps the front of the brick body of the house and contributes to a sense of importance befitting the original owner, the first mayor of Lawrence. Many of the exotic motifs of the porch could have been drawn from the pattern books that served as inspiration for several residences of the period.

## DG 08.15
### George and Annie Bell House*
*1863*
*1008 Ohio*

This modest stone home is reminiscent of many early dwellings in Lawrence. It contains two rooms per floor on each of three floors, including the one located below street level but open to a ravine at the rear. It is distinguished by the quality of workmanship of the rubble-laid limestone walls and particularly of the three-part lintels above the windows. The first owner was killed by Quantrill's raiders, reportedly while working on the house.

## DG 08.16

### Plymouth Congregational Church

*1870. John G. Haskell*
*925 Vermont*

Stylistically, the 900-seat red-brick church is difficult to classify. The architect, who was a member of the congregation and the building committee, not only must have drawn from a variety of sources, but he also prevailed on the congregation to include a number of distinctive features, invoking his often quoted dictum: "Beauty costs no more than ugliness." The particulars included stair towers flanking the sides of the main facade, which have since been removed. The building also features stained glass windows imported from England. Another smaller stone church in Lawrence designed by Haskell in the same year, the (Old) English Lutheran Church* at 1040 New Hampshire, is also worthy of note.

## DG 08.17

### Mercantile Bank
### (First National Bank)

*1969. Kivett & Myers*
*Massachusetts and Ninth Street*

This seven-story concrete and brick Modern building exemplifies the confident attitude of the time. The bank's bold geometry and crisp detailing give it a sense of abstract grace, and its honest expression of materials and structure, particularly in the lower

banking lobby wing, give it an appropriate sense of stability. The building, however, stands in sharp contrast to its otherwise harmonious small-scale surroundings.

## DG 08.18

### Barteldes Seed Company

*1865*
*804 Massachusetts*

The three-story brick commercial building fits unobtrusively in the row of storefront shops facing Lawrence's main commercial street. Although the details and proportions distinguish it from its neighbors, it represents the prevailing scale and character of many blocks of the street. The original owners, the grocers Ridenour and Baker, were among the first merchants to rebuild after Quantrill's raiders burned much of Lawrence in summer 1863. In 1888, when the grocers moved their business to Kansas City, the building was taken over by the Barteldes Seed Company.

## DG 08.19
### Lawrence Municipal Building
*1950. Louis H. Spencer*
*746 Kentucky*

This understated brick structure, characterized by shortages of materials and insatiable demand for new construction, was built to house the city's fire and police departments, though now only the former uses the building. It is reflective of the utilitarian concerns of the immediate postwar period.

## DG 08.20
### Microwave Tower
*1980. Gould Evans*
*Seventh and Vermont*

The bold geometric shapes of the brick cladding of the tower provide a welcoming beacon as one approaches Lawrence from the north. Microwave towers are beginning to compete with the ubiquitous grain elevators as the dominant vertical elements that typically mark Kansas towns.

## DG 08.21
### Fischer House*
*1860–1861. Hiram Towne (builder)*
*743 Indiana*

This two-story brick home, within the Old West Lawrence Historic District, is representative of the many well-preserved nineteenth-century residential structures in

Lawrence, still in use as such. Although relatively simple in form, both the proportions and workmanship, particularly on the surrounding wooden verandah, are admirable. The builder, who was known as a superior carpenter, probably was responsible for a number of other houses in the surrounding neighborhood.

## DG 08.22
### Lawrence City Hall
*1980. Peters Williams & Kubota*
*6 East Sixth Street*

Both its placement and its form make this four-story brick structure notable. It closes the vista at the northern end of Massachusetts Street, separating the town from the Kansas River beyond. The building emphasizes the government's administrative function rather than its symbolic role, and although its geometric form is pleasing, the city hall easily might be mistaken for a commercial office building.

## DG 08.23
### S. T. Zimmerman House*
*1871*
*304 Indiana*

The house provides an interesting example of the domestication of the Second Empire Style. The mansard roof shows the influence of this style, but the asymmetrical massing, carved woodwork, and curved tower roof

demonstrate the free appropriation and adaptation of elements from other Victorian traditions.

## DG 08.24
### Union Pacific Depot♦
*1888. Van Brunt & Howe*
*Second and Maple*

This limestone-trimmed hipped-roofed red-brick Richardsonian Romanesque building sits in an open area in a largely residential neighborhood across the Kansas River from downtown Lawrence. Its most distinctive feature, an overscaled spikelike spire, is a recently completed reconstruction of the original, which had been removed some years before. The architects moved their offices from Boston to Kansas City, Missouri, in 1887, in part because some earlier commissions to design a series of depots for the Union Pacific Railroad's route to the West had acquainted them with the potential of the rapidly developing region.

## DG 08.25
### Tee Pee
*1930*
*On U.S. 24/40 (100 yards east of U.S. 59)*

This tall, conical building is decorated to resemble an Indian tipi. Water levels from the floods of 1935 and 1951 are marked on the structure. Similar but smaller conical forms are attached to the corners of an adjacent one-story building. The deliberately eye-catching and highly symbolic qualities of the complex are typical of the vernacular roadside architecture of the early automobile age.

. . . . . . . . . . . . . . . . . . . . . . . . . . . . . . . .

# Lecompton

## DG 09.01
### Lane University*
*1857–1868*
*Halderman and Third Street*

When construction began on this two-story rectangular stone building, its sponsors hoped it would become the capitol of Kansas. Topeka, however, was selected, and the building in Lecompton remained unfinished until the structure was given to the United Brethren Church. They completed the second floor so the building could be used to house a university, but it closed in 1903. Thereafter, the structure served as a church and school before becoming a museum. Adjacent is a two-story wooden building in which the state constitution was drafted in 1855; now called Constitution Hall,* it is a National Historic Landmark.

**DG 09.02**
## Glenn House
*1879*
*On Route 1023 (two miles west of Lecompton)*

This two-story limestone farmhouse is typical of the rural vernacular I-house plan homes of the era. The quality of workmanship and the building's clarity of form are notable.

# FRANKLIN COUNTY

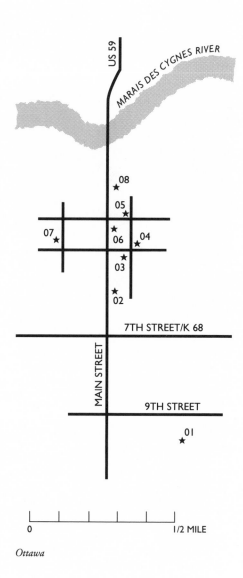

*Ottawa*

93

# Ottawa

## FR 10.01
### Tuay Jones Hall (Ottawa University)*
*1866–1869*
*Tenth and Cedar Street*

The rectangular three-story Italianate structure of local limestone is the original classroom building of the Baptist institution, where instruction began in 1866. Interest is added by the variegated colors and textures of the stone. The building has survived two major fires and continues to serve the university. The campus also contains recently completed renovation projects by Fred Truog that are of interest: the Ward Science Hall and the Wise Technology Center.

## FR 10.02
### Ottawa Public Library*
*1903. George P. Washburn*
*Fifth and Main Street*

The library, a two-story Neoclassical buff-brick building, occupies the northern end of a central city park, which also contains the 1859 Dietrich cabin,* an early log building moved to the site. The library is a simple rectangular building with a hipped tile roof; the building's ornament is concentrated around the entry, which features a pair of two-story columns supporting a pediment containing a decorative relief.

## FR 10.03
### Ottawa First Baptist Church
*1887. George P. Washburn*
*Fourth and Hickory Street*

This grand Romanesque stone church is organized around a four-story square tower, which is set at a diagonal to the facing street corner and to the remainder of the building. The geometric relationship of the building's forms is admirably resolved. A diagonal axis establishes symmetry between the adjacent gabled wings, and the east-facing gable is extended beyond to form the nave.

## FR 10.04
### Ottawa First Methodist Church
*1903*
*Fourth and Hickory Street*

The stone-trimmed red-brick church sits diagonally across from the First Baptist Church. It borrows from both Gothic and Romanesque traditions, for the window arches, though slightly pointed, lack the expected verticality. Like the nearby courthouse, the church is anchored at the corners by towered pavilions. The main entry leads through the taller tower, which faces the street corner. The education building attached to the east of the sanctuary appears to be a later addition.

## FR 10.05
### First National Bank of Ottawa
*1974–1975. Neal Hansen*
*Third and Hickory Street*

This Modern one-story brick building provides a striking contrast to the courthouse across the street. Its form is dominated by a low, sloping roof. The simple form of the building is well suited to its function; it allows the main banking hall to be lit by a continuous west-facing transom window and provides for the easy accommodation of drive-through banking.

## FR 10.06
### Franklin County Courthouse*
*1891–1893. George P. Washburn*
*Third and Main Street*

The first of the architect's thirteen courthouses in Kansas, this stone-trimmed red-brick three-story courthouse established a pattern followed in many of the subsequent structures. In form, many of the buildings were organized with towered pavilions anchoring each of the corners. In plan, dual stairs often lead to a central second-floor

courtroom that occupies the entire width of the building. In detail, the buildings often display elements from different stylistic traditions; this one is Romanesque and Queen Anne. It is among the best preserved of the remaining ten examples in Kansas. George Washburn, one of Kansas' most skillful and prolific architects of the late Victorian era, established his practice in Ottawa in 1882 after serving a four-year internship in the office of Cross and Taylor (Kansas City, Missouri). He remained in Ottawa and eventually was joined in practice by his son; he died in 1922.

## FR 10.07
### James H. Ransom House*
*1892. George P. Washburn (attrib.)*
*318 South Locust Street*

The large two-story wood-shingled house sits in a neighborhood of similarly scaled Victorian homes, but this one is noteworthy for its boldness of form. It displays the skill-

pilasters divide them into rhythmic bays. The Italianate detail found around the windows and along the cornice is noteworthy. Other buildings on the eastern side of the 200 block of Main Street are interesting and representative of commercial buildings of the late nineteenth and early twentieth centuries.

ful combination of the continuous surfaces and curvilinear forms of the Shingle Style with the formality and carved-wood detail of the Queen Anne Style.

FR 10.08
## Hamblin Building*
*1879*
*139 Main Street*

This three-story brick corner building is part of the Downtown Ottawa Historic District. It shows considerable sophistication in both composition and detail; the curved corner of the building allows one facade to flow seamlessly into the other, and stone

# Holton

### JA 11.01
## State Bank of Holton*
*1906. Alfred Meier*
*Fourth and Pennsylvania*

The two-story stone-trimmed brick bank building is a highly original adaptation of a familiar type. The bank displays classical ornament rendered with sufficient wit and irony, however, to please the sensibilities of proponents of Post-Modern architecture. Noteworthy are the interrupted curved pediments above both the main and secondary entries and the miniature building form above the bank's cornice, which attracts attention to the main entry at the corner of the building.

### JA 11.02
## Jackson County Courthouse
*1919–1921. Thomas W. Williamson*
*Courthouse Square*

The courthouse, a three-story brick and limestone Neoclassical building, is at the center of the town's main square, which is surrounded by mostly two-story storefront buildings. These buildings present a pleasing display of late-nineteenth-century ornament situated above the mostly renovated lower stories, where the original detailing

is now obscured. The courthouse remains largely intact on the outside, but the interior has been extensively remodeled.

. . . . . . . . . . . . . . . . . . . . . . . . . . . . . . . . .

# Whiting

### JA 12.01
## Shedd and Marshall Store*
*1881*
*Third and Whiting*

This two-story stone commercial building is a lonely remnant of an earlier era. It is, however, an example of a once-popular building type. The carved stonework around the windows and on the cornice displays considerable skill, both in composition and in masonry.

# Meriden

## JF 13.01
### Benedict Meyer Log Cabin◆
*1854*
*On K 4 (one mile north of Meriden)*

The one-and-one-half-story log and notch cabin is typical of the structures erected by the area's first white settlers. It is one of several buildings brought together to illustrate early Kansas life. The museum complex is located on a traditional threshing ground.

.....................................

# Oskaloosa

## JF 14.01
### Jefferson County Courthouse
*1962. Kiene & Bradley*
*Courthouse Square*

Occupying the town's central square, this flat-roofed unadorned two-story building has replaced the 1867 courthouse that was destroyed by a tornado in 1960. The disaster perhaps affected the design of the present utilitarian structure, which appears to be concerned primarily with economy and durability and thus seems somewhat out of place in its prominent setting.

## JF 14.02
### Union Block*
*1892. H. M. Hadley*
*Delaware and Jefferson*

This two-story stone-trimmed red-brick Romanesque commercial building anchors a prominent corner at the heart of town. Following a planning pattern popular in the commercial buildings of many Kansas towns, a bank occupies the ground level at the corner with its entry set at an angle, and the entry to upper-level offices is placed on the side street. Here, retail stores adjacent to the bank complete the occupancy of the ground floor.

## JF 14.03
### Old Jefferson Town
*On U.S. 59 (east of Oskaloosa)*

The town consists of a loose assemblage of small historical buildings, which have been moved to the site from around the county and are joined by some re-created structures. The group includes a one-room jail built in 1910, a replica of a traditional blacksmith's shop, a two-story wooden store building of 1887, a one-room school built the same year, a replica of a turn-of-the-century bandstand, a small frame church built in 1891, a two-story frame home built in 1890, and a metal Bowstring Bridge* from 1875. Although the buildings are of interest, their setting along a hillside meadow is unconvincing.

. . . . . . . . . . . . . . . . . . . . . . . . . . . . . . . .

# Williamstown

## JF 15.01
## Buck Creek School*
*1878*
*On U.S. 24 (two miles east of Williamstown)*

Typical of nineteenth-century rural schools in the state, this wood-shingled gable-roofed stone building sits in an open field. It is now used as a clubhouse.

# Fort Leavenworth

## LV 16.01
## Grant Hall
*1902–1904*
*Near Sherman and Augur Avenue*

The building is on an 8,000-acre reserve that constitutes Fort Leavenworth, which is located along the bluffs overlooking the Missouri River. The fort, a National Historic Landmark, was established in 1827, and it contains a number of historic buildings, including the Rookery, the oldest house in the state (1832). The fort also is home to the Command and General Staff College. One can view the fort as a city unto itself, complete with some interesting newer buildings, including Bell Hall, designed in the mid-1950s by the architectural firm of Kivett & Myers. Grant Hall's position at the center of the campus, its size and formal businesslike demeanor, and the visibility of its tall domed tower establish it as a dominant feature of a diverse complex.

. . . . . . . . . . . . . . . . . . . . . . . . . . . . . . .

# Leavenworth

**LV 17.01**

## St. Joseph Dining Hall (St. Mary's College)

*1963. Maurice Carroll / Ferris & Hamig*
*On U.S. 73 (south of Leavenworth)*

This octagonal Modern glass and stone building interjects itself into the corner of a quadrangle of larger and more traditional red-brick classroom buildings. Its purity of form and aggressiveness with respect to its neighbors, which include the original St. Mary's Hall (1870), reveal an attitude of confidence typical of its era. The spare detailing and sense of spaciousness of the main dining area are also representative of the architectural tastes of the time. The 120-acre hillside campus serves as the world headquarters of the Order of the Sisters of Mercy. A number of the structures on the campus are noteworthy, including an abstract geometric brick and steel entry gate designed in 1958 by Shaugnessy, Bower & Grimaldi and a Romanesque brick chapel designed by Wilder & Wight, built in 1915.

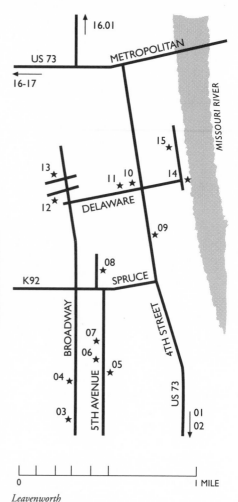

*Leavenworth*

**LV 17.02**

## Veterans Administration Center Chapel

*1893. Louis S. Curtiss*
*On U.S. 73 (south of Leavenworth)*

The unique brick and stone chapel occupies a hillside along the curving road that winds through the diverse complex of buildings constituting the campus of the Veterans Administration Center. The streetside entry leads to an upper-level chapel that serves a Protestant congregation; a chapel below, entered from the other side, serves as a Catholic worship space. The building is an en-

thusiastic and exuberant collage of freely interpreted Gothic elements; the juxtapositions of form, texture, and scale seem almost deliberately disturbing. It clearly demonstrates the boldness and inventive powers of one of the most celebrated architects of Kansas City, Missouri, of the late nineteenth and early twentieth centuries.

## LV 17.03
### A. J. Angell House◆
*1884*
*714 South Broadway*

Facing a wide boulevard with grand residences on spacious lots, this large well-kept two-story house demonstrates the variety

and flexibility of Victorian stylistic motifs. The building's unified brick mass is fractured by bays of differing shape and character and is accented by a series of individuated, articulate wooden gables, dormers, and porches.

## LV 17.04
### J. L. Abernathy House◆
*1867/1916. H. Hamblin/Wight & Wight*
*508 South Broadway*

This two-story tile-roofed Italianate stucco house sits elegantly on its broad, shaded grounds. It displays a skillful and sophisticated blending of classical and romantic traditions; the formality of the colonnaded porch seems surprisingly at home on this asymmetrical and picturesque Mediterranean villa. The diverse elements fuse into a unique and thoroughly convincing whole. The curious mixture of styles is the result of a renovation of an Italianate villa by Wight & Wight, the premier Neoclassical architects of Kansas City, Missouri, in the early twentieth century.

## LV 17.05
### Leavenworth Public Library*
*1902. M. R. Sanquist*
*601 South Fifth Avenue*

Among the first of the sixty Carnegie-financed libraries erected in Kansas; this monumental two-story gray-brick and stone Beaux-Arts building was also among the most ambitious. It features a central, Ionic-columned, pedimented entry portico set between arched, two-story window openings. Like several other Carnegie libraries across the state, notably in Lawrence, the building has been renovated to house an arts center.

LV 17.06
### Nathaniel H. Burt House*
*1895. William P. Feth*
*400 South Fifth Avenue*

This two-and-one-half-story residence sits on a rise well back from the street and combines Richardsonian Romanesque features with Neoclassical elements. The main facade is dominated by a circular bay capped by a conical roof and by an extended one-story porch supported on paired columns. It is of interest for historical as well as for stylistic reasons; its original owner was the president of a significant local manufacturing concern, the Great Western Stove Company.

LV 17.07
### Edward Carroll House*
*1858/1867/1882. George McKenna (builder)*
*334 Fifth Avenue*

The two-story sixteen-room brick Victorian home was originally constructed as a four-room cottage that was expanded to its present form through two subsequent additions. It occupies a spacious lot in a district of large, older residences. Now home to the Leavenworth County Museum, the building's interiors are an important exhibit feature. The museum also displays antique furnishings and several re-created environments, including those of a general store and barber shop.

LV 17.08
### Fred Harvey House*
*1870*
*Seventh and Olive Street*

Many features typical of the Second Empire Style popular through the third quarter of the nineteenth century are displayed in this two-story stone house. It was purchased in 1883 by Fred Harvey, the proprietor of the Harvey House restaurants that served the Atchison Topeka and Santa Fe Railroad. The building now serves as an annex to the Leavenworth County Courthouse.

LV 17.09
### Leavenworth County Courthouse
*1911–1913. William P. Feth*
*Walnut and Fourth Avenue*

The two-story Neoclassical terracotta-trimmed limestone building occupies a hilltop block to the south of the downtown district. The interior features a central rotunda with a stained-glass dome. The architect was a prominent practitioner in Leavenworth through the early years of the twentieth century. He established his practice in 1895, after returning from a decade of internship in architectural offices in Chicago and Denver.

## LV 17.10
## AXA Building*
*1905. William P. Feth*
*Fourth and Delaware Street*

This two-story red-and-tan brick structure typifies the scale and texture of the late-nineteenth- and early-twentieth-century buildings that line the city's main commercial street. Many of these structures continue to accommodate shops on the ground level with offices above. This building stands out among its neighbors because of the inventiveness of its highly articulated Neo-classical ornament, particularly along the cornice, at the second-floor bay windows, and around the lobby entry.

## LV 17.11
## Hollywood Theater*
*1937–1938. Robert Boller*
*501 Delaware*

One of the more than fifty theaters designed by the architects in Kansas, this concrete Art Deco movie theater is a good example of the style popular at the time. The facade displays the characteristic repeating, continuous patterns associated with the style. The building is now owned by the city of Leavenworth and is used as a performing arts center.

## LV 17.12
## Atchison Topeka and Santa Fe Passenger Depot*
*1887. Perkins & Adams*
*781 Shawnee Street*

The small pink-sandstone Romanesque building is typical of a number of stations built by the railroad. They reflect the influence of the Boston architect, Henry Hobson Richardson, particularly his stations of the mid-1880s for the Boston and Albany Railroad. This building is of interest for its contrasts of material and texture; the rough-faced stone is laid in a variety of interesting patterns, and the broad overhanging canopy is supported on metal brackets.

## LV 17.13
## St. Paul's Episcopal Church
*1864/1872*
*Eighth and Seneca Street*

Like other Episcopal churches around the state, notably in Atchison and Manhattan, this small Gothic stone church was adapted from buildings illustrated in the 1852 *Up-john's Rural Architecture*. This apparently effective strategy permitted each church to be unique and also to have a sense of authenticity reminiscent of historic referents. The later addition to St. Paul's extended the original three-bay rectangular structure on the north and south.

## LV 17.14
### (Old) Union Pacific Depot*
*1888. Cobb & Frost*
*123 South Esplanade*

Occupying a prominent site, this largely one-story stone-trimmed brick Richardsonian Romanesque building closes the vista at the eastern end of Delaware Street, which retains a notable row of nineteenth-century commercial buildings on the adjacent block. The depot is a highly serviceable building and has been recently renovated to serve as a multipurpose complex for the community.

## LV 17.15
### Ketcheson House*
*1874*
*309 North Esplanade*

This two-story Eastlake Style house of wood, with its triangular bay windows and curving porch, takes good advantage of its location on a street that skirts the edge of the steep bluff overlooking the Missouri River. It is one of the row of houses constituting the North Esplanade Historic District,* located from 203 through 515 North Esplanade. They provide a good sampling of the variety of styles popular in residential architecture during the latter half of the nineteenth century.

## LV 17.16
### Federal Penitentiary
*1906. Eames & Young*
*Thirteenth and Metropolitan avenues*

A long, grand, formal approach leads axially to the front of this imposing Beaux-Arts stone structure. From a distance, the building's bright dome and classical proportions symbolize the ideals of democracy, but on closer approach its cold formality and overwhelming scale make it more appropriately a symbol of governmental authority. The building, popularly known as the Big

House or simply the Pen, clearly reflects its function.

## David W. Powers Residence*
*1872*
*On U.S. 73 (two miles north of Leavenworth)*

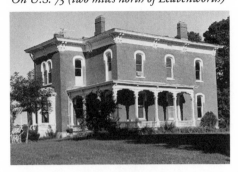

Situated among the rolling hills of the Salt Creek valley, this substantial two-story brick Italianate house is unusual for a rural setting. Powers returned to the area after having made his fortune in banking and in the cattle business in Ellsworth. The seventeen-room residence is being renovated.

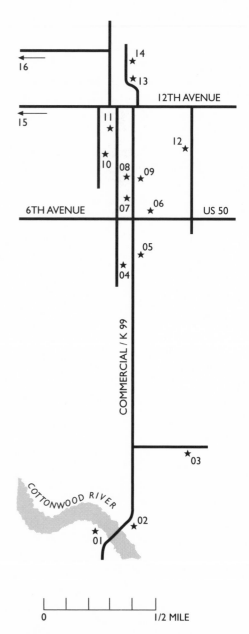

Emporia

# Emporia

## Soden's Grove Bridge*

*1924. James Barney (designer)*
*On K 57/99 (at the southern edge of Emporia)*

The concrete rainbow-arch bridge spans the Cottonwood River at the site of an 1861 flour mill. A newer bridge parallels the older one, thus making the latter one of the most visible of the seventy-six bridges of this type erected in Kansas between 1917 and 1940. The type is also known as a Marsh Arch bridge, named after the engineer who patented the design in 1911. Those bridges located throughout the state show considerable variation in the anchoring and spanning configuration. A seven-span structure built over the Kansas River at Wamego was the largest bridge of this type.

LY 18.02
## Hallie B. Soden House*

*1893. Charles W. Squires*
*802 South Commercial*

This two-story wood Queen Anne Style house is set back from the road on a generous, tree-shaded lot. Its most notable feature is a large round window on the second floor above the entry. The detail of the wrap-around lower-level porch displays the skills of local craftsmen. The architect also designed a number of other houses in Emporia, including the (1886) Iva J. Keebler house* at 831 Constitution, the (1898) Ashbel J. Crocker house at 819 Constitution, the architect's own (1895) house at 613 Exchange, the (1896) L. A. Lowther house at 617 Exchange, and the (1906) Dr. William M. Meffert house at 627 Exchange. Charles Squires, born in Long Island, New York, was trained in Columbus, Ohio, and practiced architecture in Emporia from 1879 until his death in 1934.

LY 18.03
## Richard Howe House*

*1866–1867. Richard Howe (builder)*
*315 East Logan*

Well-preserved, the two-story rectangular gabled stone house effectively represents the region's vernacular traditions. Howe, a local stonemason who contributed to the construction of a number of early buildings in the area, built it for his own use. He had learned his craft in his native Wales.

LY 18.04
## Refrigerated Fur Storage Building

*ca. 1950–1953*
*Fourth and Merchant*

A clear expression of the concerns of the time, this two-story International Style brick and stone building is straightforward and functional, using industrial-style steel-sash windows. Yet it also exhibits thoughtful enhancements through such elements as an extended canopy, a round corner, and horizontal window groupings. It is worth noting that the building survives intact, down to interior screens and counters, which is not the case for many other commercial structures of that era.

## LY 18.05
### Lyon County Courthouse
*1954. Brinkman & Hagan*
*Fourth and Commercial*

Replacing a 1901 courthouse at this location, this four-story International Style building of limestone and brick occupies an important corner site on the city's main business street. The building's sparseness of detail and tight alignment to the street help it fit unobtrusively with its neighbors, yet its geometric clarity and vertical sun screens, which are reminiscent of columns, identify it as a civic structure. The architects also designed the W. A. White Auditorium at 100 East Sixth Avenue (1938–1940), another significant public building in the city.

## LY 18.06
### (Old) Emporia Public Library*
*1905. Van Brunt & Howe*
*118 East Sixth Street*

This one-and-one-half-story Jacobethan Revival Carnegie Library of brick and stone occupies a prominent site opposite the W. A. White Civic Auditorium. It is a convincing

adaptation of an architectural style relatively rare in Kansas. Since 1979 the building has served as the Lyon County Historical Museum.

## LY 18.07
### Kress Building*
*1928. G. E. Mackey*
*702 Commercial*

The two-story commercial building displays the Gothic- and Elizabethan-inspired terra-cotta and patterned brickwork characteristic of many Kress Company stores. The building has been renovated to house a complex of offices and shops.

## LY 18.08
### Granada Theater*
*1929. Boller Brothers*
*809 Commercial*

The theater, a large Spanish Colonial Style building, is representative of the grand era of the movie palace. The architects specialized in this building type and designed theaters across the country. Although a 1952 fire destroyed much of its elaborate interior detail, the structure continued to be used for another twenty-five years.

LY 18.09
## First Presbyterian Church
*1897. Charles W. Squires*
*Eighth and Commercial*

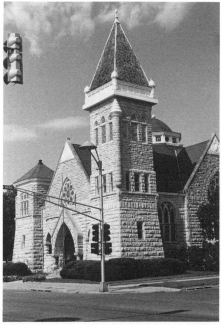

The small church features a stone base, brick walls, and wood-shingled gable ends with round windows. It follows the Akron Plan popular in the late nineteenth century, in which an L-shaped worship space surrounds a corner entry tower. This building bears a strong resemblance to the First Congregational Church in Council Grove, designed by Squires.

LY 18.11
## First United Methodist Church
*1960. J. Trevor Lewis*
*Eleventh and Merchant*

Borrowing from Classical, Gothic, and Romanesque traditions, this rough-faced stone church is difficult to classify. Despite the mixture of styles and collage of forms, the composition possesses a strong sense of unity and consistency. A massive and original corner tower dominates the design. The octagonal domed lantern, rising above the intersection of the ridge lines, suggests the presence of the cavernous centralized worship space below. The architect also designed the Christ Assembly Pentecostal Church, at Second and Merchant.

LY 18.10
## Calvary United Methodist Church
*1903. Charles W. Squires (attrib.)*
*Ninth and Constitution*

This Modern brick church complex with a low-pitched roof is organized around a courtyard that serves as an effective exterior foyer for the sanctuary since it faces the street corner. The overall utilitarian character of the building is softened by a tall stone and steel carillon tower and by elegant stained-glass windows.

LY 18.12
## William Allen White House (Red Rocks)*
*1880*
*927 Exchange Street*

The two-story Craftsman Style home of red sandstone and brick was purchased in 1899 by the Pulitzer Prize–winning journalist William Allen White. Throughout his nearly fifty years as editor of the *Emporia Gazette,* his commentary was cited regularly in national journals. When the interior of the house burned in 1920, White consulted with Frank Lloyd Wright regarding renovations, but the architect did not become involved in the project. The house is now a National Historic Landmark.

LY 18.13
## Plumb Memorial Hall (Emporia State University)
*1917. Charles H. Chandler*
*Twelfth and Commercial*

This grand four-story T-plan Neoclassical building of red brick and terracotta terminates the axis at the north end of Commercial Street. The building is a signature struc-

ture and appears on the logo of Emporia State University, an institution that begin in 1863 as the Kansas State Normal School. The 200-acre campus now contains eighteen buildings organized around a large informal quadrangle with a small lake at its center.

LY 18.14
## Morse Central Dormitory (Emporia State University)
*1952. Brinkman & Hagan*

The six-story Modern brick building is one of a row of similarly scaled dormitories that form the western edge of the parklike center of the campus. It is a good example of the functionalist approach to architecture. The building's forms reflect its constituent spaces. Of particular note are the sawtooth bays on the upper floors that provide panoramic views from the individual dormitory rooms. Another nearby building of note designed by the firm is the First Christian Church at the corner of East Twelfth and Market Street.

LY 18.15
## Anderson Memorial Library*
*1902. Charles W. Squires*
*1300 West Twelfth*

The library, a two-story neoclassical limestone building, faces the broad lawn of Way College, originally the College of Emporia. The building's notable features include a

pedimented entry portico, a central lantern and low dome, carved woodwork, and German stained glass. Financed by the steel magnate Andrew Carnegie, the library was carefully restored in the mid-1980s and received a Kansas State Preservation Award.

**LY 18.16**
## Village School
*1963/1971*
*Caudill Rowlett & Scott; addition by*
*J. Trevor Lewis*
*2302 West Fifteenth*

Although the one-story brick school is well detailed inside and out, the interior is of special interest. The school consists of three six-room clusters, each of which is organized around a sky-lit plant-filled courtyard. Those spaces form the focus of attention for the surrounding glass-walled classrooms. Two of the clusters were built originally, the third later. The original architects developed a national reputation for innovative design, particularly of schools, and became the country's largest architectural firm for a time.

. . . . . . . . . . . . . . . . . . . . . . . . . . . . . . . . .

# Hartford

**LY 19.01**
## Hartford Collegiate Institute*
*1903*

This two-story hipped-roofed stone building sits in a small park at the center of town and is a good example of the vernacular traditions of the region. Built to house a branch of Baker University of Baldwin City, it also has served the town of Hartford as a school and civic center and is used now as a library.

# Osawatomie

**MI 20.01**
## William Mills House*
*1902*
*212 First Street*

The large three-story wood frame house displays many of the features typical of the Queen Anne Style, including multitextured wood surfaces, overhanging half-timbered gables, pedimented porches, prominent chimneys, and round corner turrets.

**MI 20.02**
## John Brown Cabin*
*1854–1856*
*Tenth and Main Street*

This log cabin has been preserved as a monument to the state's most radical abolitionist. The building, originally the home of the Reverend Samuel Adair, has been moved to a rolling, shaded memorial park, the site of a battle between a proslavery force and an abolitionist group led by Brown. The procedures to preserve the cabin are somewhat unusual; it was enclosed in 1928 within a rectangular stone structure only slightly larger than the cabin, which can be viewed through large, arched windows. It operates as a museum.

. . . . . . . . . . . . . . . . . . . . . . . . . . . . . . . .

# Paola

**MI 21.01**
## Miami County Courthouse*
*1897–1899. George P. Washburn*
*Miami and Silver Street*

The three-story stone-trimmed red-brick courthouse and an undistinguished recent one-story addition occupy a full-block site near the central business district. Having a greater scale and formality than the town's other structures, the courthouse is among the most ambitious of the many designed by the architect, reflecting perhaps the expectations of prosperity stimulated by the nearby discovery of oil. The building shares many features with the architect's other courthouses, notably the one in nearby Franklin County. A 1977 renovation has restored much of the building's character, particularly that of the two-story upper-level courtroom.

**MI 21.02**
## Town Square
*Flanked by Pearl, Peoria, Silver, and Wea streets*

In scale and organization, the square is typical of those in many small Kansas towns, with its series of one- to three-story late-nineteenth- and early-twentieth-century commercial buildings surrounding it; here it is an open, landscaped central block. This square is unique, however, because in the 1960s the facades of almost all the buildings facing the park were modernized by the addition of aluminum siding, a project initiated by the chamber of commerce in a program called the Parade of Progress. The resulting appearance is quite unusual and undoubtedly annoying to architectural preservationists, but the effect is truly memorable.

## MI 21.03
### Paola Library
*1905. George P. Washburn*
*Peoria and Agate*

awkwardness of detail, the building and its site provide an appropriately meditative environment. The school was closed in 1971, but the convent continues to operate. The complex also contains a 1914 auditorium building designed by Wilder & Wight.

The hipped-roofed one-story striated brick building presents a striking composition, one different from other similarly scaled libraries in Kansas. It is well suited to its corner location. The arched recess of the entry contrasts nicely with a round turreted tower attached to an adjacent corner. An addition is sensitively subordinated to the original composition.

## MI 21.04
### Administration Building (Ursuline Sisters Academy)
*1926. Rose & Ridgeway*
*Wea and East Street*

This Neoclassical three-story brick classroom and dormitory building is set within formally organized, spacious grounds. It is composed around a central core from which originate a series of wings. Despite some

# Lyndon

## OS 22.01
**Lyndon Carnegie Library***
*1911. Keene & Simpson*
*127 East Sixth Street.*

The one-story hipped-roofed brick and stone Neoclassical building follows the typical planning strategy for the many Carnegie libraries across the state; a central entry leads directly to a raised reading room. Although the building has only the sparest of detail, careful proportioning gives it a sense of classical repose.

## OS 22.02
**Park Pavilion**
*1960. Pomona Lake State Park*
*(on K 268 east of Lyndon)*

This concrete-shell picnic structure is typical of those to be found throughout the state

park system. Cast from reusable metal forms designed by a Wichita structural engineer, they provide an inexpensive, flexible, and durable form of shelter, one ideally suited to its purpose. In some parks the roof shell is used to cover enclosed facilities such as toilets; in others, shells are combined to shelter larger areas.

. . . . . . . . . . . . . . . . . . . . . . . . . . . . . . . .

# Osage City

## OS 23.01
**Evangelical Covenant Mission Church⁺**
*1870. Topeka and Lakin*

An excellent example of the Carpenter Gothic style, this small wooden church also shows the influence of Swedish building traditions. The verticality of the tower has been somewhat compromised by the additions that bring the nave volume flush with the front of the tower.

## OS 23.02
**Osage City Santa Fe Depot***
*1911–1912*
*508 Market*

The one-story stucco and brick railroad station exhibits some characteristics of the Mission Style, perhaps to suggest the architecture native to the railroad's terminus in the Southwest. The building now houses the Osage County Historical Society.

## OS 23.03
**Citizens State Bank**
*ca. 1910–1915*
*Sixth and Market*

A relatively simple one-story terracotta-trimmed Neoclassical corner building, the bank has a sense of dignity befitting its purpose. It provides a good example of sensitive restoration work, done in 1989 by the Hagemann Design Group (now Shaw Hofstra & Associates). Original woodwork, marble work, and leaded-glass windows were restored and a sympathetically styled addition constructed.

# Berryton

## SN 24.01
**Horace G. Lyons House***
*1883*
*4831 Southeast Sixty-first Street (Berryton vicinity)*

The stone farmhouse exhibits a curious assemblage of forms that appear to have been built up over time. Some of the formal motifs bear a resemblance to those found in the Hicks Block in Topeka. A gambrel-roofed wood and stone barn forms another side of the farm complex.

. . . . . . . . . . . . . . . . . . . . . . . . . . . . . . .

# Dover

## SN 25.01
**Sage Inn***
*1865/1878*
*Fifty-seventh Street and Douglas Road*

This two-story stone building is representative of early building traditions in the area. A large wing was added to the original simple-gabled structure. Dressed stones are used for quoins, lintels, and sills, and rough stone is employed for the remainder of the walls. The house served not only as a family home but also as a hostelry.

. . . . . . . . . . . . . . . . . . . . . . . . . . . . . . . .

# Topeka

## SN 26.01
### First Congregational Church
*1948/1955. Greist Eckdahl*
*Seventeenth and Collins Street*

Sitting gently on a well-landscaped site, this small-scale brick church possesses a sense of repose comfortable with both tradition and innovation. It is reminiscent of the work of Finnish romantic modernists such as Eliel Saarinen. The sanctuary was built first, and the classroom portions of the building were added later. The architect was a 1923 graduate of Kansas State University.

## SN 26.02
### Charles R. Bennett Computer Center (Washburn University)
*1987. Horst Terrell & Karst*
*Seventeenth Street*

This one-story precast-concrete building is located along the northern edge of the 160-acre Washburn University campus. Many of the early buildings on the campus, including several designed by John Haskell, were destroyed in a 1966 tornado. The educational spaces of the Bennett Center are distributed along a skylit gallery on the north side of the building. This space provides a relief from the largely windowless classroom spaces and gives character to an otherwise unremarkable building, demonstrating that simple and inexpensive materials can be pleasingly employed. It received a design award from the Kansas Chapter of the American Institute of Architects.

## SN 26.03
### Agriculture Building
*1938. Cuthbert & Suehrk*
*Seventeenth and Topeka Boulevard*

# TOPEKA

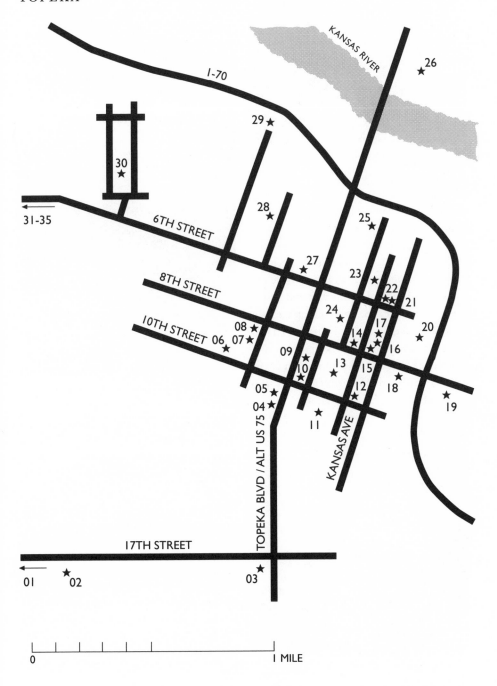

KANSAS RIVER

I-70

★ 26

29 ★

30 ★

31-35

6TH STREET

28 ★

25 ★

27 ★

23 ★

8TH STREET

22 ★★
21

24 ★

20 ★

10TH STREET  06 ★  08 ★
07 ★

17 ★
14 ★
16

09 ★★

10 ★

13 ★

15

05 ★

12 ★

18 ★

04 ★

11 ★

19 ★

KANSAS AVE

17TH STREET

TOPEKA BLVD / ALT US 75

01   02 ★

03 ★

0                    1 MILE

The Agriculture Building occupies the northeast corner of the old fairgrounds. The long, low, brick structure transcends its rather modest materials and utilitarian function. Multiple flagpoles attached to the facade are suggestive of the playfulness of the fair, and the faceted rotunda at the main entry is a reminder of its grandeur. The site is also the home of the newer and much larger Kansas Expocenter, completed in the 1980s and designed by Horst Terrell and Karst and Howard Needles Tammen and Bergendorf. The formal composition of the Agricultural Building, however, allows it to stand nobly alongside its neighbor.

### SN 26.04
### Charles Curtis House*
*1878*
*1101 Topeka Avenue*

The two-story brick mansion is representative of the fine homes that once lined Topeka Avenue. Notable features of the house are its two exotic domes; one is round in plan, the other square. The building is also

noteworthy because it was home to a man who held three different elective offices in Washington, D.C.: congressman, senator, and finally vice-president.

### SN 26.05
### Columbia Savings
### (originally American Savings)
*1964. Horst & Terrill*
*Eleventh Street and Topeka Avenue*

This small but ambitious building is a potpourri of architectural forms. The circular glass-enclosed banking lobby is capped by a folded-plate concrete roof. To this is attached a marble-clad service wing and a shading device set on trabeated arches, which continue as freestanding elements across the entry plaza. Originally, the building was surrounded by a shallow moat.

### SN 26.06
### Topeka High School
*1930. Thomas W. Williamson*
*Tenth and Polk Street*

Containing an auditorium that seats 2,500 persons, this large brick and stone Collegiate Gothic school complex occupies four city blocks. The most notable feature of the building is the tall carillon tower above the south-facing main entry. At the time of its construction it was honored by the National Education Association as the second best high school in the country. The designer of the building in Williamson's office was

Ted R. Greist, a 1923 graduate of Kansas State University.

### SN 26.07
### Bethany Place♦
*1875. John G. Haskell*
*833–835 South Polk*

Sitting amid generous shaded grounds, this simple Eclectic two-story stone building was built as the laundry for the College of the Sisters of Bethany. The college closed in 1928, and the other campus buildings (also designed by the architect) were razed to provide a site for Topeka High School. Bethany Place now houses offices of the Episcopal Diocese of Kansas.

### SN 26.08
### Grace Episcopal Cathedral
*1909–1916. Root & Siemens*
*Eighth and Polk Street*

The 1,100-seat twin-spired limestone church was patterned after English Gothic examples. The magnificent building features a

number of fine appointments, including a rose window made from glass fragments left over from the windows of London's Westminster Abbey, an altarpiece by Topeka artist George M. Stone, and a pulpit adorned with figures made by the Bavarian woodcarver, Alois Lang. The partner in charge of this commission was George M. Siemens.

### SN 26.09
### Woman's Club Building*
*1925. Frank C. Squires*
*420 West Ninth Street*

This two-story brick building with limestone trim sits immediately to the west of the capitol. Both the building's overall form and its geometric ornament suggest the influence of the Vienna Secession or perhaps more directly the midwestern Prairie Style. It now houses the State Insurance Department. The architect had worked for a number of years with the noted Topeka architect James C. Holland and for a time was his partner in the first decade of the twentieth century.

## SN 26.10
### Kansas State Office Building
*1954. John A. Brown*
*Fifth and Harrison Street*

Brown was the state architect when he designed this twelve-story Modern office building, which follows the popular idiom of the day. The long walls of the slablike structure are enclosed in a continuous curtainwall; the ends are solid and clad in stone. The lobby is of particular interest in the way visitors are skillfully directed from the corner entry to the central elevator core. An observation deck at the top of the building provides a good view of the adjacent grounds of the capitol and the city beyond.

## SN 26.11
### Kansas Judicial Center
*1976. Kiene & Bradley*
*301 Tenth Street*

The center, a three-story geometrically articulated concrete building, sits amid an open block on axis with the state capitol to the north. It is organized around a full-height central atrium with the perimeter ringed by offices. Courtrooms are located in the area between the interior and exterior zones; the appeals court is on the second floor and the supreme court on the third. The building's interior is minimally but elegantly detailed in marble and wood. The architects, strong proponents of Modernism, are also responsible for the Bank IV Building on the northeast corner of Sixth Street and Kansas Avenue.

## SN 26.12
### Memorial Building*
*1914. Charles H. Chandler*
*120 West Tenth Street*

This French-Renaissance-inspired three-story white marble building sits prominently at the southeast corner of the capitol grounds. In addition to a large second-floor assembly hall and a grand commemorative foyer containing memorial plaques to Kansas war veterans, the building once housed

the state archives and historical museum. Chandler was the state architect when the building was constructed. The similarity of this building to one proposed for Nebraska caused a stir at the time of its construction.

**SN 26.13**

## State Capitol*

*1866–1903*
*John G. Haskell & E. Townsend Mix / John F. Stanton*
*Ninth and Van Buren Street*

Modeled after the U.S. Capitol, this cross-axial building sits in the center of a ten-acre four-block landscaped park. The east wing,

which was completed in 1869 in accordance with the designs of Haskell and Mix, set the design character for the other wings, each of which is terminated in a monumental flight of stairs leading to a pedimented portico of Corinthian columns. The east wing contains the elaborately detailed senate chamber on the third floor; the west wing, added in 1880, contains the somewhat less ornate representative hall. Construction of the remaining portions of the building began three years later. The central rotunda and dome were designed by Stanton, the state architect during its construction. The building contains murals by Abner Crossman and John Steuart Curry, and the grounds contain several sculptures by Merrell Gage, a Kansan.

**SN 26.14**

## Church of the Assumption

*1924. Carroll & Defoe*
*Eighth and Jackson*

This buff-brick simplified Romanesque church complex, consisting of a twin-towered sanctuary block and a three-story classroom wing, faces the northeast corner of the capitol grounds. The bold geometric shapes of the building give it a sense of presence even among its larger and more highly articulated neighbors.

**SN 26.15**

## Thatcher Building*

*1888. John G. Haskell*
*110 East Eighth Street*

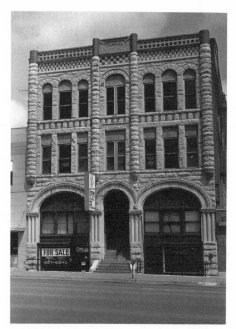

**Davies Building***

*1888*

*725 Kansas Avenue*

The rugged character of this rubble-faced three-and-one-half-story Cottonwood stone building reflects its structural solidity. It was designed with reinforced floors and wide stairs to accommodate the large equipment used by its original tenant, a lithography company. The raised placement of the main level allows storefront exposure to the basement story. The architect moved his office from Lawrence to Topeka during the time of the building's construction.

**SN 26.16**

**Topeka Bank (originally Central National Bank)***

*1927. Wight & Wight*

*701–703 Kansas Avenue*

The grand scale and careful proportions of this monumental two-story stone Neoclassical corner bank building convey an appropriate sense of stability and repose. The degree of resolution of the facades reflects the architects' training in the Boston office of McKim Mead & White, one of the nation's most widely acclaimed exponents of Neoclassicism.

This three-story brick building is typical of the many office blocks that were constructed as part of Topeka's boom years of the mid-1880s. In several of these buildings, often fifty feet wide as in this one, the entry to the upper-story offices is centered between two storefronts. Here the central bay is emphasized on the upper levels by a gently bowing protruding bay. Ornate brickwork enlivens the wall at the spandrel above the second-story windows, within the depressed arch above the third-story windows, and at the cornice.

## Central National Bank (originally Topeka Savings Association)
*1973. Eicholtz & Groth*
*Eighth and Quincy Street*

This two-story circular domed structure of precast concrete and glass is representative of the formalistic tendencies in Modern architecture of the late 1950s and the 1960s. It was modeled after a building the owners had seen years earlier in Phoenix. The design resulted from the collaborative efforts of the owners, the architects, the contractor, and the interior designer. The most distinctive feature of the glazed banking hall is a free-standing curving stair.

**SN 26.19**
## Shawnee County Department of Corrections Adult Detention Facility
*1987. Slemmons Associates*
*Eighth and Jefferson Street*

The rounded forms of this four-story brick jail are an accommodation to the concerns of surveillance and security. The forms clearly express the intentions of this ponderous, castlelike structure.

**SN 26.20**
## Shawnee County Courthouse
*1963. Raymond & Philip Cooledge*
*Seventh and Quincy Street*

Representative of the efficient, if rather uniform, stylistic tendencies of the era, this four-story rectilinear limestone and glass structure occupies a block on the eastern edge of the downtown area. The building is well ordered and cleanly detailed. The adjacent Municipal Auditorium, built twenty-six years earlier, is by Raymond Cooledge and Ted R. Greist, who was his partner then.

**SN 26.21**
## (Old) First National Bank Building◆
*1932. Thomas W. Williamson & Company*
*535 Kansas Avenue*

At the time of its construction, this fourteen-story Indiana-limestone office building was the tallest in Topeka; stylistically, it was also one of the most progressive. The bold stepback profile and Art Deco detail effectively reflected the optimism of the business community in the late 1920s. The building was demolished in 1995.

The five-story office building combines red sandstone and red brick in a collage of decorative motifs. It is representative of the eclectic borrowing that characterized commercial architecture of the time, notably from the work of the influential Chicago architects Burnham & Root. The variety of forms and textures give the facade an animated power that focuses on a single short column at the second level above the main entry, which appears to support the two-story rounded bay window above. The composition may also reflect the architect's familiarity with the work of the Philadelphia architect, Frank Furness.

*(Old) First National Bank Building*

### SN 26.22
## Columbian Block (Knox Building)*
*1888. Seymour Davis*
*112–114 West Sixth Street*

### SN 26.23
## Crawford Block*
*1888. Seymour Davis*
*501 Jackson*

The most notable feature of this brick four-story corner office block is the relatively large size of the windows, which alternate vertically between arched openings (on the first and third floors) and rectangular ones (on the second and fourth floors). A smaller bay marks the entry along the short facade. The architect had come to Topeka in 1883 to work with John G. Haskell, after having been educated at the Pennsylvania Academy of Fine Arts. He opened his own practice in 1886 and later served a term as state architect.

### SN 26.24
## Security Benefit Building
*1965/1971/1980. Eckdahl, Davis & Depew*
*Seventh and Van Buren Street*

The fourteen-story Modern office building uses a limited palette yet displays a pleasing sense of scale and proportion. The main portion of the facade is composed of a human-scaled grid of alternating, repetitive,

framed window elements. The horizontal emphasis created by the recessed glass facades at the first and fourth levels is balanced by the continuous expression of the vertical circulation elements at the ends of the building. Though constructed in three phases, the building exhibits an overall unity of form. The original Beaux-Arts headquarters for Security Benefit, designed by W. E. Glover in 1930, is immediately to the west.

## SN 26.25
### St. Joseph's Catholic Church*

*1900. Staudahar (Rock Island, Illinois)*
*235 Van Buren*

This brick church is on axis with the capitol, five blocks to the south. Although its elevation is well below that of the capitol, its twin spires play a prominent part in the Topeka skyline. The church originally served the area's immigrant German population, and until World War I German was spoken there more often than English.

## SN 26.26
### Union Pacific Depot*

*1926. Gilbert Stanley Underwood*
*Railroad Street and North Kansas Avenue*

The grand Neoclassical stone-trimmed brick railroad station contrasts strongly with the small-scale North Topeka working-class residential neighborhood surrounding it. Though now vacant, the depot remains a monument to the importance of the railroads in Topeka's development.

## SN 26.27
### Hicks Block*

*1889*
*600 West Sixth Street*

This three-story brick Victorian apartment building is a relatively rare example of nineteenth-century multifamily housing in Kansas. Each of the multiple entry points on the main facade is marked by an exterior stair leading to a covered porch and by a corresponding pedimented bay. A similarly pleasing and well-scaled composition is employed on the second street facade, and an angled turret cleverly resolves their intersection at the corner.

## SN 26.28
### Sumner Elementary School*
*1936. Thomas W. Williamson*
*300 Western Street*

Many architects working through the federal relief programs of the 1930s favored the conservative evolutionary Modern approach exemplified by this stone-trimmed two-story brick school. Here, simplified and stylized ornament replaced historically inspired ornament within fairly traditional compositions. The building is a National Historic Landmark, made notable for its role in the controversy that led ultimately to the Supreme Court decision in *Brown vs. Board of Education,* which required the desegregation nationally of schools.

## SN 26.29
### Ward-Meade House and Park*
*1870–1874*
*124 North Fillmore*

The house was built by Anthony Ward, a blacksmith who settled in the area in 1854. Two sides of the house are built of stone and the other two of brick. It has been altered over the years, most notably by the addition of a Classical portico. The house is part of a 5.5-acre historical park, which also contains a restored and relocated general store, livery stable, one-room schoolhouse, railroad depot, log cabin, wheelwright shop, drug store, and a 2.5-acre botanical garden.

## SN 26.30
### Potwin Place Historic District*
*1887–1914. Charles W. Potwin (developer)*
*Between First and Fourth streets, on*
*Woodlawn and Greenwood*

Once the western end of Topeka, this seventy-acre area of land offers an interesting display of the variety of styles in vogue in residential architecture during the late nineteenth and early twentieth centuries. It is also of interest because of its planning and landscaping. A well-landscaped circular park is located in the center of each of the intersections of the district; they not only serve to slow through-traffic but also help to give a unifying character to the diverse residences. The house shown is on the northeast corner of First and Greenwood Street. It is an example of the Craftsman Style as developed by Charles & Henry Greene in their work in California in the first decade of the twentieth century.

## SN 26.31
## Administration Building of the Topeka State Hospital
*1900. H. M. Hadley*
*West Sixth Street*

The four-and-one-half-story turreted and balconied brick building occupies a prominent site on the grounds of the former state mental institution. It reflects contemporary populist concerns for the welfare of all citizens. The nearby auditorium, built fourteen years earlier, was designed by John G. Haskell.

## SN 26.32
## Menninger Foundation (West Campus)
*1930/1974*
*W. E. Glover / Kiene & Bradley and Skidmore Owings & Merrill*
*6000 West Sixth Street*

The pleasant hilltop campus was originally developed as the Security Benefit Association Hospital. The original massive three-story hospital building was modeled after Independence Hall. In 1954 it was taken over by the world-famous Menninger psychiatric foundation. The grounds are now sprinkled with geometrically precise, small-scale residential treatment facilities arranged around informal courts and connected by curving pathways. The newer buildings were featured in leading architectural journals at the time of their construction.

## SN 26.33
## Cedar Crest*
*1928. William D. Wight*
*Cedar Crest Road*

Sitting atop a ridge in northwestern Topeka and overlooking the river valley below, the building follows the manner of late-nineteenth-century grand country houses of France. It was built for the publisher Frank MacLennan. After the death of his widow in 1955, the house was given to the state and renovated as the governor's mansion. The architect was the younger of the two Wight brothers, noted for their Neoclassical architecture. William, however, had more wide-ranging tastes than his brother had.

## SN 26.34
## Pottawatomie Baptist Mission*
*1850*
*6425 Southwest Sixth Street*

This three-story twelve-room limestone structure sits in an eighty-one-acre wooded hollow in western Topeka, adjacent to the Kansas State Historical Museum. It was built to house a community center and school. Courses were taught not only in traditional subjects for children but also in agricultural and domestic activities. It has been restored to its original condition.

**SN 26.35**

## Kansas State Historical Museum

*1981–1984. Shaefer & Associates*
*6425 Southwest Sixth Street*

The fragmented, sprawling, one-story museum of Cottonwood limestone makes effective use of the site it shares with the Pottawatomie Baptist Mission. Its human-scaled glass-covered entry canopies face the older building to the northeast; the more massive exhibit spaces face the interstate highway to the south. The building was designed around the needs of the exhibit space and was literally built around a train that is a central part of the display. A major addition, designed by Abend Singleton to house the state archives, has been completed recently.

# Southeast Region

Most of the Southeast Region consists of the hill-plain terrain known as the Osage Cuestas, a formation with plentiful limestone. The principal exceptions are the Chautaqua Hills, formed from sandstone and located in the west, extending northward in a narrow band from the border with Oklahoma, and the Cherokee Lowlands in the southeast corner. The latter held considerable mineral resources, and thus mining and smelting became truly major industries in the area during the late nineteenth and early twentieth centuries, with substantial amounts of bituminous coal, zinc, and lead extracted. The production of gas and oil also has had an important role in the region's development.

Fifteen counties constitute the region, and their settlement occurred mostly after the Civil War, progressing generally from north to south. Besides the stimulus of nearby railroad service, which for example encouraged the early settlement of the counties adjacent to the Kansas-Missouri state line, other factors also influenced where settlement occurred in the region and the growth of several of the cities. Today, 62 percent of the region's 220,000 residents are located in the five counties that form the southeast corner of the region: Montgomery, Labette, Cherokee, Crawford, and Neosho. The five most populous cities in the region—Pittsburg, Coffeyville, Parsons, Independence, and Chanute—are found in those southeastern counties (excluding Cherokee). The sector is also the location for a state university and four of the region's six community colleges.

Pittsburg (population 17,800), in Crawford County, is the largest city in the region and was established in the 1870s as a mining and smelting center for a multicounty area rich in minerals. Extensive deposits of coal were extracted, primarily through strip mining, in addition to the mining of considerable amounts of zinc and lead. Large numbers of foreign immigrants arrived to work in those industries, giving a character to the town significantly different from most of the other larger cities in the state, with the possible exception of Kansas City, Kansas. The city itself was laid out on a regular grid, with the main axis running north/south along Broadway, and the central commercial district clustering at the intersection with Tenth Street. The grid is broken by several rail lines that bisect the city at irregular angles.

An interesting architectural manifestation of the industrial history of Pittsburg is found in the proliferation of company houses (e.g., CR 09.10), which are located throughout the residential portions of the city. Though this form of development is not unique to the region, nowhere else in the state do we find so large and well preserved a sampling of the building type. Housing for executives is concentrated in the southwestern quadrant of the city and provides an interesting contrast (e.g., CR 09.08). The city is also home to Pittsburg State University on the southern edge of town (CR 09.12). Founded in 1903 as the Kansas Manual Training Normal School and later changed to the Kansas State Teachers' College, the university is now a Regents Institution.

A decidedly different set of circumstances affected the development of the next largest city, Coffeyville (population 13,000), in Montgomery County. Located in a valley at a bend on the Verdigris River, it started in 1869 as a trading center with Indian Territory to its south. The real boost for the town came from the arrival of the railroad in 1870 and a growing trade in cattle. Additional development began in the early years of the twentieth century with the opening of natural gas and oil fields in the general area, including adjacent Oklahoma. The addition of this industrial base brought great wealth to the region and to Coffeyville's economy, to which the Brown mansion (MO 20.05) is a testament.

Twenty-two miles northwest of Coffeyville by road is Independence (population 10,000 and the seat of Montgomery County). Founded in 1869, and also on the Verdigris River, it too eventually benefited first from the discovery of natural gas and then from the development of oil fields in its vicinity in 1881 and 1903, providing an economic boost that encouraged the construction of the sizable Booth Hotel (MO 21.01). In contrast, the growth of Chanute (population 9,500), the seat of Neosho County, and of Parsons (population 12,000), in Labette County, resulted from their development as regional railroad centers (see NO 22.01). Each is a pleasantly scaled small city with a shaded residential district surrounding a modest commercial core.

A far different set of circumstances influenced the founding and development of the city of Fort Scott, whose population of 8,400 makes it the sixth largest in the region. The seat of Bourbon County, Fort Scott is a place of enduring historic interest. The city started as a civilian settlement adjacent to the military Fort Scott, which had been established in 1842. The fort, and thus the settlement, lay on the military road that ran south from Fort Leavenworth in northeastern Kansas to Fort Gibson on the Arksansas River (at a site across from Muskogee, Oklahoma). The arrival of the railroad at Fort Scott in 1869 ensured the city's survival after the post–Civil War deactivation of the fort. A number of the fort's buildings were soon adapted to civilian uses, thereby preserving them. Today the buildings have been restored to their original character, and they along with a number of reconstructions represent at least the core of the old fort, which now is administered by the National Park Service as a National Historic Site (BB 03.01). Adding to the historical character of the area is the U.S. National Cemetery Number One, established in 1862 as one of the original group of twelve national cemeteries. The city of Fort Scott is quite conscious of its historical character: a number of the early buildings have been restored (e.g., BB 03.04), and some newer buildings exhibit a deference to historical patterns (BB 03.03). The downtown district stretches to the south of the fort; the more desirable residential district lies to the west of the commercial core.

The architecture located in these six cities constitutes a significant portion of the following entries in the catalog, but numerous other sites in the region are also important. For example, the small community of Girard, seat of Crawford County, merits attention as being the place where *Appeal to Reason* and later the Little Blue Books were published (CR 08.02). The map and directory locate the counties, cities, and towns in the region and provide an outline for the sequence of the entries.

# SOUTHEAST REGION

Alpha-Numeric Directory

**ALLEN (AL)**

  **01** Iola†

**ANDERSON (AN)**

  **02** Garnett†

**BOURBON (BB)**

  **03** Fort Scott†

**CHAUTAUQUA (CQ)**

  **04** Sedan†

**CHEROKEE (CK)**

  **05** Baxter Springs;

    (Columbus†)

  **06** West Mineral

**COFFEY (CF)**

  **07** Burlington†

**CRAWFORD (CR)**

  **08** Girard†

  **09** Pittsburg

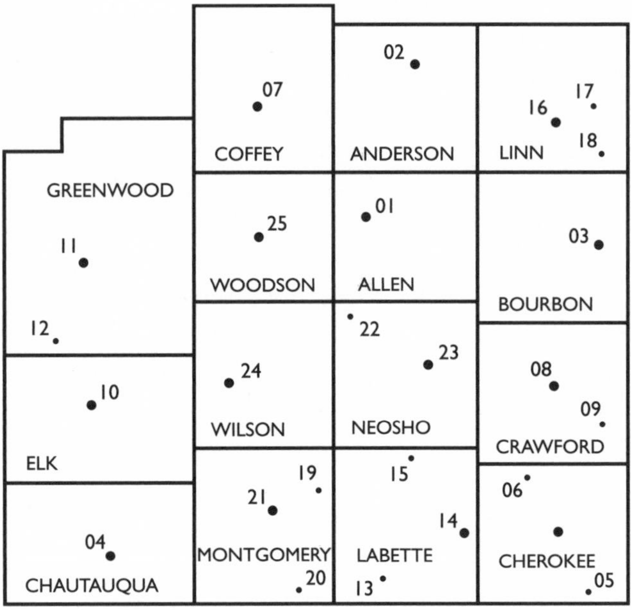

| | | |
|---|---|---|
| **ELK (EK)** | **LINN (LN)** | **NEOSHO (NO)** |
|   **10** Howard† |   **16** Mound City† |   **22** Chanute |
| **GREENWOOD (GW)** |   **17** Pleasanton |   **23** Erie† |
|   **11** Eureka† |   **18** Prescott | **WILSON (WL)** |
|   **12** Piedmont | **MONTGOMERY (MG)** |   **24** Fredonia† |
| **LABETTE (LB)** |   **19** Cherryvale | **WOODSON (WO)** |
|   **13** Edna |   **20** Coffeyville |   **25** Yates Center† |
|   **14** Oswego† |   **21** Independence† | |
|   **15** Parsons | | |

ALLEN COUNTY

# Iola

## AL 01.01
### Allen County Jail*
*1869*
*203 North Jefferson*

This two-story vernacular stone structure clearly reflects the pragmatic concerns of construction; the larger stones are placed near the bottom of the wall, and the more easily lifted smaller ones are nearer the top. The lower floor originally contained the cells; the upper floor housed the family of the jailer. The building is now operated as a museum by the Allen County Historical Society.

## AL 01.02
### Eureka Federal Savings and Loan
*1976. Abend Singleton*
*Sycamore and East Street*

The small banking facility is tucked behind a row of buildings facing the courthouse square. It resolves potential conflict between pedestrian and automobile traffic with an arcade leading from the sidewalk to the side-facing entry at the parking lot. The arcade also provides cover for a finely detailed wood wall set inside the stucco exterior shell. The building won a design award from the Kansas City Chapter of the American Institute of Architects.

## AL 01.03
### Iola State Bank (now Iola Bank and Trust)
*1908*
*Jefferson and Madison Street*

Constructed at the height of the gas boom, this two-story brick Renaissance Revival building follows a plan similar to other corner bank buildings across the state; however, stylistically it is unique. It demonstrates the clever application of a sophisticated classical vocabulary to a nontraditional building type. For example, the slight projection of the lower-level wall, framing the pair of arches that serve as the bidirectional corner entry, gives this entry precedence over an essentially similar one on the side of the building. The relationship between the upper- and lower-level windows also reveals the architect's compositional skill. The upper-floor windows on both facades are symmetrical about the building's center, yet on the lower level the symmetry is modified by the exigencies of function. The resulting syncopated rhythm gives animation to the facades.

## AL 01.04
### Jefferson Grade School
*1939. Lorentz Schmidt*
*Broadway and Jefferson Street*

This two-story concrete Modern building is representative of a style typical of structures built under the Works Progress Ad-

War hero. It is architecturally noteworthy as an example of the incremental growth of farm homes. When the Funston family purchased the house in 1864, the rectangular building contained only three simple rooms; the porches, bays, side rooms, and gables were added over time.

ministration and other depression-era federal relief programs during the 1930s. As a labor-intensive building material, concrete allowed for the maximum employment of an unskilled labor force. The simple lines, cubistic volumes, and standard metal sashes also contributed to the efficacy of the construction.

AL 01.05

## Lincoln Grade School

*1939. Lorentz Schmidt*
*700 North Jefferson Street*

A companion to the Jefferson Grade School with which it shares many features, this concrete school building illustrates how a gifted architect can provide diverse solutions to essentially the same problem while using a limited design vocabulary. In both cases, visual interest is created through the manipulation of surface and volume around the area of the corner entry. The architect's earlier work, in the Wichita area, demonstrated his sensitivity to more traditional styles. He evidently adapted quickly to changing tastes and conditions.

AL 01.06

## Funston Home*

*1860*
*On U.S. 169 (four miles north of Iola)*

The small clapboard farmhouse is historically significant as the boyhood home of Frederick Funston, the Spanish American

# Garnett

### AN 02.01
## Shelley-Tipton House*
*1871*
*812 West Fourth*

This two-story clapboard house displays many features typical of Italianate homes of the period, including a hipped roof, a tall cupola and tower, wide eaves with decorative brackets, tall windows, a gabled projecting entry bay, and a one-story porch. Here, the brackets of the porch and eaves are particularly ornate.

### AN 02.02
## Anderson County Courthouse*
*1901–1902. George P. Washburn*
*Fourth and Oak Street*

Centered in a public square, this two-story brick Romanesque Revival courthouse is sur-

rounded on three sides by handsome stone and brick commerical buildings. Of particular note is the 1883 bank building at the northwest corner of Fourth and Oak. Like many of the architect's courthouses, this one features four corner turrets and a central tower, and it bears a close resemblance to the Doniphan County Courthouse.

### AN 02.03
## Holy Angels Catholic Church
*1914–1915. Henry W. Brinkman*
*Fourth and Spruce Street*

This stone-trimmed brick church features an eclectic vocabulary of elements that combine to produce a striking image. The dominant central entry tower has a strong sense of both weightiness in its square base and verticality in its tall, octagonal spire. The interior is quite simple and consists of a single volume spanned by a series of round arches.

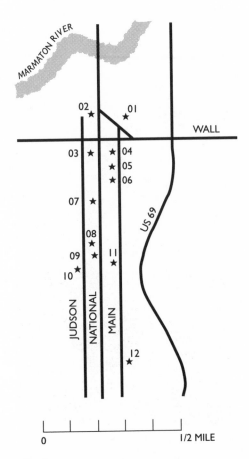

*Fort Scott*

# Fort Scott

BB 03.01
## Fort Scott National Historic Site*
*1842–1853*
*Main and Old Fort Boulevard*

The grouping of nine renovated and eleven reconstructed wood and stone one- and two-story French Colonial buildings is organized around a broad, flat parade ground (now a carefully tended lawn). The grouping comprises a hospital, which is now a visitors' center, several infantry barracks and officers' quarters, including the carefully restored Wilson Goodlander home, a stable, a headquarters building, a storehouse, a guardhouse, and a host of smaller support structures such as carriage houses, a bakery, and a blacksmith shop. The fort was originally surrounded by a stockade twelve feet high. Fort Scott served military purposes from 1843 until 1855 and again during the Civil War; after that, the remaining buildings were used for a variety of private purposes. Restoration and reconstruction of the site has been done by the National Park Service.

BB 03.02
## Crain Hardware, Eagle Block, and Hammons Realty buildings
*1888, 1888, and 1890*
*8–16 North National Street*

This group of two- and three-story commercial buildings (listed north to south) il-lustrates the range of features often found in late-nineteenth-century commercial architecture. The upper story of the Hammons Realty Building is faced in pressed metal; the other two are principally of brick trimmed in stone. Some of the original cast-iron storefronts, using thin columns to permit larger display windows, remain. The Crain Hardware Building is the best preserved of the three, and it contains many of the original store fixtures.

BB 03.03
## Microwave Tower
*1989. David Irwin, with Sverdrup & Parcell*
*National and Wall Street*

From its midblock location, the well-adorned Post-Modern tower dominates the city skyline. The historic reference to a Renaissance campanile reflects both the architectural trend of the time and the local community's awareness of the importance of its heritage.

### BB 03.04
## Union Block*
*1884*
*18–24 South Main Street*

Occupying a corner site, this three-story commercial block lies in the heart of the historic downtown district. Its east facade provides a good example of a repetitive, mass-produced cast-iron storefront construction of the sort pioneered by James Bogardus and others about the middle of the nineteenth century. The detail on the building is heightened by a modern application of paint; pale blue, rust, and pink-beige colors were selected by local architect David Irwin for a number of downtown buildings, giving the district a festive and harmonious character.

### BB 03.05
## Scottish Rite Temple
*1923–1926. William T. Schmitt*
*102–116 South Main Street*

The brick and terracotta building stands out from the surrounding nineteenth- and early-twentieth-century commercial buildings because of its large scale and exotic ornamentation. It features a 500-seat auditorium and a 1,200-seat banquet room. Its facade is adorned with a profusion of gothic elements and fraternal symbols, the most prominent of which is a stylized low-relief terracotta double-eagle, designed by Heinz Warneke of New York. Its wings stretch forty-eight feet across the front of the building.

### BB 03.06
## Moody Building*
*1888*
*Second and Main Street*

This three-story brick building combines commercial uses on the ground floor with apartment units above. The functions are well articulated on the facade. The upper two-story bay windows springing from groundfloor pilasters and capped by octagonal towers as well as the gable above the entry to the apartment units have a residential scale and character. The building has been restored recently.

### BB 03.07
## Bourbon County Courthouse
*1929–1930. Cuthbert & Suehrk*
*National and Second Street*

The courthouse, a three-story brick and limestone Neoclassical building, occupies a half block near the southern end of the downtown district. The building's limestone base and upper-level projecting frontispieces give it a sense of somber monumentality. It contains a pleasant and well-preserved barrel-vaulted courtroom on the third floor. A brick one-story law enforcement center has been added to the north.

## BB 03.08
### Fort Scott Junior High School
*1918*
*National and Fifth Street*

This massive three-story brick Collegiate Gothic school building originally housed both an elementary and a junior high school. The building's simplified English Gothic derivation followed popular models of the time.

## BB 03.09
### Congregational Church
*1873*
*National and Fifth Street*

The most prominent feature of this rectangular gable-roofed red-brick Gothic Revival

church is its corner entry tower with a tall spire. The building has been restored by the Historic Preservation Association of Bourbon County, which operates a bookstore in the building.

## BB 03.10
### Herbert Home
*1887*
*512 South Judson Street*

This large two-and-one-half-story brick Queen Anne Style home demonstrates the exuberance and inventiveness of Victorian builders. The building's rich decorative vocabulary includes porch columns of granite on the first level and plain wood on the second level; a third-level corner porch uses turned wood posts. The building also features decorative vertical-board wood panels with ornate shingled panels as well as stained glass and etched, beveled, and patterned glass. The interior contains six fireplaces and elaborate woodwork of cherry, oak, and walnut.

istration and also typifies the modestly streamlined and stylized features of much of this work.

*Herbert home*

## BB 03.11
## Martin House

*1873*
*524 South Main Street*

A hilltop corner site gives this two-story brick Georgian Revival home a commanding presence. The front facade features a full-width one-story porch, which is bisected by a two-story semicircular porch supported on full-height Corinthian columns.

## BB 03.12
## Fort Scott High School Stadium

*1939*
*Ninth and South Main Street*

The Moderne concrete and limestone seating structure runs along one side of the football field, which in turn lies between the high school on the south and a pleasant city park on the north. The stadium serves to illustrate the range of public projects done under the federal Works Progress Admin-

# Sedan

**CQ 04.01**
## Chautauqua County Courthouse
*1917–1918. Washburn & Son*
*Cherokee and Chautauqua Street*

Reflecting the taste of the time, the two-and-one-half-story stone-trimmed red-brick Neoclassical building occupies a large block to the north of the central business district. This courthouse represents a marked departure from the architect's earlier Romanesque Revival courthouses.

# Baxter Springs

**CK 05.01**
## Johnston Library*
*1872*
*210 West Tenth Street*

Classically detailed, this two-story gable-roofed rectangular brick building was built originally as the Cherokee County Courthouse. After interim uses as a city hall, jail, and junior college, in 1905 it assumed its present use as a public library.

. . . . . . . . . . . . . . . . . . . . . . . . . . . . . . . .

# West Mineral

**CK 06.01**
## Big Brutus
*1962–1963*
*On K 102 (six miles west of K 7)*

This enormous electric mining shovel is the second largest in the world, taller than a fifteen-story building. It was assembled from parts transported by 150 railcars to a site eleven miles from its present location, traveling over that distance through the course of its eleven years of operation. Renovated in 1985 to house a museum, it serves as a reminder of the importance of mining to the economic development of southeast Kansas.

# Burlington

### CF 07.01
**Wolf Creek Nuclear Plant**
*ca. 1976*
*On U.S. 75 (north of Burlington)*

Providing a striking contrast to the surrounding prairie, the complex is notable not only for its gargantuan scale but also for its geometric clarity, in which repeating simple rectilinear structures play against a larger domed form.

### CF 07.02
**Burlington Lower Elementary School**
*1990. Hight Jackson Associates*
*Seventh and Neosho*

The major addition of two-tone brick with cast-stone trim to a 1950s school building is exemplary of the Post-Modern Style popular in the 1980s. Classically inspired ornament is used in a deliberately nontraditional manner. The curving colonnade at the entry, along the bus drop-off zone, provides a notably grand gesture.

### CF 07.03
**Coffey County Courthouse**
*1964. Kiene & Bradley*
*Sixth and Neosho*

This low stone-trimmed Modern brick courthouse demonstrates an attempt to infuse symbolic importance into a building of simple vocabulary and utilitarian plan. The glazed building entry is at the juncture of an administrative wing and a slightly taller courtroom mass. The proportions of the colonnade at the entry porch are reminiscent of classical arcades.

### CF 07.04
**Peoples National Bank**
*1976. Shaefer & Schirmer*
*100 block of East Fourth Street*

The bank, a simple Modern brick building, holds interest in both its detailed resolution and its clever geometry. The banking lobby occupies a square box set within and at a forty-five-degree angle to a larger, lower, square unit. The areas outside the central interior volume and within the larger square form provide covered open spaces for the entry and the drive-through banking lanes. The basic plan for the building was outlined by Wilbert Dreiling, the client.

# Girard

### CR 08.01
## Crawford County Courthouse
*1921–1922. Tonini & Bramblet*
*Summit and Forest Street*

The three-story limestone Neoclassical building occupies a full block near the center of the small-scale business district. It is organized around a central skylit atrium.

### CR 08.02
## Wayland House*
*1886*
*721 North Summit*

Rather unassuming, the two-story wood-frame Victorian house sits well back from the road on a large, shaded lot. It is most notable as the home of Julius A. Wayland, founding publisher of the widely circulated and influential Socialist newspaper, *Appeal to Reason*. When the paper ceased publication in 1922, then publisher Emanuel Haldeman-Julius used the printing facilities to produce the Little Blue Books, a series of abridged editions of the classics. The building represents the town's disproportionate influence on the political and cultural life of the nation through the late nineteenth and early twentieth centuries.

. . . . . . . . . . . . . . . . . . . . . . . . . . . . . . . .

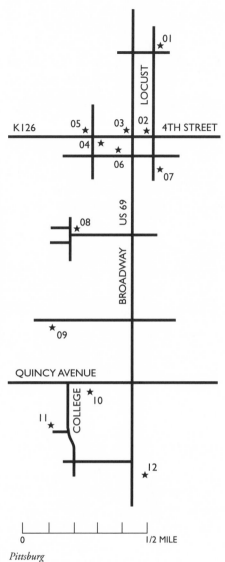

*Pittsburg*

# Pittsburg

### CR 09.01
## Our Lady of Lourdes Church
*1904*
*916 North Locust*

The Gothic Revival stone church sits on a corner, one block from the town's main street. Its nave possesses an interesting cross-section, where a central pointed arch rests

on lower half-arches on either side. The building has been recently restored.

*Besse Hotel*

### CR 09.02
## Besse Hotel
*1926*
*William T. Schmitt, J. Watson Hawk &*
*J. O. Parr*
*121 East Fourth*

A monument to civic pride, this twelve-story brick building is the town's tallest. It displays a curious mixture of motifs, including a three-story yellow-brick arch above the main door, a canopy supported by iron brackets at the side entry, and a variety of quasi-Gothic terracotta decorative panels. The building has been converted to apartments.

### CR 09.03
## Commerce Building
## (New Century Building)
*1908*
*401 North Broadway*

This four-story Renaissance Revival commercial building of brick, terracotta, and stone occupies the northeast corner of the town's main intersection; at one time similar structures were located on the other corners. The building's entry opens onto a grand stair leading to a single wide corridor on each floor. Now largely vacant, the building once housed a variety of professional offices.

### CR 09.04
## Pittsburg Public Library*
*1910. Patton & Miller*
*Fourth and West Walnut Street*

This one-and-one-half-story hipped-roofed stone building occupies a generous, shaded

corner lot. The structure is a fine demonstration of the potential applicability of the Prairie Style to institutional buildings. It retains many of the characteristic elements of that style, yet they are infused with a greater sense of permanence and formality. The interior mixes Arts and Crafts detail with formal planning principles. It is organized around an entry hall, which gives access through a series of segmented archways to the building's main public spaces.

### CR 09.05
### Mirza Shrine Temple
*1925. Thomas W. Williamson*
*Fifth and Pine Street*

The large brick Egyptian Revival building occupies a full block on Pine Street. The exotic decorative motifs in limestone are applied to an essentially classical scheme. The building was renovated in 1984 and now serves as the city auditorium.

### CR 09.06
### Red Man Hall
*1903. George G. Munn*
*112–118 West Third*

The zinc cladding of the upper floor and the segmented round-corner bay of this two-story building are typical of the many commercial buildings that once lined the downtown streets; only a few now remain. The metal was locally produced. The upper level of the building contains a hall with a seating capacity of 1,500 people and also houses a series of other club rooms.

### CR 09.07
### Hance White Building
### (Pittsburg Marble Works)
*1904. Hance White (builder)*
*202 North Locust*

This two-story stone building sits adjacent to the railroad tracks. It was built as a showroom for a tombstone and architectural ornament business and features carved stonework done by the firm's stone cutters. Hance White's home, at 512 West First Street, displays other examples of his work.

### CR 09.08
### Schlanger House
*1908. James H. Seeley*
*311 South Olive*

The house, a three-story brick and wood Queen Anne Style, occupies a prominent corner site in a neighborhood containing a number of large homes, several of which were built by executives of local mining companies. The building was recently renovated to repair damage from soil settlement caused by earlier undermining. Much of the town is laced with mine tunnels.

CR 09.09
### Edgar C. Hood House
*1913*
*303 West Jefferson*

Unusually ornamented, this two-story brick and slate shingle building sits on a quiet res-

idential street. The metal railings appear to have been salvaged from a much earlier structure. Built for the owner's young bride, it reportedly was derived from an illustration in a current ladies' magazine.

CR 09.10
### Square Company House
*ca. 1900*
*203 East Quincy*

The house is typical of many in the community that were erected by local mining companies between 1880 and 1920 to accommodate workers who were imported from many parts of the country and the world. The house originally contained four rooms, the kitchen separated from the body of the house. This plan, as was an L-shaped model, was easy to expand; consequently, many of the original stock of worker houses continue to be used, though additions made to them tend to mask (but not quite conceal) their continuing presence in the community.

CR 09.11
### Graham House
*1934. A. Staneart Graham (builder)*
*601 Grandview Heights Boulevard*

Designed and constructed by its owner, an attorney, this distinctive metal-roofed stone and concrete residence sits in an overgrown lot at the end of a cul-de-sac. It uses a variety of innovative construction techniques; the walls were made of rock assembled inside

red- and yellow-brick faces a broad lawn at the front of the Pittsburg State University campus. It forms the western end of the central academic quadrangle. Stanton was then the state architect.

wooden forms and covered with concrete; the concrete vaults of the lower roof are reinforced by rails salvaged from the Joplin Pittsburg rail line. It also features a number of forward-looking energy-saving devices, including a double roof, deep overhanging eaves, and a solar water-heating system.

CR 09.12

## Russ Hall
## (Pittsburg State University)
*1908. John F. Stanton*
*1701 South Broadway*

This imposing 235-foot-long four-story Renaissance Revival administrative building of

# Howard

### EK 10.01
## Elk County Courthouse
*1907–1908. George McDonald*
*127 North Pine*

only the bank but also a doctor's office on the ground floor, a barber shop in the basement, and five apartments on the upper floor. After the bank moved to newer quarters in 1960, the building for a time housed an electrical shop. Now vacant, a structure that was once a symbol of prosperity, through underuse and lack of maintenance, has become an indicator of changed circumstances.

The courthouse, a two-and-one-half-story freely interpreted Romanesque Revival building of buff-brick and limestone trim, occupies a full block near the center of town. The interior has been completely remodeled.

### EK 10.02
## Howard National Bank Building
*1888*
*Wabash and Washington*

This two-story corner bank building of stone, like similar buildings in other Kansas towns, signaled the center of commercial activity. Originally, the building housed not

# Eureka

### GW 11.01
## Greenwood County Courthouse
*1956. Williamson & Loebsack*
*300 block of North Main*

Set on the courthouse square, this two-story concrete-frame building emphasizes the utilitarian and administrative aspect of county government. The upper-level curtainwall, though well proportioned and detailed, gives little clue as to the function of the building. Originally the structure was L-shaped but has received subsequent additions. This courthouse replaced one from 1873 that was similar to a courthouse still in use in Chase County designed by John Haskell.

### GW 11.02
## Eureka City Hall and Auditorium
*1924. S. S. Voigt*
*300 block of North Oak*

Massively scaled, this Neoclassical brick building with stone trim is representative of a public building type popular from 1920 to 1940. Various Kansas towns of modest size built municipal buildings that combined in one structure the town's offices and (usually on the upper level) multipurpose facilities for public meetings.

### GW 11.03
## Christian and Congregational Church
*1888. John G. Haskell*
*117 East Third*

The small Romanesque Revival church, with a modified Akron Plan, was built using stone extracted from local quarries. The western wing was added in 1924 and was faced with stone removed from the original structure at the junction with the new wing. It appears that the steeple above the entry tower has been modified.

. . . . . . . . . . . . . . . . . . . . . . . . . . . . . . . .

# Piedmont

### GW 12.01
## North Branch Otter Creek Bridge*
*1928. James Barney Marsh*
*One mile west and five miles north of Piedmont*

The single-span concrete rainbow-arch bridge is representative of the seventy-six

bridges designed by the Marsh Bridge Company in Kansas between 1917 and 1940. This handsome bridge is of the tied-arch type. Here, the roadway is suspended from the arch elements. The buttresses are also worthy of note; they echo the form of the central span.

# Edna

### LB 13.01
### Grain Elevator
*Main Street*

This decaying building is located along the railroad tracks on the southern edge of town. Structures like this could once be found in nearly every town in Kansas. One of only a few remaining old style grain elevators, it is a type made obsolete after the advent of the sealed, round elevator.

### LB 13.02
### First State Bank*
*1887*
*Delaware and Main Street*

Smaller than most others of the type, this stone, two-story corner bank building is only two bays wide and three deep. The series of Ionic columns that wrap around the ground floor is another unusual feature making the building noteworthy.

# Oswego

## LB 14.01

### Smith-Hollingsworth-Thomas Log Cabin✦

*1867*
*Third and Merchant Street*

Located in a small, shaded park, this double pen (or dog trot) log cabin consists of two one-room log structures connected by a single long gable. The space between the two structures is often left open, but here it has been closed in. It is typical of the homes built by the area's first settlers and currently serves as a museum.

## LB 14.02

### Labette County Courthouse

*1948. Thomas W. Williamson & Company*
*Fourth and Merchant*

This concrete Moderne building occupies a narrow lawn between parallel streets. It mimics the disposition and proportion of earlier Neoclassical buildings but with detail rendered in a simplified, streamlined man-

ner. The structure marks a point of transition in the evolution of the building type; henceforth, architects sought inspiration from functional necessity rather than from precedent.

. . . . . . . . . . . . . . . . . . . . . . . . . . . . . . . .

# Parsons

## LB 15.01

### Parsons Carnegie Library*

*1909. F. E. Parker*
*Seventeenth and Broadway*

The library, a symmetrical stone building with a tile-hipped roof, is one of three important civic and religious buildings grouped around a prominent intersection (see LB 15.02 and .03). Although the library makes use of Classical ornament, its massing suggests other influences, including those of the Prairie Style and the Secession. In plan, it follows the format used by many of the Carnegie libraries across the state.

## LB 15.02

### First Presbyterian Church

*1906–1907. Charles W. Squires*
*Seventeenth and Broadway*

Massive and complicated, this stone structure has been described as being in the Gothic Romanesque Style. It is a curious and original assemblage of colliding forms adorned with ornament drawn from diverse sources. Unity is achieved primarily through

the uniform color and texture of the stone surface. The equally eclectic worship space was replaced in 1953 by a more orderly rectilinear treatment.

### LB 15.03

## Parsons Municipal Auditorium

*1922. Thomas W. Williamson*
*Seventeenth and Broadway*

Handsome and restrained, the stone-trimmed Neoclassical building contains the city hall as well as a 1,600-seat auditorium. The latter, which had been closed for a number of years, reopened in 1989 after a renovation. The architect had one of the largest and busiest offices in the state for much of the early twentieth century.

### LB 15.04

## Southwestern Bell Telephone Building and Microwave Tower

*1959/1980*
*Brinkman & Hagan/ Sverdrup & Parcell*
*Seventeenth and Washington*

Both the building and tower are typical of such structures across the state. The Modern building is a rather plain two-story two-tone brick box. The tower is more sculptural and distinctive, consisting of three interconnected upturned pyramids set on tall concrete masts. Microwave towers of varying configuration were built in most sizable towns principally between the years 1960 and 1980. Since that time, changing cable technology, which now allows the transmission of more information, has made microwave transmission less competitive.

# Pleasanton

## Mound City

### LN 16.01
**Linn County Courthouse\***
*1885–1886. George Ropes*
*Fourth and Main*

Occupying a full block to the east of the main business district, this two-story brick courthouse is distinctive among Kansas courthouses in both its ornament, which borrows from the Queen Ann Style, and its organization, which is more linear than most. Newer justice and health centers have been built on the rear of the site. The original two-story rectangular brick jail, built in 1868 and now used as the city hall, is located across the street.

. . . . . . . . . . . . . . . . . . . . . . . . . . . . . . . .

### LN 17.01
**Kincaid and Crocker Opera House\***
*1884–1885*
*Eighth and Main*

The two-story Italianate brick commercial structure is typical of a noteworthy building type of the time. A large, open area on the second floor above the lower-level retail spaces provided a venue for traveling shows and other nonsectarian gatherings. It is now used as a garment factory.

### LN 17.02
**Charles Hadsell House**
*1861*
*On U.S. 69 (six miles north of Pleasanton)*

The small stone cabin is built over a natural spring on the side of a hill in the midst of the Marais de Cygnes Massacre Memorial Park.\* The area is the site where in 1858 a band of proslavery activists shot eleven unarmed free-state settlers, five of whom were killed. The cabin was built by a friend of John Brown, who subsequently used the site as a fort for free-state forces. It is preserved as a museum, operated by the Kansas State Historical Society.

. . . . . . . . . . . . . . . . . . . . . . . . . . . . . . . .

**LN 18.01**
## Prescott School*
*1882*
*Third and Main*

Simple but elegant, the two-story square Italianate brick school building features a hipped roof with a gable above the entry and a square bell tower at the building's center. It was used as a school unit until 1972 and currently serves as the Prescott City Library.

# Cherryvale

**MG 19.01**
## Cherryvale United Methodist Church
*1906/1910*
*Third and Labette Street*

This brick church dwarfs its residential neighbors. The building's strong geometry allows it to address clearly its corner site. Opposing wings spring from the diagonals of the central hipped-roofed mass and enclose a corner yard. The entry tower is attached at a third corner, facing the street. The building is of interest on the interior as well. The cavernous worship space features elaborate and well-detailed woodwork. The interior work and the upper portion of the tower are part of a 1910 postfire reconstruction. Originally, the tower had a crenellated top and domed lanterns protruded from the three roof peaks.

**MG 19.02**
## Cherryvale Carnegie Free Library*
*1913. George P. Washburn & Son*
*329 East Main*

The one-and-one-half-story stone-trimmed Neoclassical building is typical of the several Carnegie libraries designed by the architect in this area of Kansas, notably the one in

Burlington done in 1912 and another in Eureka in 1914. They lack the vigor of the firm's earlier work, however, perhaps reflecting the retirement of the elder Washburn about 1907.

..................................

# Coffeyville

## MG 20.01
### Municipal Building
*1929*
*C. A. Henderson with Owen Saylor & Payson*
*Seventh and Walnut Street*

Indicative of the city's growth in the early twentieth century, this building contains city offices as well as court facilities. It is a massive three-story Neoclassical brick and limestone structure occupying a full downtown block.

## MG 20.02
### Condon National Bank*
*1890*
*811 Walnut Street*

Interestingly ornamented, the irregularly shaped brick and stone Italianate building faces a public plaza. The building's separate banking, office, and retail functions are clearly articulated in the facades. It is noteworthy also as the site of the foiled Dalton Gang bank robbery of 1892. The bullet holes from the ensuing shoot-out are still visible.

## MG 20.03
### Midland Theater
*1928–1929*
*212 Eighth Street*

This Moorish terracotta building is representative of many grand movie theaters built throughout Kansas in the early part of the century. Unlike many others, the facility has remained in continuous operation. Characteristically, the exotic motifs displayed on the exterior are carried into the relatively unchanged interior.

## MG 20.04
### First Baptist Church
*1969. Leon Ragsdale*
*Ninth and Elm Street*

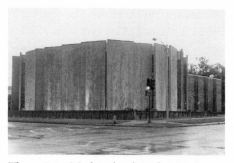

The unique Modern brick and precast concrete building occupies a prominent downtown site. The corner-facing sanctuary is formed by a curving series of vertical precast and prestressed concrete panels featuring low-relief sculptural murals by Pepe Mendez of Tulsa on both the interior and exterior. This arrangement controls the sunlight that enters the worship space through the stained-glass windows set in the slots between the panels. The remaining portions of the building are faced in brick and aligned with the street grid and are subordinated to the expressive sanctuary.

## MG 20.05
### W. P. Brown Mansion*
*1899–1906. Wilder & Wight*
*Walnut and Eldridge Street*

Occupying a parklike setting atop a tall bluff overlooking the town and the surrounding countryside, this grand Neoclassical stucco mansion has sixteen rooms. Two sides of the house feature a two-story Ionic-columned arcade, and a third side features a similarly

ornamented semicircular porte cochere. The original owner made his fortune through the discovery of natural gas; he then expanded his enterprises to include the trading of lumber and grain. Operated by the Coffeyville Historical Society as a house museum, in which many of the original furnishings remain, the mansion is perhaps the most impressive among the architects' residential commissions although they are primarily known for their public and commercial work.

....................................

# Independence

## MG 21.01
### Booth Hotel*
*1912. Frank Bender*
*201 West Main Street*

Though relatively plain, the five-story U-shaped hotel block is a reminder of an important period in the town's history, when it boomed in the late nineteenth and early twentieth centuries with the nearby discovery of natural gas in 1881 and oil in 1903. The boom ended when the gas field was depleted, soon after the construction of this hotel.

## MG 21.02
### Blakeslee Motor Company Building*
*1918*
*211 Myrtle*

Influenced by the Prairie Style, this one-story limestone-trimmed brick building is interesting as an exploration of a relatively new building type. The large windows allow an unobstructed view and abundant natural light into the large automobile showroom. It lacked the generous parking later demanded by automobile dealerships, so it now houses an electrical supply company.

MG 21.03
## Independence Public Carnegie Library*
*1907. Frederick C. Gunn*
*220 East Maple*

This two-and-one-half-story two-tone brick Neoclassical building is among the larger of the Carnegie libraries in Kansas. It has a curious sense of scale, with some elements seeming overly large and others somewhat undersized. It is still used as a library. Frederick Gunn was at one time the partner of the idiosyncratic architect Louis Curtiss.

MG 21.04
## Montgomery County Judicial Center
*1989*
*Edwards & Daniels, with Hight Jackson Associates*
*Fifth and Main Street*

The sprawling Modern brick and stone complex sits at the eastern edge of the central business district, adjacent to the 1931 Neoclassical limestone courthouse designed by Cuthbert and Suehrk. The center gives clear expression to the variety of public and private spaces contained within, yet it presents a unified image that complements the older building next door.

MG 21.05
## Dewlen-Spohnauer Bridge*
*1926. James Barney Marsh*
*On Old U.S. 160, one mile east of Independence*

The three-span tied-arch concrete bridge spans the Verdigris River. The use of multiple, repetitive spanning elements makes this system economical and easily adaptable to a variety of conditions.

# Chanute

### NO 22.01
## Atchison Topeka and Santa Fe Depot
*1902–1903*
*111 North Lincoln*

The long two-story hipped-roofed brick building reflects the importance of the railroad to Chanute, the town resulting from the consolidation of four smaller communities (Toga, Alliance, New Chicago, and Chicago Junction) that combined forces in 1870 to attract the railroad. The new town derived its name from the civil engineer, Octave Chanute, who suggested the consolidation. The depot's distinctive central tower faces away from the street and toward the tracks. The building, which served as a division headquarters for the railroad, is now vacant.

### NO 22.02
## First National Bank
*1887*
*Lincoln and Main Street*

The two-story brick and stone building represents a highly original and distinctive variant on a common Kansas building type, the corner bank building. It is an essay in ma-

sonry construction and a monument to its builder. The largely rough-stone lower level features both arched and trabeated openings, and the mostly brick upper floor features a variety of arched openings (some paired beneath relieving arches) and round windows framed in both brick and stone. The corner bay was originally capped by a copper dome.

### NO 22.03
## M. Bailey and Company Bank
*1880. Jesse Parsons (builder)*
*Highland and Main Street*

Stone-trimmed, this brick corner bank is a carefully considered and well-resolved example of the Italianate Style. It features regular window openings beneath flat stone lintels on the upper floor and segmented arch lintels on the lower floor, with a full arched opening at its corner entry. This more academic building provides an interesting contrast to the First National Bank one block to the west.

**NO 22.04**

**Chanute Public Library**

*1906. A. T. Simmons*
*102 South Lincoln*

The two-story Eclectic stone-trimmed buff-brick library is part of a complex of municipal buildings. It combines Neoclassical, Romanesque Revival, and Prairie Style elements into an asymmetrically balanced composition. The interior has been extensively remodeled.

**NO 22.05**

**Chanute Memorial Building**

*1924–1925. Schmidt Boucher & Overend*
*First and Jefferson Street*

This grand three-story brick and stone Neoclassical building sits adjacent to a grain elevator located along the railroad tracks, which bisect the town. In addition to the auditorium, it houses city offices, the police station, the fire department, and district courts. City ownership of public utilities helped to finance the building.

. . . . . . . . . . . . . . . . . . . . . . . . . . . . . . .

# Erie

**NO 23.01**

**Neosho County Courthouse**

*1962. Kiene & Bradley*
*Second and Main Street*

The courthouse, a one-story buff-brick Modern building, occupies a prominent spot along the small town's main commercial street. A colonnade of six slender concrete columns helps distinguish the building as a public facility. The architects received a number of commissions to replace aging courthouses in the region since county commissioners faced with the problems of adaptability and repair of the older structures were impressed by the architects' practical approach.

## Fredonia

### WL 24.01
### Wilson County Courthouse
*1960. Kiene & Bradley*
*Sixth to Seventh and Madison to Monroe*

This two-story Modern building of brick, stone, and glass occupies a full block in the center of town. It demonstrates the difficulty involved in placing an automobile-oriented building in a nineteenth-century context. Because of the parking spaces required, the building effectively turns its back to the north half of the square. As compensation, a tower, which mimics the vocabulary of the courthouse, is located on this side of the site. It houses the bell that was removed from the previous (1889) courthouse before it was razed.

### WL 24.02
### Dr. A. C. Flack House*
*1895*
*303 North Eighth Street*

The rambling two-story Victorian home reflects the affluence that followed the 1892 discovery of oil near Neodesha in southern Wilson County. The house consists of conventional elements though they are composed in a less than usual manner.

# Yates Center

### WO 25.01
## Woodson County Courthouse*
*1899–1900. George P. Washburn*
*Main and State Street*

The square two-story limestone-trimmed courthouse of red brick is located in the center of a landscaped square, the anchoring element of the Yates Center Courthouse Square Historic District.* The street surrounding the square is paved in red brick and is lined by one- and two-story commercial buildings of the late nineteenth and early twentieth centuries. The courthouse is similar in plan and style to others across the state designed by the architect. The cupola has been altered.

### WO 25.02
## Light Hardware Building (Stockbrand and Kemmerer Department Store)*
*1904. George P. Washburn*
*Main and Rutledge Street*

Anchoring the southeast corner of the courthouse square, this two-story stone-trimmed commercial building bears a complementary resemblance to the courthouse. The building has been renovated as a health club, winning an award from the Kansas Preserva-

tion Alliance. The more ornate metal commercial buildings in the foreground were built between ten and twenty years prior to the corner building and reflect the tastes of the late nineteenth century. Taken together, the buildings around the courthouse square form a well-preserved example of the turn-of-the-century character of a number of Kansas towns.

### WO 25.03
## Woodson Hotel*
*1887. J. T. Black*
*State and Butler Street*

The two-story Italianate hotel building sits on the northwest corner of the courthouse square. The walls topped with an articulate stone cornice are effectively treated, combining rough limestone surfaces with smooth-stone stringcourses that are connected to smooth-stone segmented arch lintels. The corner is also cleverly resolved, stepping back to allow stairs up to a main corner entry.

### WO 25.04
## Yates Center Carnegie Library*
*1912. A. T. Simmons*
*218 North Main Street*

The layout of this stone-trimmed brick building is typical of many small Carnegie libraries, with a central half-level entry giving access to the above-ground basement meeting rooms below and a reading room above. The ornament here, however, is highly original and difficult to classify; it appears to be part of the early twentieth century's search for a nontraditional vocabulary.

**WO 25.06**
## Octagonal Barn
*1910*
*On U.S. 75 (one mile north of Yates Center)*

**WO 25.05**
## First Christian Church
*ca. 1900. George P. Washburn (attrib.)*
*Washington and Main Street*

This well-preserved octagonal wood barn, situated in a farmyard near the road, is an increasingly rare example of a once-popular building form. Built around an existing silo, the supporting posts consist of undressed rough logs.

Although the forms of this small brick church are simple and residential in scale, the result bears a strong resemblance to the architect's commercial and institutional work in town, hence the attribution to George Washburn, who clearly had a strong effect on the town's character. Another building he designed is the large frame residence known as the Henry F. Stockerbrand house at 211 South Main.◆

# Northcentral Region

The Northcentral Region has a diverse topography. In the central area are the most northern elements of the Flint Hills, to their west the start of the Smoky Hills. In the region's northeastern sector we find the rounded hills and broad valleys that record the effects of the last Ice Age. As for the native flora, before the settlers arrived tall prairie grasses were dominant; but after more than a century of intensive agricultural activity and the introduction of flood control projects, the vegetation and overall character of the region have been modified significantly. The major exception is an area known as the Konza Prairie Conservancy, located a few miles south of Manhattan, where the nearly 9,000 acres still retain the tall grass cover that once characterized much of eastern Kansas. The region's fourteen counties constitute a major agricultural area, and a sizable number of the region's residents are located on farms or in small towns; yet 39 percent of the region's population of 256,300 is found in but three cities: Salina, Manhattan, and Junction City.

Salina, the seat of Saline County, is the largest (population 42,300). It is situated in the region's southwestern corner, at the confluence of the Saline and Smoky Hill rivers, in the heart of the hard-wheat country. Salina had its start in 1859 as a trading place for Indians. Later on, it became the most western settlement on the trail to the Colorado gold fields. Significant growth for the city, however, had to wait until the town gained railroad service, which occurred in 1867; by the 1880s, Salina had become one of the principal cities of Kansas. Today it ranks seventh in the state in population.

The city is situated for the most part southeast of the interchange between Interstates 70 and 135. Salina's broad main street, Santa Fe Avenue, runs approximately three miles from the campus of Kansas Wesleyan University on the south to St. John's Military School on the north. On the eastern side of the city, a notable pair of city parks, Oakdale and Kenwood, are nestled into broad curves in the Saline River. The present appearance of the city has been significantly influenced by a father-and-son team of architects, Charles and John Shaver. The former began the firm in 1915 and the latter continues in practice today; together, they designed nearly 2,000 buildings (e.g., SA 23.06 and .08). The city's economy is closely tied to the milling of wheat, and Salina is a major center for that industry. The city is also a locus for other agriculturally related business and manufacturing, and it functions as a trade center for a considerable territory.

Next in size is Manhattan (population 38,000). Centrally situated and within the Flint Hills, Manhattan is the seat of Riley County and is located about seventy miles northeast of Salina. Founded during 1854/1855 by three groups of settlers who had arrived in the area from New England and Cincinnati and then joined forces, Manhattan is located on a bowl-shaped site immediately north of the Kansas River, near its confluence with the Big Blue River. Early on, Manhattan functioned as an agricultural trading center, but its real growth, like that of Salina, came only after the arrival of railroad service. In addition to that asset, two other factors proved influential in shaping the city's development: its selection as the site for the state's land grant college and its proximity to Fort Riley (GE 05.01 to .03).

The fort had been founded in 1853, and Manhattan lay on the east side of the military reservation. The principal buildings of Fort Riley are closer to Junction City, however, and thus the fort exerts a far greater influence on that city's economy. In contrast, Kansas State University—a Regents Institution—being surrounded so to speak by the city, has played an extremely important role in the fortunes of Manhattan (RL 21.11 to .15). The university's origin can be traced indirectly to Bluemont College (affiliated with the Methodists), which had been founded in 1859. When the federal government passed the Morrill Land Grant Act in 1863, the availability of the facilities of that financially troubled college aided Manhattan in obtaining the new land grant institution, originally known as the Kansas State Agricultural College. As its mission expanded, the name received modifications: first to the Kansas State College of Agriculture and Applied Science and eventually to its current designation of Kansas State University. The last suggests the university's now comprehensive curriculum; however, Kansas State continues to place a strong emphasis on instruction and research in agriculture and engineering. Serving not only as a valuable asset for Manhattan but also for the entire state, the university and its associated agricultural lands lie to the northeast of Manhattan's downtown district, which stretches along Poyntz Avenue, at whose midpoint is a large park. The city has struggled to maintain the health of its historic core (see RL 21.01) despite pressures to develop open land on the surrounding hills. The pleasant, tree-shaded streets of the central city continue to support a viable mix of residential and commercial uses. Also contributing to Manhattan's character and economy are its regional roles as a center for trade and entertainment and as a provider of health care.

Third in size within the region, Junction City (population 20,600) is the seat of Geary County and is located at the confluence of the Republican and Smoky Hill rivers, a conjunction that forms the beginning of the Kansas River. The city's origin derived from the trading post for soldiers that had been established outside Fort Riley in 1858. Situated immediately south of the fort, the city is about twenty-five miles southwest of Manhattan, and in common with the latter the grid of Junction City stretches to fill the valley floor. Interstate 70 passes immediately to the south of town and has influenced the pattern of recent development. Another influence on the city has been the ebb and flow of military activity at the fort, which for several years has been mentioned as a candidate for closure. Yet whatever happens to the fort, its historical status is quite secure, and several of its early structures survive and help document its storied past (GE 05.01 to .03).

Two other locales in the region are places of special historical significance: Abilene and Council Grove. Abilene, the seat of Dickinson County, was platted in 1861 on the Smoky Hill River, roughly midway between Junction City and Salina. It gained notoriety after 1867 when it became—for only five years—the northern terminus for the Chisholm Trail and thus for the long cattle drives from Texas to the railhead. Abilene's reputation as being one of the nation's roughest cattle towns, however briefly, has enshrined the city prominently within the history/mythology associated with the Old West.

Today, with a population of 6,300, Abilene is a far different place from the town it was in the years immediately after the end of the Civil War. The city's main street, Buckeye Avenue, passes through a pleasant residential district as it connects the small-scale commercial district to Interstate 70 north of the city. For people wishing to sample Abilene's past, the city has re-created for visitors Old Abilene Town, complete with performances and architecture intended to bring to life the appearance and character of the city's rowdy cowtown history (DK 03.07). The city also provides the visitor with a quite different historical experience through the Eisenhower Center (DK 03.06), which honors the thirty-fourth president of the United States (and the supreme commander of Allied forces in Europe during World War II). Though a native of Texas, Dwight David Eisenhower was raised in Abilene, which provided the rationale to locate his presidential library and museum there, a complex that includes the Eisenhower family home.

A far different sort of history is found in Council Grove, located in the southeast corner of the region, on the Neosho River. Without question, it is one of the state's oldest historic places. Here in 1825 a treaty with the Indians allowed a survey party to continue peacefully in their marking out of what became the Santa Fe Trail. Council Grove's origin as a community can be traced to the trading post established in 1847 at the site of a campground for the wagon trains that traversed the 700-mile trail. Incorporated in 1858, Council Grove is the seat of Morris County; with slightly more than 2,200 residents it is the only city of size in the county. A number of structures dating back to the period when traffic on the Santa Fe Trail was still heavy survive (MR 11.01 and .05). In this respect, Council Grove is like other smaller communities in the state: one is more likely to find a higher percentage of structures of historical significance in them than in larger cities. The physical growth of larger cities, especially in the twentieth century, often came at the expense of older and smaller buildings, but such structures were more likely to remain useful in smaller cities, often continuing in their original functions (and thus serving to document for us earlier eras).

In these Northcentral cities and elsewhere in the region, many of the historically significant buildings are of local limestone. The earliest buildings often present a rather austere, utilitarian appearance since the choice of material was dictated not only by the ready availability of the stone but also by inadequate amounts of locally grown lumber, a deficiency that even led to the crafting of fence posts from stone, a solution continued farther west. After the arrival of railroad service communities began to prosper, and a richer range of building materials became available. Limestone continued to be popular but now is more likely to be shaped with greater sophistication. The interest in architectural style reflects the growing use of trained architects, who in the later years of the nineteenth century produced some impressive buildings, among which are a number of county courthouses and churches. Commercial buildings were often kept plain and practical, but here too one finds examples of design for its own sake. Some structures gain an added visual impact through a combination of brick and limestone with results that at times seem to demand our attention (e.g., CD 02.05). In the twentieth century, the range of building types and styles increased, the latter influenced by the diversification of building materials and the growing supply of architectural talent that came partly from the graduates of the state's two highly regarded schools of architecture at Kansas State University and the University of Kansas.

Within the state—as the Northcentral Region demonstrates—important town sites were frequently located on the larger rivers, often near a confluence with a tributary. Rivers not only furnished a convenient source of water but the valleys also provided easy gradients for the railroads. Moreover, the valleys held some of the choicest farmlands in the state. Unfortunately, the rivers were also subject to periodic flooding. As the sum of the flow of its many tributaries, the Kansas (Kaw) River was particularly prone to floods, causing significant damage in 1903 and 1951, especially to the two Kansas Cities, which are located adjacent to the Kaw's confluence with the Missouri River.

The 1951 flood prompted the creation of an ambitious program to protect the

Kaw valley through the creation of several large reservoirs on major tributaries. Resisted at first by many Kansans since valuable farmland would be lost to large reservoirs, the "big dam" proponents did succeed in gaining their objective and in so doing enabled a new force to affect development in the region. Today, Tuttle Creek Lake (on the Big Blue River) north of Manhattan and Milford Lake (on the Republican River) north of Junction City have become major recreational resources within the region along with serving their primary role as elements in the battle to control floods and temper the effects of drought. Still, floods can occur. In 1993, after a period of heavy rainfall, the Missouri, the Mississippi, the Kaw, and numerous other streams inundated a considerable portion of the nation's heartland; low-lying sectors of a great many towns and cities as well as considerable farmland experienced extensive damage. The lesson provided is that rivers and even minor streams continue to affect development—old and new—located near them, despite the efforts to harness the forces of nature.

As might be expected, much of the region's significant architecture is found in the five cities discussed, four of them on or conveniently near Interstate 70, which crosses the southern tier of counties. The other sites noted in the regional catalog are also readily accessible by major highways and roads, however. The map of the region and directory locate the counties, cities, and towns containing the entries and provide an outline for their organization in the catalog.

# NORTHCENTRAL REGION

Alpha-Numeric Directory

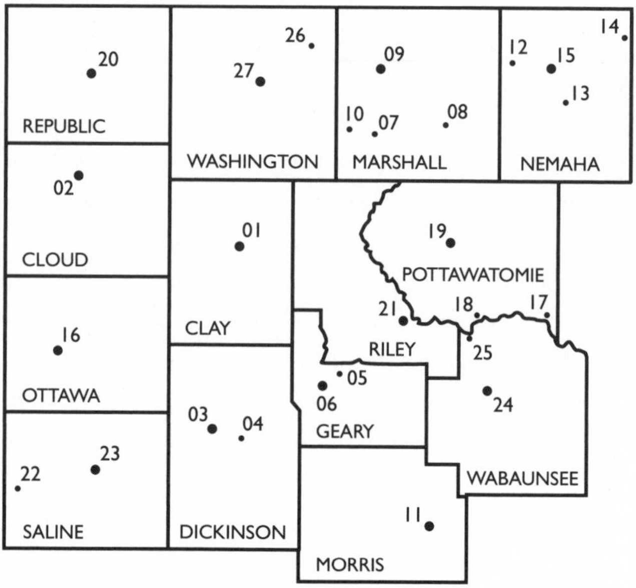

**CLAY (CY)**

  **01** Clay Center†

**CLOUD (CD)**

  **02** Concordia†

**DICKINSON (DK)**

  **03** Abilene†

  **04** Enterprise

**GEARY (GE)**

  **05** Fort Riley

  **06** Junction City†

**MARSHALL (MS)**

  **07** Blue Rapids

  **08** Frankfort

  **09** Marysville†

  **10** Waterville

**MORRIS (MR)**

  **11** Council Grove†

**NEMAHA (NM)**

  **12** Baileyville

  **13** Kelly

  **14** Sabetha

  **15** Seneca†

**OTTAWA (OT)**

  **16** Minneapolis†

**POTTAWATOMIE (PT)**

  **17** St. Marys

  **18** Wamego

  **19** Westmoreland†

**REPUBLIC (RP)**

  **20** Belleville†

**RILEY (RL)**

  **21** Manhattan†

**SALINE (SA)**

  **22** Brookville

  **23** Salina†

**WABAUNSEE (WB)**

  **24** Alma†

  **25** Wabaunsee

**WASHINGTON (WS)**

  **26** Hanover

  **27** Washington†

# Clay Center

## CY 01.01
### Garfield School
*1941. Hal Wheelock*
*Fourth and Dexter Street*

This brick two-story Moderne elementary school stands in striking contrast to its more traditional neighbors. It exemplifies many of the more progressive design motifs of the time, including curved corners and repeating horizontal trim lines. The building continues in use as a school, now housing fifth and sixth grade students.

## CY 01.02
### Clay County Courthouse*
*1900–1901. James C. Holland*
*Fifth and Court Street*

The three-story Romanesque limestone courthouse occupies an open square in the center of the business district. Despite sharing characteristics with the architect's other courthouses, this building's bilaterally symmetrical square plan and central tower are unique among them. The interior has been substantially altered.

## CY 01.03
### U.S. Post Office
*1911. James Knox Taylor*
*Sixth and Court Street*

The post office, a two-story brick and limestone Neoclassical building, occupies a prominent corner site. It is a particularly well-proportioned example of a style popular at the time, especially for governmental buildings. The nearby Clay Center Carnegie Library, built a year later and designed by H. B. Winter, is a less academically correct example of the style and provides an interesting comparison.

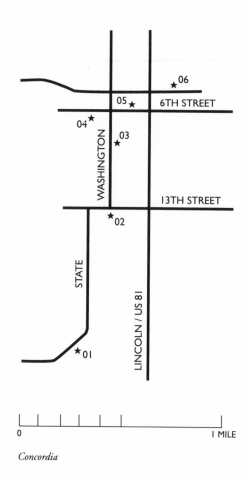

*Concordia*

# Concordia

## CD 02.01
## Cloud County Community College
*1968. Shaver & Company*
*Campus Drive*

The college's interconnected round shallow-domed brick buildings ride easily across a hillside site. They display ingenuity in the accommodation of a variety of classroom functions within a circular envelope as well as in the resolution of potentially difficult details involved in nonrectilinear buildings. The architect developed a national reputation for school design in the 1960s, a time when windowless classrooms were thought to be most conducive to uninterrupted learning.

## CD 02.02
## Nazareth Convent and Academy
*1898–1908. Wilson W. Hunt*
*Thirteenth and Washington Street*

The four-story stone-trimmed brick Romanesque Revival building is the central structure of a four-block hilltop campus operated by the Sisters of St. Joseph. The building's location on axis with Washington Street gives it additional prominence. The six-story central tower is visible from some distance.

## CD 02.03
## Cloud County Courthouse
*1958. Williamson & Loebsack*
*Eighth and Washington Street*

This Modern government building occupies a large landscaped block, the site of an earlier courthouse. The entries are set at either end of the connection between a long three-story limestone block and a one-story curtainwall building. The lower building was part of the original construction but was added to the existing plans when more administrative space proved necessary. The courtrooms occupy the upper level of the larger block, and the entry vestibules were added later. The design vocabulary is typical of commercial architecture of the time.

## CD 02.04
## Brown Grand Opera House*
*1907. Carl Boller*
*310 West Sixth Street*

The stone-trimmed brick Renaissance Revival theater, seating 1,000, is located in the heart of the downtown district. The scale of the building is a testament to the importance of the theater in the early life of the town. From the 1930s through the 1970s it served as a movie house, but in 1980 it was restored by a group of citizens and returned to its original use.

CD 02.05

## Bankers Loan and Trust Company

*1887–1888*
*W. H. Parsons & C. Howard Parsons*
*Sixth and Broadway Street*

This two-story, Queen Anne corner bank building of stone-trimmed brick follows the model of others of the time. It is distinguished by the ingenuity and playfulness of the ornament used to mark special places or circumstances on the building. Of note are the various doorways, the cornice line, the corner bay window (which most likely originally had a conical roof), and the second-story stringcourse, which is interrupted by ornamental miniature gabled building forms.

metric profile: the taller front tower is square in plan and is capped by a spire set inside the parapet, the shorter tower is capped by stone crenellations and a round turret at one corner, and a rear tower is circular in plan and is capped by a conical roof. The surface treatment reinforces the overall forms; larger smooth-faced stones outline the buttresses and edges of the elements, framing the openings, and the walls are faced in smaller rough-faced stone. The bountiful harvests at the turn of the century provided funds that allowed the addition of a bell tower, narthex, transept, galleries, and sacristy to the original church.

CD 02.06

## Our Lady of Perpetual Help Catholic Church

*1877–1880/1901–1902*
*Fifth and Kansas Street*

The stone church is notable for its clarity of form. Each of its towers has a distinct geo-

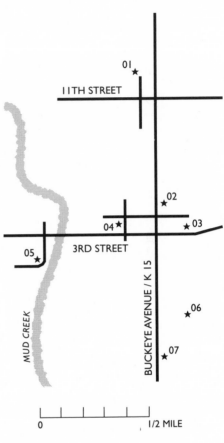

11TH STREET

01

02

04 ★ ★ 03

05

3RD STREET

MUD CREEK

BUCKEYE AVENUE / K 15

06

07

0                    1/2 MILE

*Abilene*

# Abilene

## Englehart House

*1963. Wayne Englehart*
*1206 Spruceway*

This one-story Modern wood house sits near the end of a cul-de-sac on a quiet residential street. It is representative of the straightforward and economical aesthetic of the time. Through directness of structure and simplicity of detail it achieves a measure of elegance. The architect, who practiced for many years with Jones Englehart and Gillam of Salina, built the house for his own family.

DK 03.02
## Boogaarts Grocery

*1966. Carl Ossman*
*Buckeye and Northwest Fifth Street*

Set back from the street behind a parking lot, this one-story commercial building is a good example of the integration of architec-

ture and signage. The building's most interesting feature is the series of square steel arches that emerge from the front of the structure to hold stylized letters identifying the name of the establishment.

DK 03.03
## Kirby House

*1885*
*Kirby and Northeast Third Street*

The large two-story Second Empire wood house, located on a large lot facing the Union Pacific rail line, was built for the banker, Thomas Kirby. It is a well-maintained example of the style. The restored interior now contains a restaurant.

DK 03.04
## Trinity Lutheran Church

*1878/1901*
*Cedar and Northwest Fourth Street*

The Victorian brick church, occupying a prominent corner in the town's central business district, is distinguished by its skillful brickwork and pleasing proportions. The southern portion of the building was added to the original forty-by-sixty-foot sanctuary in 1901. The wooden porches and the tower (which once had a spire) have been replaced several times.

## DK 03.05
### C. H. Lebold House*
*1880–1881*
*106 North Vine*

Located on a corner overlooking Mud Creek, this two-and-one-half-story stone Italianate home has twenty-three rooms. The house is impressive for its ambitious exuberance, particularly in its four-story central tower, and for its stonework, made of brown limestone quarried in Russell County. It was originally the home of a banker who also became the mayor. The house later served as an orphanage and a rooming house before being restored as a residence.

## DK 03.06
### Eisenhower Library
*1962. John Brink*
*201 Southeast Fourth Street*

This nearly windowless and monumental three-story stripped Neoclassical building frames the southern edge of the Eisenhower Center's broad central mall. It is faced in Kansas limestone on the exterior and on the interior features the extensive use of imported marble. The building's austere dignity seems appropriate to its function. Other buildings in the complex include Eisenhower's boyhood home* (1898/1911), a visitors' center, a museum, and a meditation chapel that contains the president's remains. Brink, the state architect at the time, also designed the chapel.

## DK 03.07
### Old Abilene Town
*Buckeye Avenue and Kuny Street*

The collection of buildings was assembled in its present location to recreate the atmosphere of a colorful era of Abilene's past. During the late 1860s and early 1870s, Abilene was the northern terminus of the cattle drives from Texas along the Chisholm Trail. The town's sheriff, James Butler (Wild Bill) Hickock, made his reputation as a gunman through his efforts to maintain order among the cowboys who frequented the town's saloons, gambling houses, and brothels.

# Enterprise

## DK 04.01
## Calene House

*1887*

*Two miles east of Enterprise on Route 452, then one-quarter of a mile south*

The two-story stone vernacular residence and an assemblage of out-buildings sit behind a stone wall among a grove of trees. It is typical of the type of construction employed by the region's homesteaders, many of whom had emigrated from Sweden. Erick Calene had established his homestead twenty years before the construction of this dwelling, and in earlier years the family had lived in a one-room cabin. The adjacent barn was built in 1908.

## DK 04.02
## Mission Church

*1881*

*Two miles east of Enterprise on Route 452, then three-quarters of a mile south*

This simple stone church occupies a lonely hilltop overlooking the rural countryside. It helps reveal the spirit of early agrarian society, much of which revolved around the church. The original steeple and bell have been destroyed, and the church has been vacant since 1934. The surrounding landscape contains the remains of a number of stone buildings erected by the area's early settlers.

# Fort Riley

### GE 05.01
## U.S. Cavalry Museum
*1857. William Pond*
*Between Sheridan and Custer avenues*

The museum, a two-story rectangular limestone building, occupies a hilltop site near the center of the original buildings on the base. It was built as a hospital only five years after the first troops were stationed at what was originally called Camp Center. The fort was established to protect settlers moving on the westward trails through Indian Territory. It later became an important training base, particularly for the artillery and cavalry and more recently for the First Infantry Division. The function of the building changed with that of the fort; in 1887, after a major renovation that included the addition of a distinctive circular bell tower, the building became the post headquarters and then the headquarters of the cavalry school. In 1957 it became the Cavalry Museum. The Main Post Area of the fort is on the National Register of Historic Places. The architect was a captain of the Quartermaster's Corps.

### GE 05.02
## Custer House (Quarters no. 24)*
*1854*
*Sheridan Road*

The simple vernacular two-story limestone residence was originally one of six identical houses built as part of the initial construction of the fort. It is believed to have been the home of Gen. George Custer when he was stationed here in 1866. Furnished as it might have been in the late nineteenth century, the building now serves as a museum, providing a view of earlier life at the fort for officers and their families.

### GE 05.03
## Church
*1897. George Ruhler*
*Barry Road*

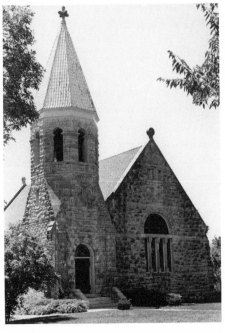

Among the fort's older residences, this modest Romanesque stone church sits back from a curving street. It is notable for the clarity and boldness of its geometry, particularly the octagonal entry tower. The drawings for the building do not bear the signature of an architect. Often in military construction at the time, national models were simply adapted to local conditions. In this case plans were drawn, as they were for most buildings on the base, to use the abundant local supply of limestone. The architect was a captain of the Quartermaster's Corps.

**GE 05.04**
## First Territorial Capitol*
*1855*
*Northeast on K 18*

This forty-by-eighty-foot rectangular two-story stone building sits alone, adjacent to the Union Pacific railroad track in what was once the town of Pawnee. It provides a clear demonstration of the construction practices of the time; the wood beams and floor planking are exposed in the undivided interior. Members of the legislature, many of whom represented proslavery Missouri interests, met only briefly in this structure, voting to relocate the capital to the Shawnee Methodist Mission in Johnson County only two weeks after the assembly first convened. The building subsequently fell into disrepair but was restored; now it is operated as a museum by the Kansas State Historical Society.

# Junction City

**GE 06.01**
## (Old) Junction City High School*
*1903. Holland & Squires*
*Adams and Sixth Street*

The three-story limestone Richardsonian Romanesque school building occupies a prominent site along one of the town's main commercial streets. Among its more remarkable features is a slightly protruding arched entry bay, which is placed off-center in an otherwise symmetrical facade. The building now houses the Geary County Historical Society Museum. One of the architects, James C. Holland, had in 1899 designed the similarly styled Geary County Courthouse.

**GE 06.02**
## Daily Union Building
*1988. Ken Ebert Design Group*
*Adams and Sixth Street*

This two-story stucco commercial building provides an interesting contrast to the (Old) Junction City High School diagonally across the street (GE 06.01). Each exhibits stylistic strategies then currently popular. The more recent building employs a historically oriented but more deliberately innovative Post-Modern approach, an endeavor less constrained by the demands of construction. Inside, the semicircular newsroom is of particular interest.

### GE 06.03
## Pentecostal Church
*1908*
*Adams and Fifth Street*

Sturdy and rectangular, the magnesium-limestone church seems particularly massive among its residential neighbors. It serves as a reminder of the quality of the local limestone as a building material and also of the diverse religious heritage of the region; it was built originally as the First Universalist Church.

### GE 06.04
## Ladies Reading Club Building
*1897*
*Jefferson and Third Street*

This one-story stone building is similar in scale to its residential neighbors but is distinguished by its quality of construction and detail, particularly in the gables. The women's group connected with it started as an organization to provide relief to the victims of the grasshopper plague of 1874 and then continued as an instrument to promote cul-

tural literacy. The building was donated by Capt. Bertrand Rockhill and his wife Julia. Their daughter Mary Rockwell Hook, then twenty years old, later became an architect and is best known for her residential work in the Kansas City Metropolitan Area.

### GE 06.05
## Christian Wetzel Cabin (Louis Kettles Cabin)*
*1857*
*I 70 and K 57 (two miles east of Junction City).*

The rustic log cabin was moved to its present location in a roadside park from a site along the nearby Clark's Creek. It is an example of a dog trot plan, in which two small cabins are placed end to end, separated by an open-air passageway, and covered with a single gabled roof. The plan was particularly popular in warmer climates, for it allowed air to circulate freely through all parts of the dwelling.

# Blue Rapids

**MS 07.01**
**State Bank**
*1871*
*Town Square*

The bank, a two-story Italianate-inspired stone building, faces the west side of the town's central open square. The contrast of differing masonry types lends interest to the wall surface: the main portion of the wall is rough-faced with prominent joints, protruding pilasters are smooth-faced, and the arched window lintels are finely finished and delicately carved.

. . . . . . . . . . . . . . . . . . . . . . . . . . . . . .

# Frankfort

**MS 08.01**
**Frankfort School***
*1902. A. W. Snodgrass*
*400 Locust Street*

The three-story Renaissance Revival building of stone-trimmed brick is set at an angle on its corner site. Its bulk and formality stand in contrast to the more modest structures surrounding it. The front and rear portions of the school are both occupied by three classrooms on each floor; the middle portion accommodates a wide hallway and

stairs at either end. It continues to operate as a school.

. . . . . . . . . . . . . . . . . . . . . . . . . . . . . .

# Marysville

**MS 09.01**
**(Old) Marshall County Courthouse***
*1891–1892. H. C. Koch*
*1207 Broadway*

This two-story red-brick and terracotta Richardsonian Romanesque courthouse and the newer courthouse on the same block anchor the eastern end of the downtown. Although the older building no longer houses court functions, the 104-foot-tall octagonal tower forms a symbolic center for the community. The building is now occupied by the county historical society. A number of interesting features in the lobby, the corridors, and the main courtroom remain intact.

**MS 09.02**
**Gas Station**
*ca. 1925*
*Twelfth and Broadway*

The small brick and stucco building is typical of early gas stations, but its Prairie Style components have been comfortably adapted to a new building type. The bracketed low-spreading hipped-roof covers both a small enclosed office and the drive-through pump bay. The scale of the building is no longer sufficient to accommodate the needs of the

contemporary gas station, and so it remains vacant. Most structures of this once ubiquitous type, if not adapted to other uses, have been demolished.

### MS 09.03
## Koester Block Historic District*

*1870 to 1929*
*Broadway, between Eighth and Ninth streets*

The well-maintained grouping of two- and three-story brick commercial buildings preserves a portion of urban fabric typical of regional centers across the state. The earlier buildings (on the left in the illustration) demonstrate the influence of Italianate principles, but the newest building shows the growing influence of the Beaux-Arts.

### MS 09.04
## Charles Koester House*

*1873*
*919 Broadway*

This two-story multigabled Italianate home occupies a well-landscaped and shaded lot near the center of town. Until 1964 the house was occupied by the descendants of the original owner; it now operates as a museum. Still containing many of its original furnishings, the house provides an effective view of life in the region in the late nineteenth century.

### MS 09.05
## Pony Express Barn*

*1859*
*108 South Eighth Street*

Located in the midst of a commercial district, this rectangular hipped-roofed stone barn is the oldest remaining building in the county and the last remaining Pony Express home station. After the demise of the Pony Express, which operated for only eighteen months, the building housed first a livery and then a produce company; it is now operated as a museum.

### MS 09.06
## South Koester House

*1904–1906*
*Tenth and Elm Street*

This highly original Victorian house, with its towered wraparound porch, takes full advantage of its prominent corner location. Stylistic elements from the Queen Anne, Shingle, and Classical Revival styles merge into a complex but unified composition. The building now houses a restaurant.

MS 09.07
## Pusch-Randall House*
*1904. Robert and Jacob Wullschleger*
*Tenth and Elm Street*

The two-story wood-frame Queen Anne house occupies a hillside overlooking the commercial district. It displays many features characteristic of the style, including a wide porch supported on Ionic columns, a protruding front gable, and a three-story octagonal corner tower. The designer/builders were brothers who had emigrated from Switzerland.

MS 09.08
## Sod House
*Tenth Street (south of Walnut on the west side)*

Built by the Marysville Kiwanis Club, this recent re-creation of an early Kansas house type that settlers constructed from the mid-nineteenth century into the twentieth century is located in City Park. It serves as a testament to the determination and ingenuity the settlers displayed in their attempt to survive in an environment characterized by harsh weather and a lack of construction

resources. City Park also contains a railroad depot, a one-room schoolhouse, and a steam locomotive.

MS 09.09
## Marysville High School
*1938. Louis H. Spencer*
*Twelfth and Walnut streets*

This stone-trimmed brick school is one of a complex of school buildings occupying four blocks. It reflects the gradual transition toward Modernism in architecture occurring at the time of its construction. The composition and massing are formal and symmetrical, but the ornament, though classical in inspiration, is highly stylized.

. . . . . . . . . . . . . . . . . . . . . . . . . . . . . . . .

# Waterville

MS 10.01
## Weaver Hotel*
*1905–1906*
*126 South Kansas Street*

Representative of a once popular building type, the three-story stone building occupies a narrow corner lot at the center of town. The structure's most notable feature is its rounded corner, capped by an elaborate bracketed cornice and decorated pediment.

## MS 10.02
### S. T. Powell House*
*1895*
*108 West Commercial*

This two-story wood-frame house demonstrates the variety of ornament found within the Queen Anne Style. Hipped, gabled, and conical roofs cover a variety of forms articulated with paneled, shingled, clapboarded, and carved wood surfaces.

# Council Grove

## MR 11.01
### Hays House*
*1857*
*112 West Main Street*

The two-story wood structure fronts the town's principal street, immediately west of the point where it crosses the Neosho River. With its continuous colonnaded one-story balcony covering the sidewalk, the building matches the stereotypical image of a commercial structure in an early frontier boomtown. It was built by the town's founder, Seth Hays, and served a variety of uses through the years. It now houses the oldest continuously operating restaurant west of the Mississippi River. The building stands as a testament to the town's importance as a stopping place along the Santa Fe Trail.

## MR 11.02
### Council Grove National Bank*
*1882. J. H. Leedy*
*Main and Neosho Street*

Facing the corner, this Italianate-influenced two-story brick building is an early example of the kind of structure that would soon become a typical feature of many growing Kansas towns in the late nineteenth century. Although it no longer houses a bank, the banking hall with its teller cages has been restored.

## MR 11.03
### Farmers and Drovers National Bank and Indicator Building*
*1892 and 1902*
*201 West Main*

Romanesque Revival elements combine with other more exotic motifs in this pair of two-story stone-trimmed brick commercial structures. The buildings' exuberance reflects the community's renewed optimism that was spurred by the coming of the railroad and the growth of the livestock shipping business. The bank building was renovated in the early 1980s and continues to serve its original purpose.

## MR 11.04
### First Congregational Church
*1898. Charles W. Squires*
*Main and Belfry Street*

This Akron-Plan church of stone and wood occupies a hilltop site near the western edge of the central commercial district. Although modest in dimension, it is noteworthy for its sense of order and proportion and for the cleverness of its detail. As with other of the architect's churches, such as the First Presbyterian Church in Emporia, the ornament is drawn from diverse sources: gothic traditions inform the stone base, and classical sources direct the wood surfaces above. The building possesses a graceful sense of repose; the base gives a sense of rooted stability, yet the shingled gable ends and overhanging roofs provide a sense of verticality. It has undergone a series of additions and renovations but continues to serve its original purpose.

## MR 11.05
### Kaw Methodist Mission*
*1850–1851*
*500 North Mission*

The two-story Federal Style stone home occupies a broad, flat site at the northern edge of town. It was built to house as many as fifty boarding students as well as teachers, missionaries, and farmers. Its construction was the result of a treaty relocating the Kaw (Kansa) Indians to a reservation that included the area of Council Grove, but the Kaw did not seek to adopt the white man's ways and were reluctant to send their children to the mission (which operated for less than four years). In 1859 the area of Council Grove was removed from the reservation, and in the 1870s the Kaw were relocated to Oklahoma. The building is now operated as a museum by the state historical society.

## Baileyville

### NM 12.01
### Sacred Heart Church
*1952. Brinkman & Hagan*
*208 Third Street*

By far the most dominant building in the collection of houses that forms the town, this stone-trimmed brick church has a sense of permanence, which stems in part from its traditional allusions. It is modeled after the Romanesque basilica form, and from that comes the clarity of its geometry and the sense of quality of its construction. For example, the round-arched wood glue-lam beams, which support the herringbone-patterned wood ceiling, seem perfectly suited both to their spatial and structural roles in the definition of space of the nave.

. . . . . . . . . . . . . . . . . . . . . . . . . . . . . .

## Kelly

### NM 13.01
### St. Bede's Church
*1913–1915. Henry W. Brinkman*

The German Gothic Revival church of dark red brick and Algonita stone sits amid a small cluster of houses on the crown of a gentle hill. The 125-foot tower is visible for miles across the surrounding fields. The interior is spacious, and the vaults of the nave and aisles rest on six cast-iron columns. The architect designed a number of simple but elegant churches for Catholic parishes throughout the region.

. . . . . . . . . . . . . . . . . . . . . . . . . . . . . .

## Sabetha

### NM 14.01
### Lanning House
*1899*
*1208 Main Street*

This two-story wood Queen Anne home occupies a double lot in a residential neigh-

borhood. A recent restoration and polychromatic repainting brings out the variety of textures and ornament characteristic of the style.

. . . . . . . . . . . . . . . . . . . . . . . . . . . . . . . . .

## Seneca

### NM 15.01
### St. Mary's Church*
*1893*
*On RR 1 (in St. Benedict)*

The 172-foot tower of this limestone church is the dominant feature of the small community. Although the exterior of the church is remarkable, mainly for its bulk, the interior is truly inspiring. The fifty-two-foot-high vaulted nave is separated from the lower, vaulted side aisles by a series of cast-iron columns. Walls, columns, and ceilings are covered by delicate decorative painted stencilwork; elaborate plaster-of-paris sculptures embellish the walls and altars; and oil-painted scenes adorn the transepts and altar area. The interior decoration was completed

in 1901, the stencil work done by G. F. Satory of Wabasha, Minnesota, and the oil painting by T. H. Zukolnski of Chicago. The interior was restored in 1979 by Joe Oswalt.

### NM 15.02
### St. Peter and Paul Church School
*1895*
*Elk Street (between Fourth and Fifth Street)*

The two-story brick building is part of a complex of buildings that surrounds the central brick church building, which was completed eight years before the school. The plans for the church were drawn by a Chicago architect named Druiding. The tower was rebuilt and a sacristy added after a tornado damaged the building in 1896. The school building is typical of many of the era: each floor accommodates four classrooms. It once housed both elementary and high school students but now operates as a grade school. Its sturdy utilitarian character is enhanced by a three-story square bell tower centered in its south facade.

### NM 15.03
### Seneca Public Library
*1867–1869*
*Sixth and Main Street*

Built as a Unitarian church, this rectangular gabled stone building has a sense of simple classical dignity. When in 1930 the church disbanded and the building was threatened

with demolition, local preservationists successfully lobbied for its preservation and transformation into the town library.

**NM 15.04**
## Nemaha County Courthouse
*1955. Thomas Harris Calvin & Associates*
*Sixth and Nemaha Street*

A Modern brick building, the courthouse is set in the midst of a spacious lawn. It is an interesting attempt at the redefinition of the building type, one that draws its eloquence from the outward expression of interior functions. The courtroom is pulled away from the office spaces and is presented as a separate volume. The entry vestibule

separates the two parts and resolves their differing floor heights.

**NM 15.05**
## First National Bank
*1890*
*Fifth and Main Street*

The two-and-one-half-story brick commercial building is an interesting variant on the familiar late-nineteenth-century small town bank building. It shares stylistic features such as a round corner tower and embedded turretlike elements on the second level with other buildings, for example the more ornate Farmers and Drovers Bank of Council Grove (MR 11.03). Here, however, the entry is not placed on the corner, which instead is reserved for an office at the base of the tower. Wood shingles provide a curious replacement for windows along the side of the first floor. The main floor is now occupied by a law office.

# Minneapolis

### OT 16.01
## Ottawa County Bank
*1887*
*Second and Concord Street*

Like many across the state, this two-story corner bank building of stone-trimmed brick anchors a main intersection. Its planning features include a bank entry facing the corner, an entry to the upstairs on the long or side-street side, and an attached storefront on the principal street. Although this building is less ornate, it shares stylistic features with the Farmers and Drovers National Bank in Council Grove (MR 11.03), notably in the embedded turretlike elements on the second story.

### OT 16.02
## Ottawa County Administration Building
*1956. Williamson Loebsack & Associates*
*Third and Concord Street*

The long two-story Modern building follows the model for contemporary office buildings as established by Eero Saarinen's General Motors Technical Center. The metal and glass curtainwall facade, which now looks conventional and mundane, must have seemed daring and innovative in its small-town context at the time.

# St. Marys

### PT 17.01
### Jeffrey Energy Center
*1971–1972*
*On K 63 (five miles north, then three miles west)*

Because of its clear geometry and sheer size, the coal-fired electrical-power-generation plant provides a dominant and orienting image within the Kansas River valley. Well lighted, it is also highly visible at night.

### PT 17.02
### Immaculate Conception Church
*1889*
*Second and Bertrand Street*

As in many of the towns founded by Catholic settlers in this part of the state, the church with its tall steeple marks the center of the community. The stately stone structure, like many churches in the area, borrows from German Gothic traditions. St. Marys was established in 1848 by the Jesuits as a mission to the Pottowatomie Indians. The connection suggests that the unknown architect probably was a Jesuit priest, for their preparation in Germany for missionary work also included instruction in architecture since among their many duties might be the need to oversee the construction of a church building.

### PT 17.03
### Immaculata Chapel
*1907–1909. Root & Siemens*

The remnants of this monumental Gothic Revival church on the St. Marys campus stand on the bluff overlooking the Kansas River valley. The image of this grand ruin is filled with power and mystery. The church burned in 1978 and was further damaged by a windstorm in 1980. Parts of the campus of the former St. Marys College are now operated as a school by the Society of St. Pius X. The architects, concurrent with their work on the church, also designed a Tudor Revival classroom building, Loyola Hall.

# Wamego

**PT 18.01**

## Old Dutch Mill*

*1879*
*Wamego City Park*

## Belleville

**RP 20.01**

## Republic County Courthouse

*1939–1940. Mann & Company*
*Courthouse Square*

The Dutch Style stone windmill sits atop an artificial hill in the midst of a well-landscaped park. It was built originally on a farm twelve miles north of town and in 1925 was moved to its present location where it is maintained by the city.

The three-story stone and metal-trimmed concrete building occupies a full block in the center of town. The building combines a number of stylistic strategies: the massing is formal and Classical, the facade composition is Modernistic, and the ornament is Art Deco. The detail of the grand stair hall is particularly impressive.

. . . . . . . . . . . . . . . . . . . . . . . . . . . . . . . .

# Westmoreland

**PT 19.01**

## Pottawatomie County Courthouse

*1884. Hulse & Moses (contractor)*

The modest two-story limestone building sits in the midst of a broad, sloping square in the center of town. Despite several additions to an originally square building and sub-stantial interior renovation, the structure is reminiscent of the earlier courthouses in the state, which in more populous counties have been replaced by modern facilities.

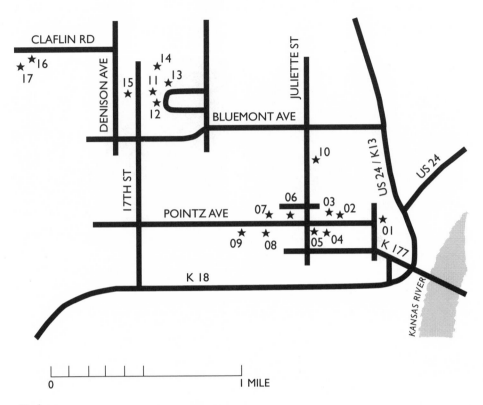

CLAFLIN RD

★ ★16
17

DENISON AVE

★14
15    11 ★ 13
★    ★
★
12

17TH ST

JULIETTE ST

BLUEMONT AVE

★10

US 24 / K13

US 24

06    03
07 ★    ★    ★ 02
POINTZ AVE    ★ ★

★    ★    ★ ★    01
09    08    05  04    ★

K 177

K 18

KANSAS RIVER

0                                    I MILE

*Manhattan*

# Manhattan

## RL 21.01
### Town Center Mall
*1986–1987. RTKL*
*Third and Pointz Avenue*

The regional shopping mall wraps around a pedestrian plaza that terminates the eastern end of Manhattan's main commercial street. It strives to harmonize with the older, smaller-scaled commercial buildings of the downtown district through the use of limestone and traditional vernacular forms and through the incorporation of portions of buildings that were demolished to make way for the new structure. The building shields the existing downtown from the larger masses of the anchor department stores and the bulk of the parking area and provides an alternative to the more typical suburban shopping mall.

## RL 21.02
### Wareham Block
*1893/1910 (theater), 1926 (hotel)*
*Boller Brothers*
*418 Pointz Avenue*

Lying at the heart of Manhattan's downtown district, these commercial structures are among the most highly detailed buildings in the area; the hotel at six stories is also one of the tallest. Originally constructed as the Coliseum Opera House, the theater was essentially rebuilt after Henry Pratt Wareham

purchased it. The marquee was added in 1938, and the interior was renovated in 1988 by Brent Bowman as a multiuse banquet facility. The hotel is notable not only for its size but also for its detail, which consists of Neoclassical terracotta ornament applied to the steel-framed brick-faced structure at the base as well as to the protruding balconies and along the cornice.

## RL 21.03
### Riley County Courthouse
*1905–1906. Holland & Squires*
*Fifth and Pointz Avenue*

The three-story Romanesque limestone building is set back from the street to form a small plaza between the Wareham Hotel on the east and the (Old) Manhattan Carnegie Library* on the west. The two-story Neoclassical stone library was built in 1909 and was designed by Henry Rose of Kansas City; it now houses a courthouse annex. The courthouse also helps to form a public open space to the rear, or north, of the building.

The courthouse was renovated and the surrounding plazas were developed in the mid-1980s in accordance with the designs of Ron Reid Associates; it was one of the ten in Kansas designed either jointly or separately by James C. Holland and his partner Frank C. Squires.

## RL 21.04
### St. Paul's Episcopal Church
*1858–1870*
*Sixth and Pointz Avenue*

The limestone Gothic Revival church and its connected parlor building form a shaded, corner-facing courtyard. The original portion of the building was modeled after Christ Church in Marlborough, New York, designed by Richard Upjohn. The completion of the parlor building along with a three-bay extension of the nave in 1930 gave the latter a somewhat awkward proportion.

## RL 21.05
### Manhattan Public Library
*1968. William R. Eidson*
*Juliette and Pointz Avenue*

This two-story library, a geometrically configured concrete-framed stone-faced building, anchors a prominent intersection. The entry, however, faces away from the street and toward a parking lot at the rear of the building. Despite its rather massive appearance on the exterior, the interior is open and filled with light. The architect, who prac-

ticed with his wife, Patricia L. Eidson, was concerned that his work reflect the spirit of the region. They also designed the First Lutheran Church at 930 Pointz Avenue.

## RL 21.06
### Robert Ulrich House*
*1868*
*121 North Eighth Street*

Modest but well-proportioned, the two-story brick Victorian home occupies a spacious, shaded lot. It was renovated in 1978 by Sweet & Habiger and now houses the offices of a travel agency.

## RL 21.07
### Women's Clubhouse*
*1911. Helfensteller Hirsch & Watson*
*900 Pointz Avenue*

The small one-story stucco bungalow is hardly noticeable among its larger neighbors. Closer examination reveals it to be a good example of the ideas of the early-twentieth-century Arts & Crafts movement. The details also reveal the influence of the Chicago architect, Louis Sullivan. The building is now used as the office of a law firm.

RL 21.08
## Manhattan Middle School
*1913 (high school), 1917 (junior high school), 1983 (renovation). Shaefer Johnson Cox & Fry*
*901 Pointz*

The three-story school complex occupies four blocks near the western end of Manhattan's central commercial district. Originally two separate schools, the buildings have been linked by a sophisticated glass-enclosed atrium to become a single school. The work done on this building was part of a comprehensive, district-wide school renovation project. The strategy of adding light-weight glazed elements to contrast with the existing massive stone elements has been employed successfully in the expansion of a number of older schools throughout the city.

RL 21.09
## Manhattan Municipal Building
*1955. Floyd O. Wolfernbarger*
*1100 Pointz Avenue*

This sprawling buff-brick and aluminum-paneled Modern building sits amid a broad lawn opposite the city's municipal park. Its spare detailing and effective use of materials make it a good example of the architectural tastes of the time. The building houses city offices, a fire station, and a municipal auditorium. Another similarly styled building by the same architect is the Manhattan Senior High School, which was completed three years later and exists in a somewhat altered state at the western end of Pointz Avenue. It won a design award from the Kansas Chapter of the American Institute of Architects.

RL 21.10
## Wolf Butterfield House
*1865*
*630 Fremont Street*

The two-story vernacular stone structure occupies a corner lot in an older residential section. It was built as a way station on the Butterfield Overland Dispatch Stage Line and contained a tavern as well as dining and sleeping facilities. It is now operated as a museum.

RL 21.11
## Holtz Hall (Kansas State University)
*1879–1884. Erasmus T. Carr*

Originally built as a chemistry building, this small one-story stone classroom structure reflects the vision of John A. Anderson, president of what was then the Kansas State Agricultural College, who hoped the campus would develop the characteristics of a prosperous farm. This and other early campus structures followed the forms of rural vernacular buildings and were irregularly arranged across a hillside on Manhattan's

western edge. Holtz Hall has since been surrounded by larger classroom buildings.

## Anderson Hall*
## (Kansas State University)
*1879–1884. Erasmus T. Carr*

This sprawling two-story stone Victorian towered building faces a wide lawn. The initial naturalistic campus plan was executed by the St. Louis landscape planner Maximilian Kern, beginning in the mid-1880s, who envisioned the campus as a botanical laboratory. This building, because of its size, formal presence, and placement, remains a dominant image for the university. Over its life it has housed a variety of functions and now is home for the central administrative offices.

RL 21.13

## Holton Hall
## (Kansas State University)
*1900. James C. Holland*

Immediately north of Anderson Hall, this two-story Richardsonian Romanesque edi-

fice faces it at a somewhat awkward angle. Despite the irregularity of the placement of campus buildings and their diversity of style, the nearly universal use of limestone—including more recent buildings—provides a sense of coherence to the campus. Holton Hall was originally built as the home of the Department of Agriculture. A recent renovation, which received a state preservation citation, was designed by Brent Bowman of Manhattan, who modified the building to accommodate the student services offices.

RL 21.14

## Farrel Library–North Wing
## (Kansas State University)
*1927. Charles D. Cuthbert*

This Collegiate Gothic limestone structure faces a central campus courtyard. Like other campus buildings constructed in the 1920s, it is representative of the stylistic preferences of the day. It features a grand north-facing vaulted reading room containing murals by David Overmyer. The library was designed, as were other buildings on campus, in consultation with faculty in the Department of Architecture. Subsequent additions have diminished the impact of the building.

RL 21.15

## Durland Hall
## (Kansas State University)
*1976/1984. Horst Terrill & Karst*

A Modern two- and three-story building, Durland Hall consists of towers made of ribbed limestone panels and infill areas of reflective glass. Built in two phases, the building centers on a three-story connecting atrium. It is representative of recent additions to campus, many of which lack the sensitivity and character of earlier buildings.

## RL 21.16
### Goodnow Home*
*1857–1861*
*2301 Claflin Road*

Well-preserved, the two-story stone house stands on the grounds of the Riley County Museum as a reminder of important aspects of the state's history. The house was purchased and completed over the course of seventeen years by Isaac T. Goodnow, an antislavery settler from Vermont, and incorporates innovative features such as a ventilation system devised by its owner. Goodnow, a teacher and politician, was instrumental in the founding of Bluemont College in 1857 and its transformation under the 1863 Morrill Act into the Kansas State Agricultural College. The house is now operated as a museum by the state historical society and is furnished with objects from the period of its early occupancy.

## RL 21.17
### Hartford House
*1855. Hinkle Gild & Company (fabricator)*
*2309 Claflin Road*

This reconstruction of a one-room one-story prefabricated frame house is adjacent to the Riley County Historical Museum. It was fabricated in six parts: four wall panels and two roof panels. An accurate replica of one of ten houses brought by a group of settlers from Ohio, the house takes its name from the steamboat on which it was loaded for the journey to Manhattan.

# Brookville

### SA 22.01
## Brookville Hotel*
*1870*
*Perry Street*

This two-story Italianate building of wood is a remnant of the town's early days and is representative of many found in similar developments at stops along the Union Pacific rail line. The hotel continues as a highly reputed restaurant.

...................................

# Salina

### SA 23.01
## John H. Prescott House*
*1884*
*122 West Prescott*

Located on a large, shaded lot, this wood two-story L-plan Second Empire house is painted to emphasize the carved wooden detail. Its most notable feature is a three-story tower set at the inside corner where the ell joins the main block of the house.

### SA 23.02
## Masonic Temple
*1922. Wilmarth & Zerbe*
*South Street and Santa Fe Avenue*

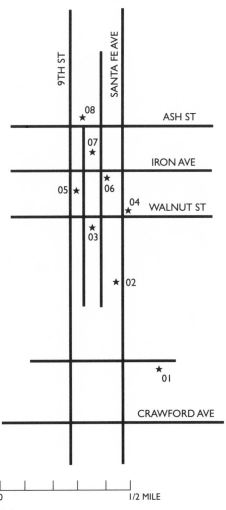

*Salina*

Massively scaled, this six-story Neoclassical Indiana limestone structure occupies a prominent corner site. The building's design, however, resulted from some compromises. The original architects were dismissed during construction, and the architects of record prepared another set of plans; apparently the contractor freely consulted both plans in completing the construction. Consequently, the building appears as if the upper story had been added later, giving the structure a curiously top-heavy appearance. It houses a 1,200-seat auditorium with two

*John H. Prescott house*

balconies as well as the offices and meeting facilities for six different Masonic Orders. Although the building's function is not readily apparent from the exterior, close examination reveals the influence of Masonic symbolism and mythology. Concurrently, the architects also designed the Eclectic Hall of Pioneers at Kansas Wesleyan University at the southern terminus of Santa Fe Avenue.

**SA 23.03**
**Lincoln School**
*1915–1917. William T. Schmitt*
*210 West Mulberry Street*

Lincoln is one of two schools occupying a full block. It has been connected to the Roosevelt School, to the south, by a walkway that makes it difficult to view the Lincoln School as originally intended. Nevertheless, both the massing and detail of this three-story stone-trimmed brick building make it one of the best examples of commercial Prairie Style architecture in the state. The mixture of geometric and figural ornament at the head of the third-storty window pilasters is particularly ingenious.

**SA 23.04**
**Fox-Watson Theater Building***
*1930–1931*
*Boller Brothers with Charles W. Shaver*
*155 South Santa Fe Avenue*

The grand Art Deco brick theater anchors the heart of the downtown district, which stretches along Santa Fe Avenue to the north and south. Unlike the central areas of other towns, Salina's downtown maintains much of its character and vitality, due partly to the streetscape improvements planned by

Charles Shaver's son, John Shaver. The theater is a good example of Art Deco design strategies; it is punctuated at strategic junctures by terracotta encrustations of repeating geometric and regularized organic ornament. The building must have been even more impressive before its tower was damaged by lightning and substantially shortened.

## SA 23.05
## Christ Cathedral
*1907. Henry Macomb and Charles M. Burns*
*134 South Eighth Street*

This English Gothic Style limestone church sits back from the street in a parklike setting. The interior is particularly striking; the woodwork is of carved black oak, and the altar is of Carthage marble. The filtered light, massive construction, and generous proportions combine to give the space a sense of quiet dignity.

## SA 23.06
## United Building
*1929–1930. Charles W. Shaver*
*Seventh and Iron Street*

The ten-story terracotta-trimmed Art Deco brick office building is typical of those built at the time in many smaller cities across the country. In the 1920s tall buildings were seen as a measure of economic and civic vitality. Although the building has been altered on the interior, it continues as a reminder of those optimistic times. A few years earlier the architect had designed another building expressive of civic pride, the monumental brick and stone Neoclassical Memorial Hall at Ninth and Ash Street. A comparison of these two buildings illustrates the changes taking place in architectural tastes during the 1920s.

## SA 23.07
## Sacred Heart Cathedral
*1951–1953. Edward J. Schulte*
*118 North Ninth Street*

The distinctive Modern limestone church forms an effective foil to the U.S. Post Office and Federal Building across the street. A cylindrical motif derived from the form of grain elevators gives consistency and coherence to the building; the forms are used to frame the windows along the east side of the building and for the tower. Interest is added through the use of low-relief sculpture on the entry vestibule.

*Sacred Heart Cathedral*

## SA 23.08
## City-County Building
*1969. Shaver & Company*
*Ash Street at Eighth Street*

This sprawling two-story Modern limestone building occupies a two-block site. On both the interior and exterior its form and detail clearly convey an attitude of efficiency with which the combined governmental functions would like to be associated. The building stands in contrast to the adjacent Saline County Courthouse, designed by Wilmarth & Zerbe in 1910, which uses a more traditional Neoclassical vocabulary. After joining the architectural office of his father Charles Shaver in 1945, John Shaver built the firm into an organization that at one time employed almost 100 people in Salina and in four branch offices. Both father and son were graduates of Kansas State University. Other buildings in Salina designed by John Shaver include the First Presbyterian Church, the South High School, and a number of buildings on the Marymount College Campus.

# Alma

## WB 24.01
## Wabaunsee County Courthouse
*1931–1932. W. E. Glover*
*Second and Kansas Street*

Located several blocks west of the central business district, this three-story building of Carthage stone occupies a sloping full-block site. The building provides a good example of the fusion of geometric Art Deco detail with Neoclassical compositional strategies; the result is a style that might be described as Federal Deco. The interior is of interest for its detail, particularly in the barrel-vaulted courtroom.

## WB 24.02
## St. John's Lutheran Church
*1908. William F. Shrage*
*218 West Second Street*

This cross-gabled stone church sits opposite the courthouse. The tower's tall octagonal spire and its extended stone finials give the building an interesting silhouette. It is impressive also for its stonework. August Peters of Alma was the contractor.

## WB 24.03
**Bank of Wabaunsee County and Kinne and Korans Merchandise Building**
*1886*
*311 Missouri Street*

# Wabaunsee

**Beecher Bible and Rifle Church***
*1859–1862*
*On K 18 (two miles west of K 99)*

*St. John's Lutheran Church*

The two-story limestone building is the most outstanding of a series of similarly scaled and constructed buildings that line the city's main street, giving it a distinctively historical character. The building also represents an interesting variant on the late-nineteenth-century small town commercial building: instead of occupying the typical corner location, it is on a midblock site. The facade cleverly resolves the problem of recognizing the principal lower-level tenants by giving each a fenestration appropriate to the significantly different purposes while maintaining a sense of symmetry for the building as a whole.

. . . . . . . . . . . . . . . . . . . . . . . . . . . . . . . .

The small rectangular gabled stone church occupies a wide yard among a scattering of rural buildings. It is worthy of note more for its history than for its form, having been founded by an antislavery group, the Kansas Connecticut Colony. The church took its name from a unique shipment received by the settlers from the famous Brooklyn abolitionist, Henry Ward Beecher; the shipment was marked Bibles but actually contained rifles.

# Hanover

### WS 26.01
### Hollenberg Ranch Station*
*1857*
*On K 243 (one mile east of K 148)*

The rectangular vernacular clapboard building sits on a hill in open country above Cottonwood Creek. It was built by a German immigrant, G. H. Hollenberg, as a service to travelers along the Oregon Trail. The station contained not only his home but also a general store, post office, and hostelry. The site was a way station for the Pony Express during its brief period of operation (1860–1861). It is now operated as a museum.

### WS 26.02
### St. John's Catholic Church
*1879*
*Church Street*

The simple limestone church sits atop the crown of a hill; its tower and steeple are visible for some distance across the surrounding valleys. The domed interior is highly detailed, featuring delicate stencilwork and intricate carved statuary.

### WS 26.03
### Hanover Methodist Church
*1895*
*North and Hanover Street*

This rectangular gabled Gothic church of wood occupies a sloping site. Its most notable feature is a corner entry tower with a distinctive roof form and an open belfry.

. . . . . . . . . . . . . . . . . . . . . . . . . . . . . . .

# Washington

### WS 27.01
### Washington County Courthouse
*1932–1934. H. G. Overend and C. F. Boucher*
*Courthouse Square*

Sitting on a landscaped square, this classically planned three-story limestone Art Deco building is located in the center of the business district. The detail in the courtroom is of particular interest, notably the silver stenciling above the windows and along the cornice.

# Southcentral and Wichita Region

The Southcentral Region incorporates several aspects of the varied terrain of Kansas. The region's eastern side is occupied by the Flint Hills, with additional hill country in the northern reaches and the southwestern corner. In contrast, much of the central area consists of the Arkansas River lowlands and to their west is a segment of the High Plains that characterizes much of western Kansas.

The twelve counties that constitute the region together have a population of nearly 700,000 people. More than half reside in Sedgwick County, primarily in the city of Wichita, thus placing the county—and Wichita—first in the state in population size. In sharp contrast, Chase County in the northeastern corner of the region, with a population just slightly more than 3,000, is near the bottom of the list. Even so, Chase County is home to some notable buildings, such as the 1873 county courthouse made from local stone (CS 03.02), a favored building material in that area of the Flint Hills.

The region supports a diversified economy. Agriculture is an important component, with wheat, especially in the western sector, and cattle production in the Flint Hills assuming major roles. Indeed, wheat is grown in sufficient quantity to have encouraged the development of quite sizable storage facilities and processing mills in the region, particularly at Hutchinson in Reno County. The extraction of minerals within the region also contributes significantly to the economy; petroleum and natural gas production became truly important after 1915, especially in the vicinity of El Dorado in Butler County. The Southcentral Region is also known for the production of salt through direct mining and by the brine process; Reno County is an important center. Other valuable mineral products are sand and gravel, used extensively in construction. The region is also home to considerable manufacturing, most notably in Wichita, where the aircraft industry is of national importance as well as contributing significantly to the state's economy (SG 24.48).

Settlers began to arrive in the region during the territorial period, leading to the organization of Chase, Marion, and Butler counties prior to 1861. McPherson, Sedgwick, and Cowley counties were organized during the 1860s; but not until the arrival of railroad service in the 1870s did settlement in the region increase to the point that urban centers began to take shape, and the remaining six counties were formed. Before the railroads the movement of animals, goods, and people occurred primarily along established trails, the Santa Fe Trail becoming heavily traveled years before 1854 when Kansas became a territory. That trail crossed through the northern portion of the region in the area now occupied by Marion, McPherson, and Rice counties. Its presence there, however, did not by itself provide a direct influence on town-building, but when the right-of-way of the Santa Fe Railroad approximated that of the trail (and in Rice County, west of Lyons, essentially overlaid it), matters changed and towns quickly appeared.

A somewhat different history developed from the Chisholm Trail, along which Texas cattle were driven north to a railhead at Abilene, beginning in 1867. When rail service reached the trail farther south in 1871, that junction displaced Abilene as the terminus for the cattle drive and stimulated the founding of Newton and the organization of Harvey County. Newton as the new railhead shortened the cattle drive by nearly seventy miles, and when Wichita—already a stop on the trail— received its rail service in 1872, it in turn displaced Newton as the place to transship the cattle, helping boost Wichita's development (e.g., SG 24.20).

The creation of settlements did not necessarily depend on the railroad or a major trail. Another source came from group colonization, especially that of German-speaking people who emigrated from southern Russia in search of religious freedom and to escape compulsory military conscription. A great many were Mennonites, and they settled primarily in the northern portion of the region in Reno, Harvey, McPherson, and Marion counties. The Mennonites are principally credited with bringing into Kansas a hardy strain of winter wheat known as Turkey Red, making possible the extensive wheat production for which the state is now famous. Hillsboro, in Marion County, is a major center for the Mennonite Brethren, and North Newton, in Harvey County, is home to the Mennonites' oldest college (1887), Bethel (HV 11.07). The Swedish Lutherans also created some colonies in McPherson County (and in Saline County in the Northcentral Region). Lindsborg, in McPherson County, was organized in 1868 and is home to their denominational Bethany College (1881). These settlers were essentially agriculturists, as were many others who came into the region. Yet urban centers were founded, and today the majority of the region's population are city dwellers. Three of those urban centers, centrally located, early on grew notably larger than the average: Newton, Hutchinson, and Wichita.

Newton, the seat of Harvey County, is the smallest of the three with a population slightly under 17,000. Founded in 1871, Newton's status as a cattle boomtown lasted only a couple of years after it replaced Abilene as the railhead, for it soon ceded that role to Wichita, twenty-eight miles to the south. Fortunately for Newton, in 1873 the railroad selected it to be a main division point, quickly helping the community to grow and prosper (see HV 11.03 and .04). The railroad tracks pass diagonally through the city, breaking the grid of the streets; the intersection of the tracks with Main Street marks the center of the downtown district.

Hutchinson (nearly 40,000), the seat of Reno County, is substantially larger than Newton. Located on the Arkansas River, thirty-five miles due west of Newton, Hutchinson's incorporation in 1872 also can be credited to the arrival of the Santa Fe Railroad, whose main line then continued west paralleling the river. Hutchinson's economy has depended heavily on grain storage and milling and on the extraction of salt, but the development nearby of oil and gas wells also has provided important contributions to the community's growth, reflected in its substantial courthouse (RN 21.06) and an elegant Art Deco theater (RN 21.05). Hutchinson is also home to the annual Kansas State Fair, which is located toward the northern end of the city's Main Street. This street passes south through the central business district, which consists primarily of one- to two-story buildings, and across the Arkansas River. Residential districts spread east and west, with storage and processing facilities clustered along the rail line that bisects the city in this direction.

The dominant city within the Southcentral Region is Wichita, the seat of Sedgwick County. Since 1950 it has ranked as the largest city in the state (current population 304,000). Wichita originated from James R. Mead's trading post established in 1864 near the Wichita Indians, who had been relocated to the area that year. Mead had some help from Jesse Chisholm, who marked out the trail in 1865 that bears his name. The trading post was located east of the confluence of the Little Arkansas and the Arkansas rivers, and the trail passed nearby. Even though the Indians were again forced to migrate (in 1865), Mead's trading post somehow managed to survive and evolve into a small settlement.

With the creation of Sedgwick County, the Wichita Town and Land Company was organized in 1868 and two years later officially platted the town. Wichita also succeeded in gaining the county seat, and although the status helped the town it could not automatically guarantee significant future growth. Thus, local efforts began almost immediately to attract the cattle trade and to underwrite the construction of a rail link for Wichita. A spur from the main line at Newton became operational in May 1872, and in due course Wichita became the principal railhead for the transfer of cattle that had been driven up the Chisholm Trail. With these developments, business trade rapidly increased in Wichita, indicated by the establishment of more banks and grocery stores and in the continuing construction of housing for a growing population. Another measure of the impact of the cattle trade, however, is found in a concurrent increase in saloons and bordellos within the city.

Wichita's cowtown prosperity was temporary, and its decline was reinforced by a quarantine ordered in 1876 to protect northern livestock from a fever carried by the Texas cattle. Though Texas-based cattle drives to Kansas continued, their destination was moved many miles to the west to Dodge City. Furthermore, Wichita not only lost the cattle trade, but it also had to cope with the effects of the nationwide financial panic of 1873 and then with the damage caused by a widespread plague of grasshoppers in 1874. The piling up of such complications affected the city's economy negatively and the size of its population, which began to drop. Wichita, however, had a number of energetic and even visionary civic leaders who were determined to ameliorate the situation. Their solution focused on adding railroad connections, and by 1883 they had succeeded to the point that the city experienced a major real estate boom. By 1885 the city's population had reached 8,000; more impressive buildings soon followed, such as the Cary House Hotel (SG 24.08) and a number of substantial residences (e.g., SG 24.24 and .29).

Wichita, of course, had numerous competitors who were also courting the railroads and who would experience the heady sensation of being a center of intense real estate speculation for several years. Yet, such speculation balloons inevitably were subject to abrupt collapse, with obvious negative effects. Wichita's came in mid-1887, by which time the population had approached 34,000, the number of business firms and industries had increased noticeably, and several private colleges had been founded. When the boom burst, the city's economy quickly worsened, the population dropped substantially, and the colleges foundered. Nevertheless, Wichita continued to work at achieving physical improvements, including a start on a modern sewer system and the construction of new public buildings (e.g., SG 24.23). Even so, by the turn of the century Wichita's situation seemed far less encouraging than it had a dozen years earlier, and its future appeared inexorably tied to the uncertain fortunes of agriculturally related enterprises.

Physical evidence of the era before the boom is best witnessed in the Old Cowtown Museum located in Sim Park, which is nestled between the two rivers just north of their confluence. Consisting of both restorations and reproductions, the more than forty buildings that make up the museum village—including the city's first residential structure (SG 24.32)—are representative for the period 1865 to 1880. As for the boom years, ever more substantial buildings were being erected, many of which are still standing. These include a good sampling by the firm of Proudfoot and Bird, who came to Wichita in 1885 but then left after only five years, when the surge of construction initiated by the boom had clearly come to an end. In Wichita, the firm's work ranged from residential structures (SG 24.58) to major public and academic buildings (SG 24.03 and .37).

The new century brought changes, and Wichita's economy finally took a decided upturn from 1908 to 1910. Soon thereafter promoters began encouraging the infant aircraft industry, which grew substantially after the conclusion of World War I. Another boost came from major discoveries of oil in the region in 1915, most particularly in adjacent Butler County. With aircraft production companies finding the area suitable for the manufacture and testing of aircraft and for air meets, by 1927 the city with some justification began to promote itself as the Air Capital of the U.S.

Along with the growth of aviation and other industries in the 1920s, the city introduced professional planning to guide its development, including the passage of a zoning ordinance in 1922. Though the depression years of the 1930s restricted development, Wichita's deserved reputation as an aviation center made it a magnet for important defense contracts beginning in 1940, the year the city's population reached 115,000. By 1943 the population had increased to 135,000, reflecting the notable increase in the manufacture of aircraft for the military. Indeed, during World War II literally half the city's residents depended on the aircraft plants for their livelihood (see SG 24.48). The increase in people required a collateral increase in housing, which was constructed as an adjunct to the defense industry.

With the return of peace came a reduction in manufacturing and a decline in population, but only temporarily. Wichita's manufacturing capacity could now be reoriented to products that would serve a variety of needs pent-up during the many years in which the nation had first had to cope with the Great Depression and then with a global war. Recovery was comparatively swift, and by 1950 Wichita's population passed 190,000, growth that made the city the largest in the state. Increases continued, not only in physical size and population but also in urban amenities, which included a variety of educational and cultural institutions. In addition to Wichita State University (SG 24.54–.57), a Regents Institution since 1966 whose origins reach back to the 1895 Fairmont College that became Wichita Municipal University in 1926, higher education in the city is also provided by Friends University and the Kansas Newman College. Important cultural institutions include the All American Indian Center Museum (SG 24.33), an art museum (SG 24.31), a science center, a county zoo and botanical gardens, and a historical museum (SG 24.03).

Wichita's past is clearly reflected in its present form. The downtown district, which occupies approximately ten blocks in either direction, lies principally between the Arkansas River on the west and an elevated rail line on the east (SG 24.04). The commercial, civic, and religious structures of this area mirror Wichita's periods of rapid growth, with two- to six-story limestone Romanesque buildings from the 1880s (e.g., SG 24.13), eight- to twelve-story brick Neoclassical buildings from the 1920s (e.g., SG 24.14), similarly scaled Modern buildings from the 1950s (e.g., SG 24.16), and a variety of recent buildings (e.g., SG 24.17). The combination gives the area a vibrant and cosmopolitan atmosphere. Wichita's sense of urbanity is heightened by a series of city parks that rest in the curves of the Arkansas and Little Arkansas rivers, and that contain many of the city's cultural institutions (e.g., SG 24.31) and civic improvements (e.g., SG 24.30). Although the city has grown in all directions, the most prestigious residential areas have spread eastward. They also reflect the city's periods of substantial growth. A drive from west to east through the center of the city provides an instructive view of the settlement patterns of the late nineteenth century, early twentieth century, the postwar period, and contemporary urban sprawl. The easternmost developments, built in the last twenty-five years, contain not only residential areas and supporting neighborhood commercial developments but also major corporate employment centers (e.g., SG 24.50) similar to those that have arisen in Johnson County (see Metropolitan Kansas City Region). Wichita's industrial areas have concentrated in pockets near the rail lines in the northern section of the city and around McConnell Air Force Base (SG 24.47) in the southeastern quadrant.

Sedgwick County, with a population that now exceeds 400,000, anchors the Wichita Metropolitan Statistical Area, consisting also of Butler and Harvey counties. The area is served by Interstate Highways 135 and 35, the latter providing not only convenient access to Topeka and the Metropolitan Kansas City Region but also to major cities in Oklahoma and Texas. Wichita's ascendance occurred while Kansas City, Kansas, once the state's largest and most industrialized city, lost momentum and eventually population. A different sort of rival has arisen, however: rapidly growing Johnson County in the eastern part of the state. Johnson County, with many more service workers than blue-collar employees, is expected soon to surpass Sedgwick County in population, but Wichita apparently will remain secure in its ranking as the state's largest city and as a prominent force not only in the Southcentral Region but also in the state generally. A case in point is Wichita's support in the development of several important architectural practices and in the construction of a number of notable modern buildings; the consistently high-quality work produced by Robert Shaefer and his associates is particularly significant.

Wichita also provides a rich variety of architecture. Given the number of examples from other locales in the area, the visitor to the Southcentral Region will have access to a diverse representation of building types and architectural styles, ranging from the old to the new and including everything from modest vernacular examples to work by architects of consequence. The map of the region and the directory serve to locate the counties, cities, and towns containing these buildings and to provide an outline for the organization of the catalog entries for the region.

# SOUTHCENTRAL & WICHITA REGION

Alpha-Numeric Directory

**BUTLER (BU)**

01 Augusta

02 El Dorado†

**CHASE (CS)**

03 Cottonwood Falls†

04 Elmdale

05 Strong City

**COWLEY (CL)**

06 Arkansas City

07 Winfield†

**HARPER (HP)**

08 Anthony†

09 Harper

**HARVEY (HV)**

10 Halstead

11 Newton†

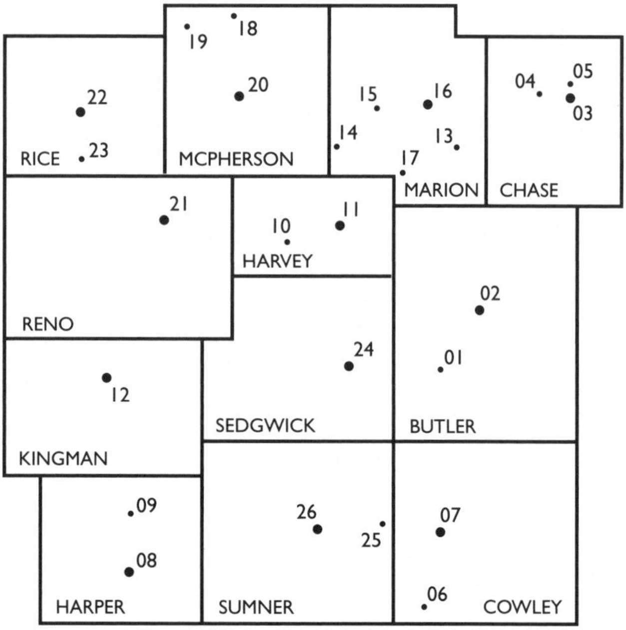

**KINGMAN (KM)**

12 Kingman†

**MARION (MN)**

13 Florence

14 Goessel

15 Hillsboro

16 Marion†

17 Peabody

**MCPHERSON (MP)**

18 Lindsborg

19 Marquette

20 McPherson†

**RENO (RN)**

21 Hutchinson†

**RICE (RC)**

22 Lyons†

23 Sterling

**SEDGWICK (SG)**

24 Wichita†

**SUMNER (SU)**

25 Oxford

26 Wellington†

# Augusta

**BU 01.01**
## C. N. James Cabin*
*1868*
*303 State Street*

The one-and-one-half-story log building provides insight into the state's early architecture. Although clapboards cover only the upper gable portion of the facade, early log structures were in time often covered completely by clapboard siding in order to protect underlying structure or to add another barrier to the elements. This cabin, like many early buildings, served multiple uses in the pioneer community; it has been a store, Masonic hall, church, and again a store. Now it houses the Augusta Historical Museum.

. . . . . . . . . . . . . . . . . . . . . . . . . . . . . . . . .

# El Dorado

**BU 02.01**
## Butler County Courthouse
*1908–1909. George P. Washburn & Son*
*Central and Gordy streets*

Located on a broad, open block just to the west of the main business district, this three-story red-brick Romanesque Revival courthouse bears many similarities to the five

other Kansas courthouses designed by the architect in the first decade of the twentieth century. They vary primarily in the shape of the corner pavilions, the central tower, and in the ornament, especially around the main door. This building, the last in the series, is unique in that it features a pedimented entry porch supported on two-story Ionic columns. It marks a change in the firm's work, which later favored Neoclassical motifs. Portions of the building have been altered, but significant details, such as an interesting metal stair, remain.

**BU 02.02**
## El Dorado Carnegie Library*
*1912. John F. Stanton*
*101 South Star*

The small tile-roofed two-story rough-stone library sits across a lawn west of the county courthouse. The simple geometric stone ornament on the pilasters flanking the central half-level entry provide a Prairie Style character to the building.

**BU 02.03**

## Eureka Federal Bank / Metropolitan Federal Bank

*1977. Cary Goodman*
*Central and Gordy streets*

Facing the front of the courthouse, this exuberant one-story building, despite its modest size, demands attention because of the sheer profusion of architectural elements in the composition: a freestanding curved masonry wall, a half-conical skylight, faceted glazing, and exposed steel framing. Its playful if unresolved forms are representative of the spirit of architectural exploration characteristic of the time.

# Cottonwood Falls

**CS 03.01**

## Samuel N. Wood House*

*1867*
*One mile east of Cottonwood Falls on county road*

The limestone farmhouse demonstrates the durability of local vernacular building traditions. The house and its attendant outbuildings continue to serve their intended purpose. The irregular disposition of the house would seem to suggest the building has received alterations and additions. Samuel Wood was influential in the settlement of the state, first as a leader of the free-state movement in Lawrence, then in 1858 as a founder of Cottonwood Falls, and later as a combatant in the struggle to establish the county seat of Stevens County.

**CS 03.02**

## Chase County Courthouse*

*1871–1873. John G. Haskell*
*Broadway (south end)*

This impressive three-story Second Empire limestone structure is the oldest Kansas courthouse continuing its original function. The building is a remarkable display of the architect's talents; the sophistication of the

# Strong City

## Lower Fox Creek School*

*1882*
*On K 177 (three miles north of Strong City)*

A well-preserved reminder of early life on the frontier, this one-room stone schoolhouse sits as a lonely sentinel on a hilltop amid broad fields. The building's carefully cut quoins, lintels, and arches as well as the joinery of the adjoining rough-stone walls provide a dramatic demonstration of the artistry of the stonemason. The building was in use as a school until 1947.

CS 05.02

## Spring Hill Ranch*

*1881*
*On K 177 (three miles north of Strong City)*

The complex of stone farm buildings, which includes a house, barn, silo, smokehouse, carriage house, and several storage sheds, occupies a stone-terraced hillside. The two-story Second Empire farmhouse takes ad-

composition reveals his training in a Boston architectural office and his education at Wesleyan Academy and Brown University. The siting of the building atop a hill at the end of Cottonwood Falls' main commercial street makes the composition even more striking. The most notable feature of the building's interior is a continuous three-story cantilevered curving stair.

. . . . . . . . . . . . . . . . . . . . . . . . . . . . . . .

# Elmdale

CS 04.01

## Clover Cliff Ranch House*

*1860/1883*
*On U.S. 50 (four miles southwest of Elmdale)*

The two-story Italianate limestone house was built only two years after the formation of the county. Although the building is not ornate, its stature points to the early prosperity of the region.

. . . . . . . . . . . . . . . . . . . . . . . . . . . . . . .

vantage of the sloping site; entry is from the lower level on the front and the upper level at the rear. The house features corner pavilions capped by tall mansard roofs set at an angle to the main body of the house. Efforts are under way to establish the ranch as a national park.

COWLEY COUNTY

# Arkansas City

**CL 06.01**

## Old Arkansas City High School*

*1890. Charles Sedgewick*
*300 West Central*

This majestic stone Richardsonian Romanesque school building occupies a prominent corner at the edge of the business district. It presents a complex and sophisticated set of interpenetrating gable forms that unites with a dominant entry tower to produce an effect that is both weighty and vertical. The building is now being used by the Cowley County Community College.

**CL 06.02**

## Union State Bank*

*1883*
*127 South Summit Street*

The two-story stone-trimmed brick corner bank lies at the heart of the Arkansas

City Commercial Center Historic District,* which stretches for several blocks in each direction along Summit and Fifth streets. Buildings in this area display considerable variety; they range from one to five stories in height and date primarily from the period between 1880 and 1930. Though many of them are individually noteworthy, taken together they form an impressive study of late-nineteenth- and early-twentieth-century small town commercial architecture.

. . . . . . . . . . . . . . . . . . . . . . . . . . . . . . . .

# Winfield

### CL 07.01
## Cowley County National Bank*
*1886*
*820–822 Main Street*

This stone corner bank anchors the heart of Winfield's downtown district. Subtle adjustments in the rhythm of the facade, refinements of detail, and an interesting mansarded attic story set this building apart from the many similar structures in towns throughout the region.

### CL 07.02
## Winfield Public Carnegie Library*
*1912. E. C. Smith and J. O. Parr*
*1001 Millington Street*

Similar in organization to many other small Carnegie libraries across the state, the symmetrical rectangular brick building's entry is placed at the half level, the main reading room occupies the upper floor, and meeting and service rooms are placed on the lower level. The building is distinguished by the highly original treatment of the area around the round-arched doorway, which is flanked by tall stone pilasters, ornate decorative medallions, and bracketed cornices. The structure reveals a kinship to the work of the Prairie Style architects in that the building appears to be a deliberate experiment in new ornamental devices.

### CL 07.03
## Cowley County Courthouse
*1962*
*Caton Yadon & Potter with Stitzel & Thoma*
*400 block of Ninth Street*

Horizontal and well-detailed, this Modern two-story metal curtainwall building occupies a landscaped block near the center of town. It reveals a changing attitude toward government, one that values efficiency over prestige. The building might be mistaken for a suburban commercial office building. The most notable feature is a map of the county incised in a stone mass that protrudes through the main block, marking the building entry.

without windows, the building has a pleasing human scale appropriate to its urban corner location. A thin horizontal canopy wrapping around the structure helps to mediate its height and focuses attention on a corner entry accented by dark stone panels. Many of the features of the building, including vertically accented windows and inset glass block, are typical of commercial buildings of the era.

## CL 07.04
### Winfield City Building
*1926. Schmidt Boucher & Overend*
*Ninth and Mullington streets*

Despite its modest proportions, this narrow two-story Neoclassical brick building achieves a surprising presence. A well-composed corner pavilion featuring stone-trimmed corner pilasters, a raised stone cornice, and a two-story Palladian arched entry mark the civic importance of the building. The structure demonstrates how simple adjustments can transform a building's nature.

## CL 07.05
### Southwestern Bell Telephone Company Office
*1953–1954. Oliver D. Howells*
*Ninth and Millington*

The two-story brick building houses both offices and switchgear. Despite the requirement that much of the space be designed

# Anthony

### HP 08.01
## Harper County Courthouse*
*1907–1908. George P. Washburn*
*900 North Jennings*

Located one block north of the center of town, this simplified red-brick Romanesque Revival building occupies a full block. The interior public spaces remain intact, making it one of the best preserved of the architect's thirteen Kansas courthouses. The floor-tile patterns and decorative iron railings are of particular interest.

### HP 08.02
## Anthony Municipal Hall
*1934*
*Main and Anthony*

Anchoring one end of Anthony's main commercial block, the building houses a variety of assembly functions, from theater productions to sporting events. Terracotta ornaments reflective of the transitional phase between traditional and modern expression add interest to this simple two-story brick box.

### HP 08.03
## Anthony Theater*
*ca. 1936. S. S. Voigt*
*Main and Kansas Avenue*

This building stands at the heart of Anthony's main commercial strip. It is among the better preserved of the Art Deco movie houses that were built at the time throughout the state. The awkwardly exuberant marquee continues to demand attention.

### HP 08.04
## Anthony Public Carnegie Library*
*1908–1911*
*John Lawrence and Edwin A. Anderson*
*104 North Springfield*

The building is typical of the smaller examples among the fifty-eight Carnegie libraries built in Kansas. Often they were simple rectangular one-story symmetrical structures built on a raised podium and judiciously rendered in a variety of mostly revival styles. Anthony's library is given a Jacobethan look through the addition of stone trim around the central raised doorway of the mostly brick structure.

. . . . . . . . . . . . . . . . . . . . . . . . . . . . . .

# Harper

### HP 09.01
### Thompson-Wohlschlegel Barn*

*1912–1913*
*Take U.S. 160 three miles east of Harper, then head south one-half mile*

This seventy-five-foot-tall, eighty-foot-diameter domed round barn has begun to suffer serious decay; already the center portion of the roof has collapsed. The building is interesting because of its overall construction and form and because it features a two-story wooden gabled vestibule compressed between two circular stone silos with conical roofs.

### HP 09.02
### Chaparral High School

*1970. Shaefer Schirmer & Eflin*
*On K 14 (one-half mile south of U.S. 160)*

The Modern brick school building is composed of simple but massive geometric forms with deep set window openings. The scale of the elements is appropriate to the rural open site. The various forms house separate functional areas that are arranged around a central corridor. It is typical of a popular, contemporary approach to school design.

# Halstead

## HV 10.01
## Bernard Warkentin Homestead*
*ca. 1874–1885. John G. Haskell*
*140 East North Street*

The complex of buildings consisting of a house, barn, shed, pump house, and silo is a National Historic Landmark, located on the banks of the Arkansas River where it passes through Halstead. Both the individual buildings and the spaces between them are typical of the more affluent late-nineteenth-century farmsteads in the region. The two-story wood-frame is a solidly built example of the then popular Queen Anne Style. The two-story wood barn is a long rectangular building with a single gabled roof running its entire length. A series of small, well-proportioned windows and carefully detailed twin cupolas give the barn scale and character. Although simple in overall form, the building is a strong presence in the landscape. The brick silo adds a vertical emphasis to the entire composition. The complex is also of interest because Bernard Warkentin was one of the first German Mennonites to settle in Kansas after fleeing Russian persecution. He then encouraged many of his relatives to settle in the region and later organized one of the area's larger grain-milling operations.

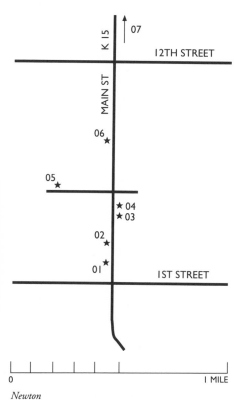

*Newton*

# Newton

## HV 11.01
## Carnegie Library*
*1903–1904. William W. Rose*
*203 Main Street*

Carnegie libraries were often the most significant cultural repositories in places that were little more than emerging frontier settlements. The scale and ornament of this three-story Neoclassical brick and stone library speak proudly of its civilizing ambitions. The classical referent helps connect the building to the long tradition of Western learning. The focus of this library is the central entry portal, which is framed between monumental brick pilasters and Ionic columns and is capped by a wide stone entablature and tall attic.

## HV 11.02
### Warkentin Mill*
*1879*
*Third and Main streets*

The mill complex consists of a rectangular four-story brick building with a mansard roof and an irregular one-story brick wing in front of the larger block, extending toward Main Street. The complex has been renovated to house a variety of commercial spaces, including a restaurant that occupies the one-story portion.

## HV 11.03
### Santa Fe Depot*
*1929–1930. E. H. Harrison*
*414 North Main Street*

The two-story brick station serves as a clear reminder of the importance of the railroad in the development of central Kansas. The ornate Jacobethan stone trim and lively profile mark the building as an important destination, from both the track and street sides. The building sits at an angle to Newton's main commercial street, so both sides are clearly visible.

## HV 11.04
### (Old) Railroad Building and Loan Building*
*1925. Greenbaum Hardy & Schumacher*
*500 North Main Street*

The handsome two-story Neoclassical building is distinguished by its careful proportioning and skillful detailing. The shorter three-bay side of the building faces Main Street, and the longer eleven-bay side faces the Santa Fe Railroad Station across a secondary street. The bays are framed by monumental Corinthian pilasters. Within each of the front bays and the first seven of the side bays a double window is set above a tall, arched window. The triple windows of the four rear bays of the side elevation reveal the presence of a mezzanine in this portion of the building. The interior of the building has been remodeled to house a restaurant and multiple tenant office spaces.

## HV 11.05
### Samuel A. Brown House*
*ca. 1878*
*302 West Sixth Street*

This generous frame house is of interest for its overall form as well as for a number of interesting details. It offers a variety of shingle types and textures, curving brackets beneath the broad porch, and most notably a round corner bay that seems to grow from the porch roof and culminates in a bullet-shaped, shingled, domed roof.

## HV 11.06
### St. Mary's Catholic Church
*1902–1904*
*William and George Hanna (builder)*
*Eighth and Main Streets*

Both in its form and inception, this sturdy brick church is typical of many built by early Catholic congregations. In this case the priest, Moses McGuire, wishing to build a new church, drew upon the construction skills within his congregation. Using the recently completed church in Florence (Marion County) as their guide and perhaps drawing on skills developed in their native Ireland, the Hanna brothers accepted the challenge. The resulting church shows their skill and inventiveness. A school building was added in 1909 and a rectory in 1914. The church was remodeled in recent years and continues to serve its congregation.

## HV 11.07
### Administration Building (Bethel College)*
*1887–1893*
*Proudfoot & Bird / Dumont & Hayward*
*North Newton*

The massive three-story building continues to anchor the main campus quadrangle. In addition to administrative and classroom spaces, it contains a large chapel located in a wing that extends perpendicularly behind the main block of the building. The most dominant feature of this rough-stone Richardsonian Romanesque structure is a large arched entry portal set between two towers, one round and the other octagonal. Originally the building was to have a fourth story, but the end of the real estate boom in 1889 forced a change in design. Also as result of the faltering economy, Proudfoot & Bird elected to move their office from Wichita to Salt Lake City and asked the firm of Dumont and Hayward to oversee the remainder of the construction. The change affected the building's profile, which lacks the striking character of other Proudfoot & Bird buildings, notably the Administration Building of Friends University in Wichita (SG 24.37).

# Kingman

**KM 12.01**
### Kingman County Courthouse*
*1907–1908*
*George P. Washburn & Son*
*120 Spruce Street*

The three-story red-brick courthouse occupies a half block, one block east of the main business street. It follows the rather individualized stylistic formula of several other of the architect's courthouses, notably the one designed nearly a decade earlier for Woodson County (WO 25.01). The interior has been extensively remodeled; a dropped ceiling and fire corridor have compromised the space of the original courtroom.

**KM 12.02**
### Kingman City Building*
*1888*
*Main Street and Avenue C*

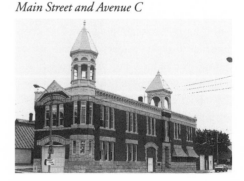

The two-story brick and stone building incorporates a variety of civic functions within a strikingly well-ordered composition. The lower floor originally housed the fire department and the upper floor a courtroom in the front and city offices in the rear. The corner is marked by a tall octagonal tower that was used by the fire department for drying their hoses, and the public entrance is marked by a square bell tower set in the center of the long side of this rather narrow structure. The building now serves as a museum.

## KM 12.03
## First National Bank Building◆
*ca. 1888*
*Main Street and Avenue A*

Standing proudly at the center of town, this three-story brick and stone commercial block recalls a time of optimism in the region, corresponding to the arrival of the Santa Fe Railroad in 1884 and the Missouri Pacific Railroad in 1887. The building is a highly original variant of a familiar type, achieving a sense of unity yet giving expression to the variety of functions that once were housed in the building, which, in addition to the bank, included a store, a hotel, and a Masonic lodge. Each of the functions is proclaimed by a slightly raised, carefully composed portion of the facade capped by an elaborate, pedimented stone cornice piece.

## KM 12.04
## Doney-Clark House*
*1885–1886*
*817 West Sherman*

The simple one-story T-shaped four-room cottage of red brick occupies a shaded site at the western end of Sherman Street and is representative of a modest, popular house type of the late nineteenth century. It features front and rear porches supported on turned wood posts located at the inside corners of the main body of the house. It is distinguished by the quality of the masonry work, which includes a belt course of black brick at the lintel level. Mathias Doney, the builder and original owner, operated a local brickyard.

## KM 12.05
## Hugo Oeding House
*ca. 1990*
*On U.S. 54 (one mile east of Kingman)*

Set into the south side of a gentle swell in the midst of a broad field, this concrete and glass house reflects the growing awareness of the need for the conservation of expendable natural resources. The earth covering provides insulation, the extensive south-facing windows gather the heat of the sun, and a windmill provides supplemental energy. Ironically, the building represents a return to the values of the early settlers of the region who built earth-sheltered houses of a different sort. It was designed and constructed by the owner, based on his study of similar houses in other parts of the country.

# Florence

## MN 13.01
**Harvey House***
*1876*
*204 West Third Street*

This broad and welcoming two-story wood frame structure serves as a reminder of an important chapter in Kansas' history. The building is the original portion of what became the second Harvey House dining facility and the first to offer lodging. Frederick Harvey ultimately operated dining facilities serving passengers throughout the Santa Fe Railroad system. He is credited with providing a civilizing influence in the frontier territory, both through the quality of service offered in his establishments and through the young women he attracted to the region to work in his facilities. After the Harvey House closed in 1900, the building was moved several times and served a variety of uses. In 1951 the original portion of the building (first built as the Clifton Hotel) was moved to its present location; it now houses a historical museum operated by the Florence Historical Society.

# Goessel

## MN 14.01
**Freisen House (Mennonite Heritage Museum)**
*1911*
*North Poplar Street*

The compact two-story wood frame house is one of a collection of structures brought together from around the region to illustrate the lives of early Mennonite settlers. Other buildings grouped around the central lawn of the museum complex include the Krause house (1874), the Bloomfield School (1875), the Schroeder barn (1902), the Goessel Preparatory School (1906), the Goessel State Bank (1910), and a contemporary exhibit building.

## MN 14.02
**Alexanderwohl Mennonite Church**
*1886*
*On K 15 (one mile north of Goessel)*

Sitting alone in a rural landscape, this two-story Neoclassical wood church was built originally of lumber from earlier settlers' cabins and has received a number of additions. The austere central worship space faces the front of the building; the almost cubic volume is surrounded on three sides by narrow balconies. It is the most impressive of the remaining early Mennonite worship spaces in the state.

. . . . . . . . . . . . . . . . . . . . . . . . . . . . . . .

# Hillsboro

**MN 15.01**
## Music Education Building (Tabor College)
*1990. John Thessen*
*On U.S. 56*

The Modern geometric brick building helps to form the edge of a campus composed primarily of traditional Neoclassical buildings. Landscaping is used to soften the contrast between the building and its neighbors. An earth berm conceals the lower half of the building, which also helps to isolate it acoustically. A tall tower marks the main entry to the public auditorium.

**MN 15.02**
## Peter Loewen House*
*1876*
*501 South Ash*

The gable-roofed one-story pioneer adobe house of seven rooms and the attached barn display the ingenuity of the region's Mennonite immigrants. The structure represents an essentially European building type constructed from readily available local materials. Now housing a museum, it exhibits household articles and farming equipment used by the settlers.

. . . . . . . . . . . . . . . . . . . . . . . . . . . . . . .

# Marion

**MN 16.01**
## Marion County Courthouse*
*1905–1907. Holland & Squires*
*601 East Main*

This stone Richardsonian Romanesque building occupies a full block just south of the main business district. It is nearly identical to two other courthouses in Osborne and Riley counties designed at the time by the architects and is similar to two courthouses in Geary and Mitchell counties designed by J. C. Holland before he entered partnership with Frank Squires. The building has been somewhat modified on the interior.

**MN 16.02**
## Hill Grade School*
*1873 (south portion), ca. 1890 (north portion)*
*601 East Main Street*

The two-story stone building sits in a meadow atop a wooded hill; the tower is visible above the surrounding trees. Although the two parts are similar in massing and fenestration, the differing dates of construction are clearly evident in the quality and texture of the stonework.

**MN 16.03**
## Presbyterian Church of Marion◆
*1874*
*610 Lawrence*

*Hill Grade School*

The simple rectangular gable-roofed stone church occupies a prominent corner on a hill. The most distinguishing feature is the bell tower, which rises above the main entry. The form of the roof would seem to indicate a Scandinavian influence.

**MN 16.04**
### Elgin Hotel*
*1886. Third and Santa Fe streets*

The size of this three-story building serves to anchor the central intersection of the down-

town district. The hotel was built in the year the town was laid out although settlement had begun twenty-five years earlier. It is built of stone from local quarries, like many other buildings in the city, and it now contains apartments.

**MN 16.05**
### City of Marion Municipal Building
*1938. W. E. Glover*
*Third and Santa Fe streets*

The multiuse municipal building houses city offices as well as a municipal auditorium and fire station. Many local governments were able to build such structures with the assistance of the federal government's programs to relieve unemployment during the Great Depression. The stylized classical stone ornament on this boxy brick structure is characteristic of the architecture that resulted from the government building program and is sometimes referred to as Depression Modern.

## MN 16.06
### Stone Barn
*1921. G. W. Penland (builder)*
*U.S. 56 (two miles west of Marion)*

With its wood-shingled gambrel roof this stone barn is a well-preserved example of a sight that was once typical in the rural sections of this portion of Kansas. The lintels above the small windows reveal the surprisingly high degree of care taken by the building of the utilitarian structure. Much of the stone used in the barn came from a dismantled mill.

. . . . . . . . . . . . . . . . . . . . . . . . . . . . . . .

# Peabody

## MN 17.01
### Peabody Township Carnegie Library*
*1914. Anthony A. Crowell*
*214 Walnut*

The organization of this two-story Neoclassical brick library is typical of many other similarly sized Carnegie-financed libraries of the time. The symmetrical entry, which is framed by brick pilasters and capped by a stone entablature and cornice balustrade, is located at the half-level. In the particularly well-preserved interior, the entry opens directly into a large, light-filled reading room that occupies the entire upper level. Tall bookcases fill the spaces on the exterior walls between the generous windows; the interior of the room features only low, desk-height furnishings, thereby maintaining a sense of openness.

## MN 17.02
### Alva Burton House
*1922. Scott Brothers Construction (builder)*
*502 North Walnut*

The two-story Prairie Style brick residence stands out among the many fine homes that line Peabody's primary street. The stature of the houses reflects the affluence resulting from the oil boom of the 1920s. The Burton house takes features typical of the Prairie Style, including corner piers, broad overhangs, and horizontal window groupings, and moulds them into a highly original and unusually solid composition. The interior is notable as well, featuring impressive inlaid woodwork.

## MN 17.03
### Kansas State Bank
*1887. W. H. Traver (builder)*
*Walnut and Second streets*

# Lindsborg

**MP 18.01**
## Bethany Lutheran Church
*1874/1880/1904*
*300 North Main Street*

As in many small towns around the state, the most important downtown intersection is anchored by a solidly built stone bank building with a corner entry addressing both streets. Typical of the building type is this two-and-one-half-story Romanesque Revival structure, whose functions are clearly evident on the facade; large arched windows mark the main banking hall, and a separate entry gives access to the commercial space available above the first-floor bank.

**MN 17.04**
## Stone Barn
*ca. 1900*
*On U.S. 50 (one mile east of Peabody)*

The simple gabled stone barn stands proudly among a clutter of metal outbuildings. The overall proportions and the central arched opening give it a sense of repose. Ironically, it stands on the grounds of a retailer who sells the sort of prefabricated agricultural buildings that have made earlier stone barns obsolete.

This stuccoed stone church occupies an open site near the center of town. The central portion of the church, begun in 1874 by members of the congregation who had emigrated from Sweden only five years earlier, is hidden beneath a tower and steeple added to the front in 1880 and by the transepts added to the sides in 1904. The form of the church reflects the Scandinavian heritage of the congregation, and inscriptions on the buildings are in Swedish.

**MP 18.02**
## Swedish Pavilion*
*1904. Ferdinand Boberg*
*120 Mill Street*

Located in the county's Old Mill Park, this hipped-roofed wooden building is part of a museum complex. Also included are a three-story brick roller mill built in 1886, a log cabin built in 1870, and an 1880s Union Pacific Railroad depot. The Swedish pavilion was prefabricated in Sweden and originally erected at the 1904 St. Louis World's Fair. It was then given to Bethany College, where it was used as a classroom building and later donated to the Smoky Valley Historical Association, who moved it to its present site. The building reflects the growing National Romanticism in Scandinavia at the turn of the century. It currently houses a display of Swedish and local arts and crafts memorabilia. The architect, who practiced in Stockholm, enjoyed an international reputation as a twentieth-century exponent of traditional architectural styles.

. . . . . . . . . . . . . . . . . . . . . . . . . . . . . .

## Marquette

**MP 19.01**
### Washington Street Historic District*
*1886–1910*
*Washington Street, between Second and Third streets*

As in most of the smaller towns in Kansas, Marquette's image tends to be dominated by the height, bulk, and distinctive form of the ever-present cylindrical grain elevators. Yet Marquette also provides a view of earlier times, for many of the buildings along the town's main street have been restored by owners conscious of the street's historic character.

. . . . . . . . . . . . . . . . . . . . . . . . . . . . . .

## McPherson

**MP 20.01**
### McPherson County Courthouse*
*1894–1895. J. G. Haskell and J. F. Stanton*
*Maple and Kansas streets*

The castlelike stone courthouse, a three-story Romanesque building, occupies a half block immediately west of the central business district. Originally, the building contained county offices on the first floor, the main courtroom on the second floor, a meeting room on the third floor, and service spaces in the basement. Although the interior has been considerably altered, the exterior remains largely as originally designed. The most prominent features are a 105-foot clock tower centered on the primary entry facade, octagonal towers at each of the four corners, and a pair of chimneys united in a pedimented bay on the rear (west) facade.

**MP 20.02**
### McPherson Opera House*
*1889. George Shaffer*
*221 South Main*

Although modestly detailed, the size and proportions of this three-story brick building remain noteworthy, and at the time of construction it must have seemed impressive. The building suggests an early hunger for culture, and often such structures were among the earliest built in towns in the newly settled territory, providing space for musical or theatrical performances.

MP 20.03

## McPherson High School

*ca. 1965. John Shaver*
*East First Street and North High Drive*

Unusually shaped, the sprawling one-story Modern building occupies a broad, flat site in a suburban residential neighborhood. The complex consists of two principal building forms: the gymnasium portion, which is round in plan, and the hexagonal classroom portion. The round portion is covered by a low dome, and each of the classrooms is marked by a low, curving concrete shell roof that protrudes through a larger flat roof.

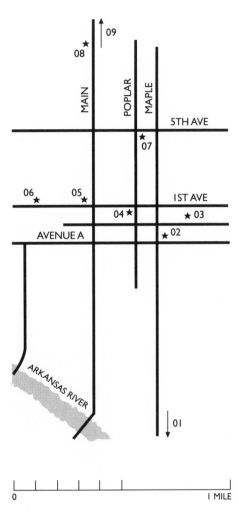

Hutchinson

# Hutchinson

## RN 21.01
### Carey Memorial
*1935*
*Carey Park*

The triple-arched Stripped Classical stone memorial marks the entry to a large urban park along the Arkansas River. It honors Emerson Carey, owner of a large local salt company, who donated the land to the city for the park. The memorial forms a back-drop to an elaborate formal fountain. Both the memorial and surrounding park are grand manifestations of similar monuments and landscaped areas in cities across Kansas.

## RN 21.02
### Sherman Middle School
*1983. Mann & Company*
*Avenue A and Maple Street*

This four-story monolithic brick box represents a rather unusual expression of its building type. School buildings in recent years most often carry a lower, more horizontal form than does this structure. Only the playful positioning of the windows begins to reveal the building's function.

## RN 21.03
### Houston Whiteside House•
*1880*
*504 East Sherman*

A pleasing example of the influence of the English Arts and Crafts Style, this two-story stucco house received a major addition to the right side in 1915 that compromises the lines of the original structure. The 500 block of East Sherman Street provides an interesting view of the variety of styles used by architects in the late nineteenth century, with good examples of Neocolonial (511), Shingle (512 and 544), Queen Anne (525 and 528), and Greek Revival (526).

## RN 21.04
### John Brown House
*1874*
*First Avenue and Poplar Street*

The two-story brick mansion is an early example of Victorian Italianate design. Built only two years after the railroad reached Hutchinson, it is of brick and artificial stone made in a recently opened local brick plant. The building was purchased in 1924 by the architect W. E. Hulse, who converted the home into six apartment units and constructed a block of apartments connected to the rear of the original house. Hulse's interior remodeling was extensive; on the exterior he extended the original porch and replaced its original wooden posts and arched brackets. The building now serves a commercial use.

### RN 21.05
### Fox Theater*

*1930–1931*
*Boller Brothers, with Mann & Company*
*18 East First Avenue*

This major downtown theater building provides a classic example of the exuberance of the Art Deco Style Complex syncopated stepped-relief patterns in the brick and a variety of boldly decorated terracotta inserts give interest to what is essentially a windowless box above the store windows on the ground floor. The decoration on the exterior gives promise of a fantasyland within. The Boller brothers gained a reputation as theater designers, and they worked in many parts of the country.

### RN 21.06
### Reno County Courthouse*

*1929–1931. William Earl Hulse*
*102 West First Avenue*

The courthouse, a massive six-story stone building, sits aloof from its downtown surroundings. The step-back massing and simplified incised conservative-modern ornament give it an imposing feeling, much like Bertram Goodhue's Nebraska state capitol. The interior of the courthouse is one of the most distinctive in Kansas. The entry leads directly to the second level and a large, double-height central space filled with the desks of various administrators. Public circulation is separated from the administrative area by low partitions skirting the large, columned hall. On the third floor, a formal central hall provides access to two symmetrical courtrooms; the hall and courtrooms contain murals. The fourth floor houses the juvenile courts, and the upper stories accommodate the offices of public works and the jail. A one-story, city-county law enforcement building, designed by Miller Holt Dronberger Arbuckle & Walker, was added to the west side of the courthouse in 1971.

### RN 21.07
### St. Theresa Catholic Church*

*1910–1911. Emmanuel L. Vasqueray*
*211 East Fifth Avenue*

The grand Romanesque Revival church of stone-trimmed brick towers above its residential surroundings. The vaulted interior

features an ornate Del Prado altar. The church was built as part of a deliberate expansion campaign by the Wichita Diocese, and fifty-two churches were constructed in the first twenty years of the twentieth century. The architect, noted for his church designs, has examples located throughout the Midwest, including St. Mary's Cathedral in Wichita (SG 24.21).

**RN 21.08**

## Hutchinson Public Library

*1949/1985*
*English Miller & Hockett / Miller*
*Dronberger Arbuckle Walker & McLain*
*Ninth Avenue and Main Street*

The earlier (southern) portion of the building is a good example of the postwar Americanized version of the International Style. The clearly defined interpenetrating volumes, glass corners, and horizontal windows of this style are moulded to the specifics of use and rendered in largely traditional materials. Even though the entry has been moved to the newer portion of the building and the interior functions have been modified, the materials and details of the original building's interior, including the terrazzo floors, wood-paneled walls, and metal stair rails, remain as thoughtful examples of an era's popular design motifs.

**RN 21.09**

## Kansas State Fairground

*Since 1913*
*Main to Plum streets and Twenty-ninth to Twenty-seventh avenues*

The fairgrounds spring to life each year to showcase the people and products of the state. In the many weeks between the fairs, the grounds have an eerie, desolate quality. Unless filled with crowds of people, the buildings seem too large and the spaces between them too great. Most of the buildings are utilitarian sheds; however, several are worthy of note, including the Capper Pavilion (1913), which retains the feeling of the original fair although it has been enclosed and has had its cupola removed (pictured above), and the Encampment Building (1933), which is a simple dormitory but suggests an appropriate sense of frivolity.

# Lyons

### RC 22.01
## Rice County Courthouse
*1910–1911. J. C. Holland & Son*
*Courthouse Square*

The three-story stone-trimmed brick Romanesque Revival building occupies a traditional courthouse square at the center of the business district. It represents a departure from the architect's many earlier courthouses, most of which were built entirely of stone. The structure is more compact and centralized than many earlier courthouses, probably in response to the constraints of the site. The interior has been substantially altered.

### RC 22.02
## Methodist Church
*1915. Charles D. Cuthbert*
*West Comm and South Pioneer*

This stately Neoclassical brick building underscores the universal popularity of the idiom in the late teens and early twenties of the twentieth century. Indeed, the shape and proportions of the church, the broad stairs leading to an inset entry set behind paired Ionic columns on the front, and the full-height arched windows of the side are characteristics frequently associated with civic buildings such as a municipal auditorium rather than with a church.

### RC 22.03
## Presbyterian Church
*1906*
*West Lyon and South Pioneer*

A corner-towered cross-gabled Eclectic brick building, the church weaves together a variety of diverse forms and dissimilar ornamental motifs. The battered entry tower of brick features a pedimented doorway, above which is an encircling ornamental frieze. Each side of the tower is punctuated by a single narrow-arched window. The tower roof is separated from the brick base by a squat Romanesque arcade. Despite the variety, the building maintains a sense of unity among its well-proportioned parts. The similarly quirky interior has been substantially modified. Overall, the building bears a strong resemblance to the work of Charles Squires.

. . . . . . . . . . . . . . . . . . . . . . . . . . . . . . .

# Sterling

### RC 23.01
### Cooper Hall (Sterling College)*
*1887. Seymour Davis*
*Broadway and Cooper Avenue*

Built of Strong City limestone, this three-story 17,600-square-foot Romanesque Revival classroom building lies at the heart of the Sterling College campus. The school, a Presbyterian institution originally called Cooper College, was founded the year before the building was erected. Cooper Hall, whose central tower was removed in 1948 after it was struck by lightning, has served a variety of uses until 1988, when it was closed due to structural problems. A renovation of the building is planned.

### RC 23.02
### Sterling Masonic Temple
*1901*
*Broadway and Jackson*

The two-story brick building fronts on the town's main commercial street. The temple is distinguished by two round corner turrets

with conical roofs and by an interestingly ornamented pediment and entablature. The lower floor contains a single large meeting room, but the upper floor is divided into a series of smaller offices.

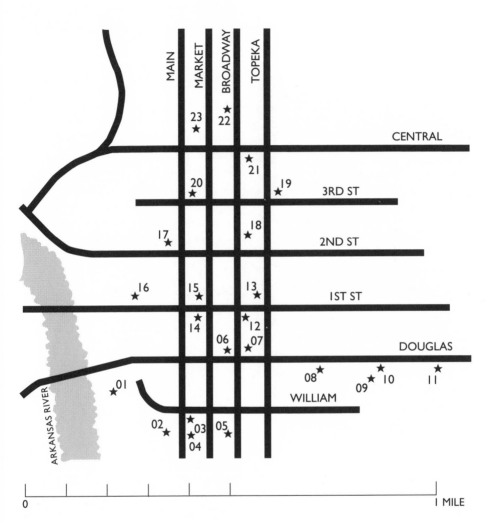

Wichita–Central

# Wichita-Central

## SG 24.01
## Century II Civic Center
*1966–1969. John Hickman*
*Douglas Avenue and Main Street*

The circular form and the mammoth domed roof clearly indicate that this building is a large exhibition hall. The complex, however, also houses the city's primary theater and concert hall. The articulation of the facades is consistent with the form of the building; they also reveal the architect's interest in the later work of Frank Lloyd Wright, with whom he studied. Although the building's bold form gives identity to an important civic space along the Arkansas River in downtown Wichita, it fails to organize the space for pedestrian activity.

## SG 24.02
## Wichita (New) Public Library
*1965. Shaefer Schirmer & Eflin*
*200 block of South Main Street (west side)*

The three-story Modern building relates effectively to the Richardsonian Romanesque Old Wichita City Hall (SG 24.03) and to the old Beaux-Arts public library (SG 24.04) across Main Street, thereby helping to form a well-defined public space. The new library, though informal in composition, is unmistakably civic in character. The exposed concrete structure, vertical concrete shading fins, and deep-set windows give the building

a sense of massiveness akin to its neighbors, yet the horizontality of the overhanging third floor and uninterrupted cornices give it a sense of lightness and accessibility. The Brutalist materials and forms of the facade are carried consistently through the building's interior. The design appears to have been inspired by the 1961 Boston City Hall project by Kallmann McKinnell & Knowles.

## SG 24.03
## Old Wichita City Hall*
*1889–1892. Proudfoot & Bird*
*204 South Main*

Known as "the palace of the plains," this Richardsonian Romanesque structure remains a symbol of the dramatic economic boom and population expansion of the 1880s. Clad in carefully cut rough-faced Cambridge limestone, the tall four-story mass is marked at each of the four corners by a round tower and is capped by a central clock tower. The building can be entered from either of the streets flanking its corner site. It has been renovated and now houses the Sedgwick County Historical Museum.

## SG 24.04
### Old Wichita Carnegie Library*
*1915. Anthony A. Crowell*
*220 South Main Street*

The classical symmetry of this Beaux-Arts composition helps to frame an important civic space, flanked also by the new library and the old city hall. The green tile roof over the central pavilion provides significant punctuation for the space. Currently, the building houses an omnisphere and science center.

## SG 24.05
### Petroleum Building
*1929. Overend & Boucher*
*221 South Broadway*

This eight-story terracotta office building, which uses modern Art Deco motifs mixed with traditional Mission Style elements, reflects the transitional aesthetic of the time. The building is representative of the cautious but timely work of an architectural firm that had a significant impact on Wichita and Kansas. Harry Overend's and Sy Boucher's sensibilities are also reflected in the nearby seventeen-story Allis Hotel (200 South Broadway), completed the following year.

## SG 24.06
### S. H. Kress and Company Building*
*1929–1932. Edward F. Sibbert*
*224 East Douglas Avenue*

The five-story Neo-Gothic terracotta structure is similar in material and style to other though usually smaller Kress stores built in the 1920s in many Kansas towns. Because of its consistent application, this type of building came to symbolize the Kress chain of retail stores.

## SG 24.07
### Fourth Financial Center / Bank IV
*1974*
*Skidmore Owings & Merrill, with Shaefer & Associates*
*Broadway and Douglas Avenue*

The nine-story glass and concrete Modern building occupies a site on Wichita's most prominent commercial intersection. The center's most notable feature is a full-height atrium that stretches across the southern portion of the structure. The space may have been inspired by the winter garden of Roche & Dinkeloo's 1967 Ford Foundation building in New York. Here, however, instead of being filled with vegetation, the space is largely vacant with the exception of a mobile by Alexander Calder.

## SG 24.08
### Carey House / Eaton Hotel*
*1886. Terry & Dumont*
*525 East Douglas Avenue*

The six-story brick commercial block is as impressive for its bulk as for its details, which refer to the then popular Second Empire Style. Even in its somewhat decrepit condition the building reflects the spirit of optimism that surrounded the city's rapid growth in the mid-1880s. The smaller buildings that occupy the remainder of the block and that are part of the Carey House His-

toric District♦ (501 to 515 Douglas) are typical of commercial structures of the first decade of the twentieth century.

## SG 24.09
### Union Terminal
*1906–1912. Louis S. Curtiss*
*701 East Douglas Avenue*

Sitting beside the elevated tracks that run through downtown, this building stands as a reminder of the importance of the railroads in Wichita's early history. The classic Beaux-Arts composition of the principal facade befits the building's civic stature, and the freer composition of the terminal's rear portion uses a more progressive vocabulary expressive of the building's structure. The stylistic contrast discloses much about the spirit of eclecticism. Ironically, it is the terminal's more utilitarian portion that reveals this notable architect's more significant contribution to architectural history. Louis Curtiss has been credited with the early use of several technical innovations, including caisson foundations for buildings and curtainwall construction, and is remembered for his stylistic innovation. The interior spatial quality of the terminal has been compromised by a recent renovation for the offices of a cable television company.

## SG 24.10
### Rock Island Depot*
*1887. J. T. Long*
*729 East Douglas Avenue*

The two-story hipped-roofed Romanesque Revival train station forms the western edge of the forecourt to the later and much larger Union Depot. It also provides an interesting contrast to the Union Depot's more formal character, but it too has been renovated for office use.

## SG 24.11
### Wichita Eagle and Beacon (addition)
*1970. Charles McAfee*
*825 East Douglas Avenue*

Though containing primarily storage and distribution facilities, the crisp geometries and board-formed concrete surface texture of this major addition to the offices of the *Wichita Eagle and Beacon* elevate a service structure that might have been merely utilitarian into the signature portion of the complex. The building received an award from the Kansas Society of Architects.

## SG 24.12
### Bell Telephone Company Building (addition)
*1970. Shaefer Schirmer & Eflin*
*First and Broadway*

This eight-story glass curtainwall Modern building, containing 180,000 square feet, is representative of a common design approach of the time. It is distinguished from other all-glass buildings by the subtle and skillful patterning of the windows. Like many other buildings designed in John Shaefer's office, it received an award from the Kansas Chapter of the American Institute of Architects.

## SG 24.13
### Scottish Rite Temple*
*1887–1888/1907/1956*
*Proudfoot & Bird / Thomas Harris Ash &*
*Mason / Overend & Boucher*
*First and Topeka streets*

Built originally as a YMCA, the four-story stone building became the Scottish Rite Temple in 1897. The 1907 addition, to the north, contains the main auditorium and dining room. The most striking feature of the building is the round corner tower, which once carried a two-story conical roof.

## SG 24.14
### Old Wheeler / Kelly / Hagny Building*
*1920. Richards McCarty & Bulford*
*120 North Market Street*

The seven-story brick building is typical of commercial structures being built at the time in downtown Wichita. It features a straightforward brick facade graced with Renaissance Revival stone ornament concentrated around its base and cornice. A similar approach is evident in the Lassen Hotel at Market Street and First Avenue, designed two years earlier by the same architects. The office building has been renovated to accommodate a board of trade center.

## SG 24.15
### Kansas Gas and Electric Building
*1953, remodeled 1969*
*Thomas Harris & Calvin*
*120 East First Street*

The nine-story International Style office building is a prime example of the functionalist approach to architecture popular at the time. The portion containing anonymous office functions is ringed by continuous uniform horizontal window bands, and the end containing the elevator core is marked by a separate vertically articulated block.

## SG 24.17
### Epic Center
*1989. Platt Adams Braht & Associates*
*Second and Main*

This building displays the full range of Modernist vocabulary and reveals the adaptability of the style. The structure responds to the demands of function, the size of its floor plate is varied through its seven levels, yet the urban context is respected. For example, there is a pedestrian arcade at the sidewalk, and the street edge established by older buildings is maintained. Although the building lacks singularity, it bears closer examination because of the effective use and integration of a variety of materials. The same architects were responsible for the (New) Sedgwick County Courthouse (525 Main Street); this building, although different in form and purpose, displays similarly skillful detailing.

## SG 24.16
### Colorado Derby Building
*ca. 1955. W. I. Fisher*
*First and Water Street*

At 320 feet, this is the tallest building in Kansas, containing almost 400,000 square feet of office and retail space and a parking garage for 680 cars. The most notable features of the regularized facades of the twenty-two-story Modern building are a glass reveal, which runs up the corner of the building, and the top, which appears to have been sliced at an angle across the diagonal. The two features combine to produce a silhouette that adds to the distinctiveness of the Wichita skyline.

## SG 24.18
## First United Methodist Church

*1961. Glen Benedick*
*300 North Broadway*

Even with its diverse elements, this building nevertheless achieves a pleasing sense of balance. The massiveness and singularity of the round-domed sanctuary block plays against the repetitive smaller-scale elements of the education wing. The primarily horizontal composition is set against a tall, simple, crown-capped obelisk, and the stylized mosaic that covers the front of the sanctuary mass complements the character of the building.

## SG 24.19
## St. John's Episcopal Church

*1887–1893/1961. Dumont & Hayward*
*North Topeka and East Third*

This nicely scaled Romanesque Revival limestone church faces a busy downtown intersection. The surprisingly sympathetic ed-

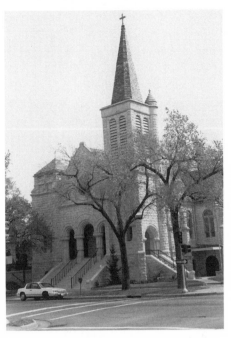

ucation wing, added in 1961, was designed by Shaefer Schirmer and Eflin.

## SG 24.20
## Occidental Hotel*

*1874*
*300 North Main*

The three-story Italianate brick building is one of the oldest remaining structures in the city and is a reminder of the years when Wichita served as the rail-head destination for the Texas cattle drives. After serving as a hotel for almost 100 years, it has been converted to office use.

## SG 24.21
## St. Mary's Cathedral

*1912. Emmanuel L. Vasqueray*
*Central Avenue and Broadway*

The massive but graceful Renaissance Revival stone church features three copper domes; the larger one is above the crossing and the smaller ones are on the two towers flanking the main entry. The entry itself is marked by a pedimented portico featuring four massive granite columns. The building, which was inspired by the twin churches of the Piazza del Popolo in Rome, reveals the breadth of the architect's background. Raised and trained in France, he practiced in the offices of the distinguished New York architects Carrere & Hastings as well as with Richard Morris Hunt before beginning his own firm.

### SG 24.22
### First Presbyterian Church
*1910. Badgley & Nicklas*
*Broadway and Elm*

The limestone Gothic Revival church is impressive for its scale as well as for the quality of its details. The centralized interior worship space is organized around a tall octagonal lantern. Light from large stained-glass windows at the perimeter, designed by A. A. Leyendecker, offers a pleasant balance to the illumination provided by the lantern. The adjacent classroom building, added in 1936, was designed by Glenn H. Thomas.

### SG 24.23
### Old Sedgwick County Courthouse*
*1888. W. R. McPherson*
*504 North Main*

The stone exterior of this prominently sited Neoclassical structure remains strikingly true to its original appearance. Interior renovations undertaken to accommodate mod-

ern offices, such as the 1978 work by Stanford Roberts, have altered many of the interior spaces. The original stair, manufactured by Stewart Ironworks of Wichita, remains and is of particular interest. The new courthouse, by Thomas Hams & Calvin (1956), is located at 525 Main Street.

. . . . . . . . . . . . . . . . . . . . . . . . . . . . . . .

# Wichita-West

### SG 24.24
### William Sternberg Home*
*ca. 1886–1887. William Sternberg*
*1065 North Waco*

This ornate frame house is a well-preserved example of Queen Anne, a style first explored in Great Britain by Richard Norman Shaw and his contemporaries and popularized in this country through pattern books. The availability of precut moldings facilitated the proliferation of Queen Anne residences through the final two decades of the nineteenth century.

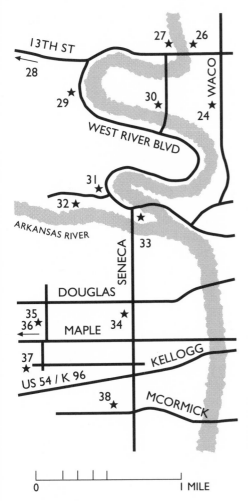

13TH ST

28

29

30

24

27

26

WACO

WEST RIVER BLVD

31

32

ARKANSAS RIVER

33

SENECA

DOUGLAS

35
36

MAPLE

34

37

US 54 / K 96

KELLOGG

38

MCORMICK

0 ——————— I MILE

*Wichita—West*

Identical repetitive concrete frames are used to form a variety of structures within an urban park: restroom facilities, concession stands, open pergolas, and a swimming pool bathhouse. The thoughtful design strategy produces objects that are interesting in themselves and that provide an overall identity to the park. The project received recognition for excellence by the Kansas Society of Architects. The level of creativity displayed here typifies much of the work of this talented architect, one of only a few black architects in the state of Kansas.

## SG 24.26
## Wichita High School (North)
*1928. Glenn H. Thomas*
*Thirteenth and Rochester streets*

The massive brick building reflects the conservative modern tradition of Eliel Saarinen and Bertram Goodhue as well as that of the Prairie Style. Ornate polychrome terracotta decorations by Bruce Moore of Wichita display inspirational scenes and proverbs. The building consisted of a U-shaped classroom block flanked on one end by an auditorium and on the other by the gymnasium; however, an infill addition has altered the character of some of the interior spaces. The school continues in its original use.

## SG 24.25
## McAdams Park Bathhouse
*1970. Charles McAfee*
*Thirteenth and Ohio*

## SG 24.27
## Minsa Bridge
*1932. Glenn H. Thomas*
*Thirteenth Street*

Spanning the Little Arkansas River, the ornate stone and terracotta bridge was designed to harmonize with the adjacent North Wichita High School Building, which the architect had designed several years earlier. As with the school building, the sculptor was Bruce Moore.

SG 24.28
## Northwest High School
*1978. Shaefer & Associates*
*Thirteenth and Tyler*

Low and sprawling, this one-story Modern school is typical of suburban school construction in the 1970s. It is centered on an atrium that connects the wings of the building. Each wing houses a different discipline whose function is revealed through the exterior expression of specialized spaces. The building is notable not only for the clarity and expressiveness of its plan but also for its careful and effective detailing. The structure consists of nicely related jumbo buff-brick boxes that are incised with well-proportioned dark glazed openings and enlivened

by contrasting elements characterized by dark skeletal metal framing.

SG 24.29
## B. H. Campbell House (Crumm Castle)*
*1886–1888*
*1155 North River Boulevard*

The imposing limestone building occupies a prominent site along the Little Arkansas River. Modeled after a Scottish castle, it is unique in the region. The most prominent feature is a five-story crenellated round tower that anchors one corner of the irregular two-story mass of the house.

SG 24.30
## Park Villa
*1912. Ulysses Grant Charles*
*Riverside Park*

Consisting of a central enclosed room surrounded on all sides by a broad porch, this substantial and distinctive stone pavilion is located in one of a series of parks that follow the Little Arkansas River. The parks, designed by L. W. Clapin and Alfred McDonald, were modeled after the work of Frederick Law Olmsted. The adjacent bathhouse, designed by Glenn H. Thomas and built in 1935, is also of interest. The tiny building is like an architectural sampler, exhibiting fragments of a variety of popular stylistic motifs of the day.

## SG 24.31
## Wichita Art Museum

*1935/1962–1963/1976–1977*
*Clarence S. Stein / Shaefer Schirmer &*
*Eflin / Edward Larrabee Barnes*
*619 Stackman Drive (in Sim Park)*

The original concrete museum building featured polychrome sculpture depicting Indian arts and crafts by Lee Lawrie, a long-time collaborator with the influential architect Bertram Goodhue. The sculpture was removed in connection with an addition, which itself was removed in conjunction with a second expansion project. The original building is still visible in altered form within the new museum structure that surrounds it. The new museum, a dark-brick building, assumes a modest stance behind landscaping and berms in its attempt to disguise the bulk of its simple geometric forms.

## SG 24.32
## Darius Sales Munger House
## (Historic Wichita Cowtown)*

*1868–1869*
*1717 Sim Park Drive (in Sim Park)*

The restored house is part of an assembly of over forty structures brought together to recreate the atmosphere of the Wichita area from 1865 to 1880. The museum, which occupies over seventeen acres, provides a convincing if not entirely accurate view of nineteenth-century life in Wichita. The collection of buildings furnishes a sampling of the types found in early Kansas settlements, from sod huts and small Stick Style Victorian houses to commercial structures and grain elevators. The Munger house is shown as originally built; siding had been added to protect the exterior walls. When it was built, the house was Wichita's most substantial building; it served not only as home for Munger's family but also as a small hotel, a post office, and a church.

## SG 24.33
## All American Indian Center

*1974. Shaefer & Associates*
*650 North Seneca*

The building generates interest through a clear expression of a simple but sophisticated plan order. The center consists of a single-story triangular board-formed concrete building, which houses exhibition spaces, and a taller steel-framed glass-enclosed open square performance area set into the long side of the triangle parallel to the opposite faces of the building. The plan order sets up an interesting series of spatial experiences that begin in a well-landscaped parking area, move through the variously open and closed spaces of the entry and exhibition halls, and culminate in the large open performance area, which looks upon a carefully composed vista consisting of an exterior performance area and the Little Arkansas River beyond. The integration of the building into the landscape, the reliance on geometric form, and the focus on ritual activity make the building appropriate to its function.

## Masonic Home
*1917*
*Maple and Seneca*

Stretching behind an open lawn, the broad two-story concrete retirement home faces a busy intersection. From this vantage point, the building presents a bold and arresting image. The smooth whitewashed walls and convincing Mission Style articulation stand in stark contrast to Wichita's architectural context. The building reflects the resurgence in interest in Spanish Colonial architectural traditions, which followed in the wake of Bertram Goodhue's buildings for the 1915 Panama-California Exposition in San Diego. The use of this style is also a natural expression of the building's concrete structure. Built as a replacement for a structure that had burned, the owners encouraged the use of nonflammable materials.

SG 24.35
## Gus Johnson House
*1887. Proudfoot & Bird*
*133 South Charles*

This house is simpler in form than other residences by the architects. A single large gabled roof encompassing the second floor

covers the entire house. Still, it is a clear demonstration of the skillful manipulation of the Shingle Style vocabulary. The home was built for a stonemason and contractor who worked on several of the architects' buildings.

SG 24.36
## Christ the King Parish Church
*1968. Hanney-Sanders*
*4413 Maple (at Young Street)*

The building is distinctive in both form and detail. The inspiration for the forms appears to have come, at least in part, from Pacific Island cultures. The exterior is marked most significantly by a cantilevered exterior breezeway and the curved conical roof of the worship space. The interior forms echo those of the exterior. The altar is at the center of the sanctuary and is lighted from above by a lantern held aloft by exposed curving wood beams. Even the detailing of the pews reflects the building's specific character.

## SG 24.37
**Davis Hall / University Hall (Friends University)***

*1886–1888. Proudfoot & Bird*
*2100 University Avenue*

This building was originally constructed to house Garfield University, a college operated by the Christian church, but despite a sizable endowment the school went bankrupt after only a few years. The building remained vacant until 1898, when it was purchased and donated to the Society of Friends and became the central building of Friends University. It now serves as the school's administrative headquarters. The commission for the building prompted the architects to locate in Wichita. The hall is impressive because of its ornate Richardsonian Romanesque brick and stone detail and because of its massive scale: it is 232 feet long and 150 feet wide, covering three-quarters of an acre.

## SG 24.38
**McCormick Elementary School***

*1890/1910. Proudfoot & Bird*
*855 South Martinson*

The limestone school building originally contained only two classrooms per floor; the rear portion was added in 1910. The simple structure is distinguished by its facade treatment around and above the central entry. The oldest remaining schoolbuilding in Wichita, one of its classrooms is maintained as it might have appeared when the school was first opened. It is one of nine area schools designed by Proudfoot and Bird.

. . . . . . . . . . . . . . . . . . . . . . . . . . . . . .

# Wichita-East

## SG 24.39
**Hillcrest Apartments**

*1927. Schmidt Overend & Boucher*
*Douglas Avenue and Rutan*

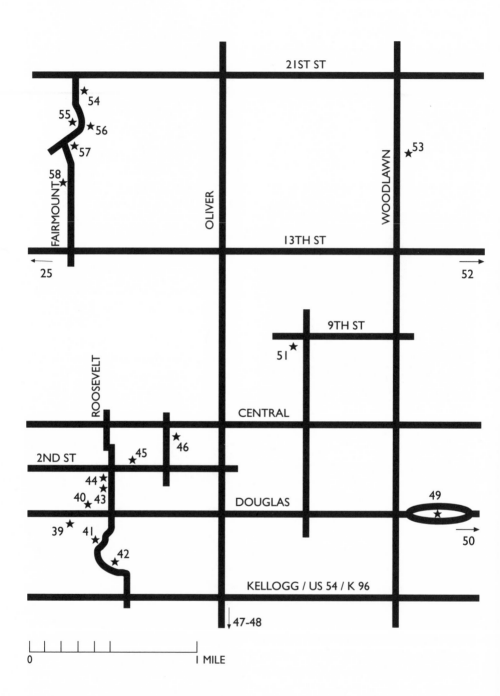

The distinctive half-timbered top floor of this ten-story Neo-Tudor apartment building is visible for some distance above its primarily small-scale residential surroundings. The convincing adaptation of the symbolically significant architectural vocabulary helps the eighty-eight-unit building retain its original elegance. The wood-paneled lobby possesses a hushed dignity suggestive of cultured living.

## SG 24.40
### St. James Episcopal Church
*1925. Schmidt Overend & Boucher*
*Douglas Avenue and Yale*

The L-shape of this Gothic church effectively shields the serene interior spaces from the traffic of the busy intersection outside. As with the nearby Hillcrest Apartments, the architects effectively adapted early English precedents to contemporary use. The designer, Lorentz Schmidt, who practiced first with Overend & Boucher and later with McVey & Peddie, was a talented and influential architect in the city throughout the first half of the twentieth century. He was the first Kansas architect to be elected to the American Institute of Architects' prestigious College of Fellows.

## SG 24.41
### Hillside Cottage / Willis T. Proudfoot House*
*1887. Proudfoot & Bird*
*303 Circle Drive*

Set on a prominent corner site in the College Hill neighborhood, the house is composed of a curious eclectic mixture of elements: a ground floor of rough stone, a wood-shingled gambrel-roofed upper floor, a round-ended porch on one side, and a two-story pedimented porch on the other. Despite the diversity of elements, the house, originally the clubhouse of the Wichita Country Club, is tightly massed and compositionally unified.

## SG 24.42
### The Aviary / George Bird House
*1887. Proudfoot & Bird*
*330 Circle Drive*

The house displays a synthesis of features typical of Shingle Style dwellings. It draws inspiration from Queen Anne, Colonial Revival, and Richardsonian Romanesque traditions and is similar in form to Riverside Cottage (901 Spaulding), also designed by Proudfoot and Bird in the same year. Both residences employ the playful contrast of a stone lower story and a more fluid shingled upper story capped by a complex hipped roof. Though the massing of the main block of the two houses is nearly identical, the different handling of the fenestration, particularly on the gables, and of the detailing, notably on the porches, demonstrates the richness of expression available within the Shingle Style vocabulary.

SG 24.43

### Warren G. Brown House

*1925. Keene & Simpson*
*Roosevelt and First*

Though larger than most, the palatial Renaissance Revival tile-roofed brick house is representative of the residences in the College Hill neighborhood. The original owners of many of the houses, as in this instance, achieved their income subsequent to the discovery of oil in the region.

SG 24.44

### Henry J. Allen Home*

*1917–1919. Frank Lloyd Wright*
*255 North Roosevelt*

The building is a late example of the type of Prairie Style house developed by Frank Lloyd Wright in the suburbs surrounding Chicago in the early years of the twentieth century. It represents a culmination of those efforts and is an effective demonstration of key compositional principles. As in many of these houses, cross-axial masses pivot around a central masonry chimney. The structure clearly demonstrates the architect's

ability to integrate the building with its site, providing a sense of security and enclosure while maintaining an openness between interior and carefully defined exterior spaces. Much of the original furniture, designed by the architect and fabricated by George Niedecken (Milwaukee), remains in the house.

SG 24.45

### Gill House

*1922. Don Schuler*
*Bluff and Second*

The two-story brick house displays a variety of interesting Prairie Style features. It demonstrates the interpretation of Frank Lloyd Wright's mannerisms by one of his apprentices. The architect came to Wichita as the construction supervisor for the Allen house and stayed for several years, designing a number of similar houses before moving to Kansas City and then to Alabama to continue his career.

SG 24.46

### Parks House

*1918–1919. Myron Hunt*
*334 North Belmont*

The simple two-story brick cottage sits modestly in a similarly scaled residential neighborhood. It is of interest as an early building by an architect whose reputation rests largely on work executed after his move to Southern California.

## SG 24.47
### Administration Building (Building no. 1), McConnell Air Force Base*

*1930. Thomas & Harris*
*Southeast George Washington Boulevard and South Oliver Street*

The building reflects the late 1920s' movement away from a strict reliance on historical precedent and toward a more abstract system of ornamentation. Although largely completed by 1930, the building did not open as Wichita's airport terminal until five years later. The side wings were added during World War II. The facilities served as Wichita's airport until a new one, designed by a successor architectural firm, Thomas Harris and Calvin, opened in 1954 on the west side of the city. The structure is now being renovated to house an aerospace museum.

## SG 24.48
### Boeing Assembly Buildings

*Oliver and MacArthur Road*

The Boeing Assembly Plant seems to be in the process of ongoing reconstruction. A survey of these buildings provides an instructive view of the evolution of American factory buildings in the years since World War II. Some of the buildings are interesting in their own right for both their form and their massive proportions, but the juxtaposi-

tion between the forms can be breathtaking. Of particular note is the company's original administration building, designed by the Austin Company in the early 1930s but later substantially altered.

## SG 24.49
### Wakefield House

*1938–1939. William Caton*
*Huntington and Mission*

Like other residences in the affluent Eastborough area, this large stone cottage occupies a generous, well-landscaped site. Although it references traditional English country houses, most notable is its clear, well-proportioned geometric massing. The house is typical of the work of this regionally significant residential architect.

## SG 24.50
### Pizza Hut Headquarters

*ca. 1975. Shaefer & Schirmer*
*101 South Webb Road*

Minimally detailed, the concrete and glass Modern office building occupies a heavily landscaped suburban site and is representative of a type that is replacing the downtown high-rise office building as a symbol of corporate success. The soaring glazed lobby is clearly intended to impress. Other interesting examples of suburban offices in Wichita are the Metropolitan Life Insurance Company computer facility (2600 North Woodlawn), by the same architects, and the Rent-A-Center Corporate Headquarters (Thirty-seventh and North Rock), designed by Gossen Livingston.

## SG 24.51
## Ford Rockwell Branch Library
*1976. David A. Haines*
*5939 Ninth Street*

This small building is representative of its era. The forms begin to allude to historical building types, which are reduced through geometric abstraction. The interplay of bold simple shapes creates interest on the dark monochromatic brick exterior. Vaulted ceilings and large windows facing semienclosed courtyards give the interior a surprisingly spacious feeling.

## SG 24.52
## Country Club Park
*1990. Gossen Livingston*
*1313 North Webb*

The two-story Post-Modern building of cast-stone trimmed brick occupies a heavily landscaped parklike setting. A custom office building for three primary tenants, it is the first phase of a much larger development. Representing an interesting attitude toward business environments, the building is disguised as an over-scaled traditional English manor house.

## SG 24.53
## Hebrew Congregation
*1962. Herbert L. Berger*
*1850 North Woodlawn*

Sitting on a broad grassy suburban site, this low, sprawling building is characterized by the juxtaposition of forms and materials. Brick, stucco, aggregate-stone panels, and metal-framed glass window walls are composed in an innovative fashion. The result is surprisingly coherent and expressive.

## SG 24.54
## Education Building (Wichita State University)
*1959. Frank Lloyd Wright*

The building was completed by Taliesin Associates after the architect's death, and though not among his most notable designs it reflects some of his ongoing concerns, such as the integration of a building with its site. Here the two building masses are arranged to make use of the existing topography and to create significant outdoor space. The structure also reflects some of the preoccupation of the architect's later years, such as the use of circular geometries, which here occur primarily in the building details. A second building was planned for the site but never built.

## SG 24.55
## Wideman Hall (Wichita State University)
*1982. Shaefer & Associates*

This 400-seat brick-and-cast-stone Modern recital hall attempts to harmonize with

the Neo-Colonial buildings of the central campus. The three grand arched portals on the structure's front draw attention away from the windowless building's austere geometric mass. The interior of the hall is most impressive; it was designed around a 4,000-pipe organ built by Marcussen and Sons for the space.

## SG 24.56
## Morrison Hall
## (Wichita State University)
*1938. Ed Forsblom*

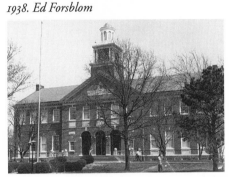

The red-brick Neo-Colonial building occupies a spacious lawn along the central curving drive of the campus. The hall's central tower provides a strong symbol for the university. The building was erected under the Works Progress Administration to house the library, but now it contains administrative offices. The architect was also responsible for the adjacent, similarly styled Jardine Hall as well as for the more Functionalist Duerksen Fine Arts Center built in 1956.

## McKnight Fine Arts Center and the Edwin A. Ulrich Museum (Wichita State University)
*1974–1975. Charles McAffee*

The most notable exterior features of this pair of crisp geometric structures are the two glass-enclosed bridges that connect them and the full-height mural, designed by Juan Miro, covering the south side of the museum building. The buildings form a striking vista as one approaches the university from the south on Fairmount Street. The fine arts center is organized around a dramatic four-story atrium capped by an intricate skylight. The buildings were much heralded when they were new; they won awards from both state and regional components of the American Institute of Architects. The small building directly to the east, Fiske Hall (1905), is also of interest; it was designed by the Chicago architects Patton & Miller.

## SG 24.58
## Fairmount Cottage*
*1888. Proudfoot & Bird*
*1717 Fairmount Avenue*

The large Queen Anne residence features a rough-cut limestone ground story and a wood-shingled upper story and roof. The house was built originally for A. S. Parks, a prominent Wichita businessman. By the 1970s it was being used as a rooming house and had fallen into disrepair; however, it is now restored as a single-family home.

# Oxford

### SU 25.01
### Old Oxford Mill*
*1876. D. N. Cook and John Hewitt (builders)*
*Go north on Sumner Street one mile past U.S. 160, then east one mile, and then one-quarter of a mile south*

The three-story stone mill was built along a three-mile race dug beside the Arkansas River. Although converted to electricity, the mill continued to operate until fairly recently. It is now in the process of restoration by owners who hope to open a restaurant in the building.

. . . . . . . . . . . . . . . . . . . . . . . . . . . . . .

# Wellington

### SU 26.01
### Memorial Auditorium
*1922*
*700 block of Washington*

The large brick building was erected as a memorial to the veterans of World War I. The central assembly hall accommodates a variety of civic activities, from basketball games to festivals and dances. The building bears a striking resemblance to Albert Kahn's Hill Auditorium of 1913. In both cases, a five-bay stone classical facade is

Deliberately modest, this stucco building occupies a prominent site on Wellington's main street. It is notable because of its pleasant interior and clever sectional organization: the building takes the form of a wedge. The lower end houses private offices, with additional offices above teller stations on the higher side of the building; public spaces occupy the intermediate zone.

framed in the center of a larger, more freely ornamented brick facade.

SU 26.02

## Sumner County Courthouse

*1951. Thomas Williamson & Victor Loebsack*
*500 block of Washington*

Reflective of the architects' stylistic evolution, this simplified classically disposed stone building occupies an entire block along Wellington's main street. Returning to Kansas from the University of Pennsylvania in 1912 to begin his practice, Thomas Williamson throughout his extensive early career favored classical designs. He was joined in the business after World War II by his son-in-law, Victor Loebsack, who preferred more straightforward utilitarian designs. The courthouse shows the influence of their individual concerns.

SU 26.03

## First Federal Savings Bank / Panhandle Credit Union

*1973. Shaefer & Associates*
*Ninth and Washington*

# Northwest Region

The western half of the Northwest Region is part of that larger area we now call the High Plains. In the mid-nineteenth century, however, the High Plains were labeled on maps as the Great American Desert, despite the extensive grasslands and the presence of rivers and streams. Being located west of the 100th meridian, this region with limited rainfall and a deficiency of trees led the early explorers to assume it was unable to support agricultural practices of the sort common farther east, hence their designation of the High Plains as desert country. Consequently, the migration of homesteaders into western Kansas proceeded slowly, and those settlers willing to try did indeed have to cope with some serious setbacks. Today, the region remains thinly populated, and the dependable production of crops requires irrigation.

Early settlement in the region received encouragement when railroad service began in the late 1860s, which, coupled with what proved to be a rare period of above-average rainfall, understandably raised homesteaders' expectations of success. Once on the land, however, they had to figure out which crops the soil would grow and how best to cultivate them. Progress in the settlement of the region moved rather methodically, from east to west. Locations proximate to the larger rivers and creeks were favored, making the area between the Saline River and Big Creek especially attractive. Those streams run more or less due east, as does the Solomon River to their north and the Smoky Hill River to their south. The presence of the Union Pacific (Kansas Pacific) Railroad—the earliest to traverse the region—within much of the area occupied by the Smoky Hill River system enhanced the value of that sector of the Northwest Region.

The terrain through which these rivers flow includes elevations that range from well over 3,000 feet in the High Plains of the west to about 1,400 feet in the Smoky Hills, in the eastern part of the region. One sector of the Smoky Hills contains a limestone formation that is easy to quarry and then to shape for the construction of all sorts of buildings and more imaginatively for use as fence posts. The formation is often found in thin (six-to-ten-inch) layers. By driving rods into closely spaced holes in the ground in parallel lines about eight inches apart, settlers could easily extract long postlike sections of the rock, a product that proved extremely useful for farmers trying to develop their lands in a region largely bereft of local lumber sources (see RH 25.01, Southwest Region).

Prior to 1870 only five of the twenty-two counties constituting the region had been organized: the easternmost tier plus Ellis County; the remaining counties were organized by 1890. Three army forts, built in 1865, encouraged settlement in their general vicinity; they were Fort Hays in Ellis County on Big Creek, Fort Harker in Ellsworth County, and Fort Wallace in Wallace County, both on the Smoky Hill River. They were intended to provide protection against Indian raids, and indeed the region became the setting for the skirmishes that have been called the Indian Wars, conflicts particularly frequent during the second half of the 1860s. During that time the Indians were viewed as serious impediments to the progress of civilization, but today we recognize that the Native Americans truly had legitimate grievances. They had been subjected to a variety of abuses, including the systematic destruction of the great herds of bison on which they depended to sustain their traditional lifestyle. By 1870 the army had succeeded in generally pacifying the region, but conflict with the Indians had retarded settlement there, which in its far western portion also carried the burden of meager annual rainfalls.

The eastern half of the region, in contrast, managed to achieve a moderately dense agricultural settlement, including groups of European colonists such as the Russian (Volga) Germans—both Protestant and Catholic—who occupied sizable portions of Ellis and Russell counties (as well as sections of the Southcentral Region). They were a deeply religious people who evidently made great sacrifices to build in their otherwise modest communities magnificent church buildings; the St. Fidelis Church (EL 06.01) is a clear example. They and other settlers, including African Americans seeking better opportunities than those available to them in the South, arrived in the 1880s, creating a comparatively diverse population for the Northwest Region. Nevertheless, they had to share some common problems, such as the great grasshopper plague of 1874 and periods of severe drought—particularly in 1880 and again in the early 1890s—and some bitter winters, notably in 1886. These natural calamities caused many settlers to give up and leave the region, and western Kansas still remains for the most part rather sparsely populated. Thus there are few cities of size, with the largest serving as the principal market and service centers for the region, whose economy remains quite dependent on agriculture.

The twenty-two counties of the Northwest Region have a population of about 125,000, but nearly 21 percent reside in Ellis County. Hays, the county seat and the largest city of the region by a substantial margin, has a population approaching 18,000. Located on Big Creek, roughly midway between the Saline and Smoky Hill rivers, Hays came into existence as a civilian satellite of Fort Hays (EL 05.04). The city grew rapidly after gaining service from the first railroad line to penetrate the region. When the fort was closed in 1889, the state received the 7,000-acre tract with the proviso that it be used for educational and scientific purposes. A portion became the campus of what is now Fort Hays State University, and a larger section became an agricultural experiment station.

Hays and a number of other county seats also prospered from the discovery of oil fields in their general proximity, thus adding an industrial component to their economies. Although none of the other county seats even approximates the size of Hays, several have populations in the 4,000 to 5,000 range, with Colby in Thomas County approaching 5,500. Colby's prominence was aided significantly by the construction of Interstate 70, which followed the track of Highway 40 until Oakley and then shifted northward to Colby on Highway 24, from where it proceeded into Colorado.

At one time a location on or near a railroad was absolutely necessary to ensure at least stability if not steady growth for a community; today, the interstate highways provide much the same benefit—or pain if too far removed. Interstate 70 is the only east-west freeway to cross the entire state, entering Kansas at Kansas City, moving more or less due west through Lawrence, Topeka, Junction City, Salina, and Hays and then across the High Plains and through Goodland before entering Colorado. Beyond Hays, the city of Colby (and Thomas County) have clearly benefited from proximity to the freeway; however, other communities also close to that highway seemingly have not. Obviously, other factors will affect the urban-growth equation, such as the number and types of jobs available. Then too, cities everywhere require dependable sources of water, as do the farmers. Furthermore, within a largely agricultural region the character and quality of the soil, rainfall averages or access to suitable irrigation sources, and decisions about land use definitely affect the distribution and density of the population and thereby the number of cities needed to serve that population. The initial location of towns and their present status truly reflect such circumstances though the consolidation of farmsteads and ranches as well as the improved road systems also have had their effect.

As for the towns themselves, those in the Northwest Region tend to follow a familiar organizational pattern; commercial buildings are typically ranged along several blocks of a single main street, and residential structures are similarly aligned behind the business structures. Unlike the pattern in eastern Kansas, where courthouses are usually given a central placement, here they tend to occupy a site either at the end of the commercial strip or in a location proximate to the residential section. Clearly, various factors such as the size and the density of a county's population along with the percentage who choose to live or work in an urban setting directly affect the number and types of buildings erected. Consequently, the architecture of this region, as with the other regions, provides a mirror in which we can view some of the historical development and the character of the area. The following regional map and directory locate the counties, cities, and towns of the region and furnish an outline for the sequence of the catalog entries, which constitute a representative selection of the region's architecture.

Alpha-Numeric Directory

**CHEYENNE (CN)**

01 St. Francis†

**DECATUR (DC)**

02 Leoville

03 Oberlin†

**ELLIS (EL)**

04 Catherine

05 Hays†

06 Victoria

07 Walker

**ELLSWORTH (EW)**

08 Ellsworth†

09 Kanopolis

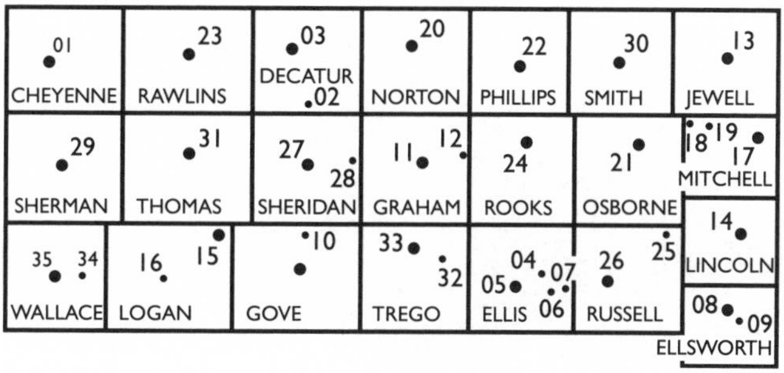

|  | | | | | | |
|---|---|---|---|---|---|---|
| 01 CHEYENNE | 23 RAWLINS | 03 DECATUR .02 | 20 NORTON | 22 PHILLIPS | 30 SMITH | 13 JEWELL |
| 29 SHERMAN | 31 THOMAS | 27 28 SHERIDAN | 11 12 GRAHAM | 24 ROOKS | 21 OSBORNE | 18 19 17 MITCHELL / 14 LINCOLN |
| 35 34 WALLACE | 16 15 LOGAN | •10 GOVE | 33 32 TREGO | 04 07 05 06 ELLIS | 26 25 RUSSELL | 08 09 ELLSWORTH |

**GOVE (GO)**

10 Grainfield [Gove†]

**GRAHAM (GH)**

11 Hill City†

12 Nicodemus

**JEWELL (JW)**

13 Mankato†

**LINCOLN (LC)**

14 Lincoln†

**LOGAN**

15 Oakley†

16 Russell Springs

**MITCHELL (MC)**

17 Beloit†

18 Cawker City

19 Glen Elder

**NORTON (NT)**

20 Norton†

**OSBORNE (OB)**

21 Osborne†

**PHILLIPS (PL)**

22 Phillipsburg†

**RAWLINS (RA)**

23 Atwood†

**ROOKS (RO)**

24 Stockton†

**RUSSELL (RS)**

25 Lucas

26 Russell†

**SHERIDAN (SD)**

27 Hoxie†

28 Studley

**SHERMAN (SH)**

29 Goodland†

**SMITH (SM)**

30 Smith Center†

**THOMAS (TH)**

31 Colby†

**TREGO (TR)**

32 Ogallah

33 Wakeeney†

**WALLACE (WA)**

34 Sharon Springs

35 Wallace†

# St. Francis

**CN 01.01**

## Cheyenne County Courthouse

*1924–1925. Thomas W. Williamson*
*Dennison and Washington Street*

a gymnasium covered by a low arched concrete-shell roof, and it is connected to the south end of the main building by a glazed entry corridor. Despite the stylistic discontinuity, the addition is related to the original building through the use of common materials and a compatibility of scale.

This three-story stone-trimmed Neoclassical structure faces the town's broad central commercial street. The building is distinguished on the exterior by six giant columns supporting the protruding entablature at the main entry and on the interior by the detail and proportion of its spaces, notably the grand stair and spacious hallways. With the exception of the insertion of an elevator, it remains in its original condition.

**CN 01.02**

## St. Francis High School

*1927/1934/1955/1966. Mann & Company*
*College and Washington Street*

The simplified brick Collegiate Gothic Style school terminates the vista at the rise on the eastern end of the town's central street. The geometric detail of the brickwork and stone trim, particularly the pistonlike pilasters, gives the building a contemporary quality while conveying the historical stylistic intent. This vocabulary was used through the first two additions, but the Modern third addition departs from the pattern. It houses

# Leoville

### DC 02.01
### Immaculate Conception Church
*1923. Brickman & Hagan*
*Main Street*

The stone-trimmed brick Romanesque Style Catholic church is the dominant structure in the community. The twin bell towers, which flank the entry and are topped by segmented domes, are visible from some distance across the surrounding countryside. Many of the architects' Catholic churches of the period are marked by a cautious but confident interpretation of traditional styles, just as this building is.

# Oberlin

### DC 03.01
### Decatur County Courthouse
*1926–1927. Squires & Ross*
*Hall Street and South Penn Avenue*

The rectangular three-story Neoclassical brick and limestone building is located in the downtown district. Representing the most popular mode in courthouse design in the 1920s, the ground-level story, dressed in limestone, provides a base for the upper floors, which are united by two-story stone columns and pilasters and by contrasting red-brick walls.

### DC 03.02
### Bank Building
*ca. 1888*
*Hall Street and South Penn Avenue*

The two-story stone-trimmed brick Italianate structure follows the most popular model for similar late-nineteenth-century corner bank buildings throughout the state. Of particular interest are the rhythm of the fenestration, notably the doubling of the windows on the upper story, and the careful detailing of the stonework, especially around the corner entry.

# Catherine

### EL 04.01
## St. Catherine's Church*
*1890. A. Druiding*

Like the other Catholic churches in the small towns of Ellis County and the surrounding counties, the Gothic-inspired stone church was built by German-Russian immigrants who were among the region's earliest settlers. The most striking aspect of St. Catherine's is its tower, which features a crownlike octagonal lantern and tall spire set on a square base. The sculptured angels in front of the chancel, executed by the Kaletta studios of St. Louis, were added in 1955.

. . . . . . . . . . . . . . . . . . . . . . . . . . . . . . . .

### EL 05.01
## Ellis County Courthouse
*1940–1942. Mann & Company*
*1204 Fort Street*

Built as a Works Progress Administration (WPA) project, this three-story Classical Modern granite-trimmed limestone courthouse shares a block near the central business district with other public buildings. The scale of the stone blocks on the facades, the simplicity of the detail around the window openings, and the proportions of the stepped massing give the building a sense of purposeful severity. It has been extensively remodeled.

### EL 05.02
## Southwestern Bell Telephone Company Office and Microwave Tower
*1979–1980. Sverdrup & Parcell*
*Tenth and Fort Street*

The octagonal steel microwave transmission tower rises above the downtown district. The rings encircling the tower bring to mind the form of cylindrical grain elevators, and in fact, several of Southwestern Bell's towers in the state were constructed using slip-form-concrete methods often used to construct silos.

the campus, though individually undistinguished, form a pleasing ensemble, united through the common use of limestone and grouped to form well-scaled shaded courtyards.

**EL 05.04**

## Fort Hays Officers Quarters

*1867*
*Frontier Historical Park*

**EL 05.03**

## Comeau Catholic Campus Center

*1984. Stecklein & Brungardt*
*Sixth and Park Street*

A two-story Modern brick building, the center is in a residential neighborhood at the edge of the Fort Hays State University campus. The building's broken massing helps it to fit comfortably into its smaller scale surroundings. It houses a variety of functions, including a worship space, a lounge, and individual sleeping rooms. The adjacent eighty-acre campus is part of the original area of Fort Hays. The buildings of

Sheathed in wood clapboards and facing a formal parade ground, the hipped-roofed two-story duplex is one of the few surviving buildings of the original thirty-eight that constituted Fort Hays. In 1889, when protection from Indians was no longer necessary, the fort was closed. Its land has since been used for a variety of purposes, including a golf course. At one time the remaining octagonal stone blockhouse was used as a clubhouse. The complex is now preserved as a museum, illustrating military life at the time of the fort's operation.

**EL 05.05**

## Walter P. Chrysler House*

*1889/1897*
*104 West Tenth Street (in Ellis,*
*13 miles west of Hays)*

Gabled and L-shaped, this one-and-one-half-story clapboarded vernacular house is representative of many similar homes of the time. It is noteworthy as the boyhood home

of the founder of a major automobile company. Chrysler was born in Wamego in 1875.

. . . . . . . . . . . . . . . . . . . . . . . . . . . . .

## Victoria

EL 06.01
### St. Fidelis Church*
*1908–1911*
*John T. Comes, with Joseph Marshall*
*Tenth and Cathedral Avenue*

Sometimes called the cathedral of the plains, the monumental limestone Romanesque Revival Catholic church towers over its small-scale surroundings. The body of the church is 73 feet wide and 220 feet long, and it seats 1,700 people. Its twin towers are 141 feet high and are visible from a great distance. A landmark to travelers, the building is impressive for its refinement as well as for its size. The arched interior features polished granite columns, extensive stencilwork, and elaborate, carved altars.

. . . . . . . . . . . . . . . . . . . . . . . . . . . . .

# Walker

EL 07.01
## St. Anne's Church
*1904*

The rustic stone Gothic Revival church is the most substantial structure in the small settlement. The town, like many in the area, was settled by German-Russian Catholics who were the descendants of Germans invited to settle in Russia in the eighteenth century but who in the late nineteenth century found themselves unwelcome in their adopted homeland. They were an industrious and deeply religious people whose lives centered on the church; St. Anne's is a testament to their commitment and fortitude.

# Ellsworth

**EW 08.01**

## Ellsworth County Courthouse

*1956. John G. Seitz Associates*
*First and Kansas streets*

A symmetrical two-and-one-half-story Classical Modern building of two-tone stone, the courthouse occupies a block near the center of town. It is entered on a half-level and is organized around a central divided stair.

**EW 08.02**

## Perry Hodgen House*

*1875*
*104 West Main Street*

The two-story L-shaped vernacular building of rich brown Dakota sandstone occupies a site abutting the Smoky Hill River. It now houses the Ellsworth County Museum. A stone livery stable, a wooden schoolhouse, and a country church are also located on the site.

**EW 08.03**

## Arthur Larkin House*

*1884–1885*
*On K 14 (one-quarter mile south of Ellsworth)*

Overlooking the town of Ellsworth to the north, this two-story Italianate stone home sits atop the south bluff of the Smoky Hill River. Although the building is in need of repair, its original grandeur is evident; the carved stone window surrounds are notable as are the stone sidewalks.

. . . . . . . . . . . . . . . . . . . . . . . . . . . . . .

# Kanopolis

**EW 09.01**

## Abandoned Home

*On K 140, one mile west of K 141*

This one-story red sandstone home with a shingled hipped-roof sits on a rise in an open field and is a testament to the durable quality of locally quarried stone. It is also representative of the abandoned farmsteads that dot the Kansas landscape. Families departed their farms in early days often as a result of negative variations in growing conditions, particularly rainfall, and more recently because of the consolidation of agricultural lands.

**EW 09.02**

## Fort Harker Guardhouse

*1867*
*Wyoming and Ohio Street*

Now operated as a museum, this red sandstone two-story hipped-roofed rectangular structure sits among a loose assemblage of small buildings. It was built as the jail for the

fort, which for a time was among the most significant of the western outposts. Between its establishment in 1867 and its closure in 1872, the base was the supply headquarters for all the forts in Colorado, New Mexico, Arizona, and northern Texas. After it was closed, the land was sold by ambitious speculators who promoted the town of Kanopolis, in overly optimistic hope that it would become a major city and perhaps even the capital of Kansas. Two officers' quarters, a barracks, and the guardhouse are all that remain of the fort.

# Grainfield

### GO 10.01
**Grainfield Opera House***
*1887*
*Third and Main Street*

The two-story brick and metal Italianate building is a remnant of the once larger town center. The ornate front facade is rendered in sheet metal on the upper level and on the lower level is supported by cast-iron columns manufactured by Mesker Brothers of St. Louis. The building is largely vacant and in need of maintenance.

### GO 10.02
**St. Agnes Church**
*1949. Brinkman & Hagan*
*Cedar Street (between Second and Third Street)*

The two-tone brick Eclectic Modern church with limestone trim occupies an open flat block in a small-scale residential area on the western edge of town. It illustrates the cautious introduction of a Modern architectural vocabulary. Although many of the detail features are innovative, the overall form of the building follows that of the traditional basilica. The architects employed similar forms in a more sophisticated manner three years later in the Sacred Heart Church in Baileyville (NM 12.01).

# Hill City

### GH 11.01
### Graham County Courthouse
*1958. Mann & Company*
*East Cherry and North Pomeroy*

Occupying a low open site in the midst of the downtown district, this sprawling U-shaped one-story building provides a demonstration of characteristic Modern compositional strategies. First, the different functions of the building are clearly articulated: the administrative operations are expressed by a simple repetitive window pattern; the larger volume of the courtroom is visible on the exterior; and a covered walkway leads to a glass-enclosed public entry space. Second, the building's expressed concrete frame structure contrasts with the brick and glass enclosing walls. Third, the appointments and finishes, notably the light fixtures, convey an aesthetic of elegant efficiency.

### GH 11.02
### Hill City Presbyterian Church
*1890*
*Fourth and Oak Street*

The simple vernacular L-shaped stone building, which occupies a hilltop site in a residential area, is representative of the many elegant stone structures built by the region's early settlers. The church's quiet dignity is a reminder of the fortitude and character of its builders.

**GH 11.03**
## Sanger Service Station
*1939/1946. A. T. Sanger (builder)*
*On U.S. 24 (ten miles west of Hill City, near Morland)*

The red, green, and white rock structure, with an adjacent house, sits amid open fields on a rise above the present highway, which has been moved away from the building. The original unit, built as a gas station modeled after a similar smaller one in Beloit, is the front of the building; the rear unit was added when the station became an automobile dealership. The structure was built from stones found at three different local quarries, along with some acquired by the owner in his travels across the country. Some of the construction was done by passing motorists, whose labor helped to pay for their gasoline. The building, when new, was advertised as "the prettiest station in all the nation." It is now vacant.

. . . . . . . . . . . . . . . . . . . . . . . . . . . . . . . . .

# Nicodemus

**GH 12.01**
## Nicodemus AME Church*
*1884*

The simple gabled stucco church is among the scattered, decaying buildings that form Kansas' only remaining black settlement. The town was founded in 1877 by approximately 500 freed slaves, who migrated north to Kansas. The church and the town are a source of pride to the descendants of the early settlers, many of whom return for an annual celebration.

# Mankato

### JW 13.01
**First National Bank***
*1887*
*Commercial and Jefferson*

Like other buildings of the type throughout the state built in response to the period's prosperity, this brick and stone Romanesque Revival building occupies the town's most prominent intersection. The bank's construction is clearly expressed; the stone arches serve both a decorative and structural function. It is well preserved and continues to serve its intended purpose; the original teller cages are still in use.

### JW 13.02
**Jewell County Courthouse**
*1936–1937. Radotinsky & Mertz*
*Commercial and Madison*

Geometrically massed, this two- and three-story symmetrical Modernistic building marks the northern end of the town's main commercial street. The structure, which is amost devoid of ornament with the exception of carved panels at the entrances, relies for interest on the rough texture of its stone walls. The stone was quarried in the southeastern part of the county, near Randall. The architects, who secured the commission

through friendship with the county attorney, were also responsible for the design of another federal-relief-sponsored project, the (Old) Mankato High School (1939) at the eastern end of Madison Street.

### JW 13.03
**Saint Theresa Church**
*1959. Brinkman & Hagan*
*Commercial and Monroe*

Sitting opposite the county courthouse, this well-scaled Gothic-inspired stone-trimmed brick church demonstrates the dual sensibilities of the architects, who were the most prolific designers of Catholic churches in the state through much of the twentieth century. On the exterior, historical elements are rendered with modern precision; contemporary elements in the interior, including curved laminated wood beams, are used to create a traditional ambience.

# Lincoln

### LC 14.01
### Lincoln County Courthouse*
*1899–1900. Charles W. Squires*
*Third and Lincoln Avenue*

The two-story Eclectic limestone building occupies an open block on the eastern edge of the downtown district. It features the architect's characteristic freedom of quotation as well as several of his favored forms, including the round conical roofed bays and the square stepped tower. The exterior stone walls clearly show the marks of their quarrying.

### LC 14.02
### Commercial Building
*1881*
*Third and Lincoln Avenue*

Particularly noteworthy is the stonework of this two-story restrained Renaissance Re-

vival commercial corner building of limestone. The carefully carved smooth-arched stone lintels contrast with the rough-faced stone of the walls. The stone itself, exhibiting a uniform striated gray to brown color variation, is also of interest. The area is noted for its limestone and quartzite quarries.

### LC 14.03
### Lincoln Carnegie Library*
*1913. C. A. Smith*
*203 South Third Avenue*

This stone one-and-one-half-story hipped-roofed Prairie Style building follows the model for smaller Carnegie libraries: the entry is centered in the facade and set at a half-level between an upper-level reading room and lower-level meeting rooms. The financing also followed the typical pattern. The Carnegie Foundation paid the cost of construction with the provision that the town provide an annual operating budget of 10 percent of that cost.

### LC 14.04
### Bank Building
*1886*
*Fourth and Lincoln Avenue*

The town's primary intersection is marked by this two-story two-tone stone multipurpose commercial building. It makes good use of the variety of locally available stone. The dentils beneath the cornice, a second-

# Oakley

### LG 15.01
## Logan County Courthouse
*1965. Kiene & Bradley*
*West Second and Cherry Avenue*

story stringcourse, and the imposts and key-stones above the windows carry dark stone accents, thereby calling attention to the eclectic Italianate structure. The variety in the fenestration suggests the building was intended to accommodate multiple uses.

The low and sprawling nature of the one-story Modern brick building is well suited to its rather suburban site. It is distinguished as a public building only by the medallion over the main entry and the flag poles in front of it. A comparison between this structure and the earlier courthouse in Russell Springs (LG 16.01) provides an instructive view of changes in the building type.

### LG 15.02
## (Old) Methodist Church
*1921*
*Fourth and Central*

This Eclectic one-and-one-half-story building of stone-trimmed red brick and stucco faces the town's broad main street and demonstrates the free and effective adaptation of motifs from a variety of historical sources, notably English Gothic prototypes. It bears a strong resemblance to several churches in the state designed by Ernest O. Brostrom, which are illustrated in a 1919 brochure of his work on churches.

. . . . . . . . . . . . . . . . . . . . . . . . . . . . . . . .

**LG 16.01**

## (Old) Logan County Courthouse*

*1887. Alfred Meier*
*Main Street*

The loose scattering of buildings that constitute the town surround this rectangular two-story limestone and brick Victorian building on a hilltop. The architect's more flamboyant predilections are revealed only in the detail of the short, central tower (note the State Bank of Holton, JA 11.01). The citizens of Oakley, the county's most populous community, made several attempts before successfully gaining the county seat in 1963, thus making the older courthouse redundant. It is now maintained and operated as the Butterfield Trail Museum, but the original character of the building is still evident.

# Beloit

**MC 17.01**

## Mitchell County Courthouse*

*1901–1902. James C. Holland*
*Main and Hersey*

The two-story Richardsonian Romanesque stone building occupies a full block on the eastern edge of the commercial district. It is one of five nearly identical courthouses designed by the architect around the turn of the century; similar structures were designed for Geary, Marion, Riley, and Osborne counties.

**MC 17.02**

## St. John the Baptist Catholic Church*

*1904*
*701 East Court Street*

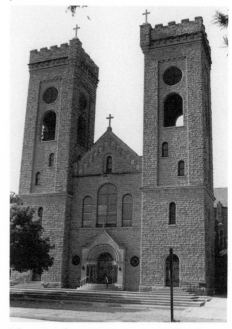

The pair of massive square crenellated towers anchors firmly to the land this rusticated limestone Romanesque Revival structure. It follows the traditional Latin cross plan: the nave is flanked by symmetrical side aisles and transepts, and there is a full apse. The light-filled vaulted interior is more finished than the exterior and features polished granite columns. The forms of the church are similar to those employed during alterations to Our Lady of Perpetual Help Catholic Church in Concordia (CD 02.06).

### MC 17.03
### F. H. Hart House*
*1880. Asa Beebe Cross*
*304 East Main Street*

The two-story stone Victorian home sits amid a grouping of mature trees. Using elements from several currently popular traditions, it exhibits the mason's considerable skills. The house is among the relatively few remaining residences designed by one of Kansas City's earliest and most prolific architects.

. . . . . . . . . . . . . . . . . . . . . . . . . . . . . . . .

# Cawker City

### MC 18.01
### Wisconsin (Street) City Historic District*
*1871–1927*
*700 block of Wisconsin Street*

The series of two-story brick and stone commercial structures represents the sort of unassuming buildings that lined the main street of many agriculturally based towns across the state in the late nineteenth century. Such buildings are more likely to survive in smaller towns where development pressures have been moderate.

. . . . . . . . . . . . . . . . . . . . . . . . . . . . . . . .

# Glen Elder

### MC 19.01
### E. W. Norris Service Station*
*1926/1929. Frank A. Slack*
*Market and Main Street*

This one-story distinctively castlelike limestone building occupies a prominent corner in the center of town. Its rather curious form derives from the owner's memories of German castles seen during his service in World War I and was used to attract the attention of passing motorists. The through-highway now bypasses the town, and the building is vacant.

## Norton

**NT 20.01**

### Norton County Courthouse

*1929. Cuthbert & Suehrk*
*Main and Kansas*

This three-story limestone-trimmed brick Neoclassical building occupies an open block near the central commercial district. It is organized around a central hallway, which is connected to a formal stair opposite the entry leading to a grand pilastered and vaulted courtroom on the third floor. The courthouse is nearly identical to the one the architects designed concurrently for Bourbon County (see BB 03.07, Southeast Region).

# OSBORNE COUNTY

## Osborne

### OB 21.01
### Osborne County Courthouse
*1907–1908. Holland & Squires*
*Fourth and Main Street*

The two-and-one-half-story Richardsonian Romanesque limestone structure is among the better preserved of the several similar courthouses designed by the architects. On the main level, offices are arranged along a corridor paralleling the front facade; a stair adjacent to the entry leads to a centralized second-floor corridor giving access to the main courtroom located at the rear of that floor. In the years of their partnership (1903–1910), James C. Holland and Frank C. Squires were responsible for the design of four Kansas courthouses.

### OB 21.02
### Osborne Public Carnegie Library*
*1913. N. W. Penland (builder)*
*Third and Main Street*

The library, a one-and-one-half-story Neoclassical brick building with a tiled hipped roof, occupies a spacious lot near the center of town. It is a handsome and straightforward interpretation of the standard plan for Carnegie libraries. Both this building and an identical one in Stockton were copied from a building designed for Dewitt, Iowa.

### OB 21.03
### First National Bank
*1885*
*Second and Main Street*

Occupying a prominent corner site, the simple two-story Italianate limestone commercial building follows a custom common to Kansas' corner bank buildings: its longer dimension is oriented to the side street. In this case the relative prominence of the facing street is emphasized by the degree of finish of the stonework. Frequently, an adjacent building continues the treatment of the principal facade, and in this instance a law office building, completed the following year, uses similar ornament but employs altered proportions.

# Phillipsburg

**PL 22.01**
## Phillips County Courthouse
*1912. Ruel A. Curtis*
*301 State Street*

The three-story classically composed Beaux-Arts building of limestone sits in the center of an open square that forms the core of the town's commercial district. The courthouse is bilaterally symmetrical with four identical facades, each of which carries a central full-height entry portal flanked by massive Doric columns and topped by a cornice arching above a prominent clock. The building has received several additions and has undergone substantial alteration.

**PL 22.02**
## Methodist Episcopal Church
*1921. Charles W. Shaver*
*Third and G Street*

Nearly filling its corner lot, the church is a three-story stone-trimmed dark-brick Neoclassical building. Unlike most structures of its type, its form is determined primarily by exterior rather than interior forces; expression of the interior volumes is sublimated to the welcoming gesture of the curving corner porch and stairs. The worship space nearly fills the building's upper stories. The entry leads under a round balcony toward the altar at the opposite corner.

## PL 22.03
## Phillipsburg Grade School
*1953. Mann & Company*
*Third and Nebraska Street*

The Modern school of brick, glass, and stone is a successful piece of urban design in that it terminates the vista at the south end of Third Street. A focus is created through the axial placement of a massive vertical brick pier that conceals the building's boiler stack; the space is resolved through the school's angular placement, which creates a triangular entry court. Also, the structure's mass and form relate well to adjacent residences and playing fields.

# Atwood

## RA 23.01
## Rawlins County Courthouse
*1906–1907*
*Eisentraut Colby Pottinger Company*
*Sixth and Main Street*

The square three-story Eclectic limestone and brick building occupies a block at the eastern end of the business district. The tower above and the trim around the main entry enhance this otherwise sturdy but plain structure. The courthouse has been substantially remodeled, as evidenced in the sealed openings on the tower.

# Stockton

### RO 24.01
## Rooks County Courthouse
*1921–1924. Frank C. Squires*
*North First and Walnut Street*

The courthouse, a rectangular four-story Neoclassical stone building, occupies a corner lot behind a row of commercial buildings facing the town's main street. Its height is masked by the careful proportioning of an Ionic colonnade set on a full-story base that appears on each of the building's principal facades. The interior is appointed with white marble wainscoting.

### RO 24.02
## St. Thomas Catholic Church
*1950. Brinkman & Hagan*
*Main and Oak Street*

The stone church, along with a rectory completed ten years later, occupies a prominent site on the town's main commercial street. The buildings have a timeless quality; details are borrowed from traditional models but combined in novel ways, and they are rendered with a geometric precision consistent with Modern tastes. Both structures appear solid and convincing.

# Lucas

### RS 25.01
### Garden of Eden*
*1906–1932. S. P. Dinsmoor (builder)*
*Second and Kansas*

The fantastic assemblage of stone and concrete buildings and sculpture is a product of the creative obsession of a folk artist, S. P. Dinsmoor, a disabled Civil War veteran. He began the complex with his home, which is made of stone but is modeled after log construction. Over the next twenty-two years he added a series of concrete allegorical sculptures derived from the Bible or addressing contemporary issues; he also added several unusual outbuildings. His embalmed but slowly decomposing body is visible in a glass-topped concrete coffin set within a stone-log ziggurat-shaped mausoleum.

. . . . . . . . . . . . . . . . . . . . . . . . . . . . . . . .

# Russell

### RS 26.01
### Tower Building
*1937. Charles W. Shaver*
*Main and U.S. 40*

This Moderne building that once housed a service station and cafe is a good example of the forward-looking aesthetic of the time. The tan brick structure features horizontal bands of black brick and a rocketlike tower that once was trimmed with neon lights. The establishment offered full service for both cars and people and included several well-equipped automobile service bays, a dance floor, an orchestra shell, and an early form of air-conditioning in the cafe. The building has been altered over the years and now houses a used-car dealership.

### RS 26.02
### Russell American Legion Hall
*1950. Mann & Company*
*Third and Main Street*

The tall stone obelisk adjacent to the front door of this one-story Modern brick building marks its presence on the town's broad central street. The obelisk balances well with the building's clear cubistic volumes and their horizontal glass-block windows. The architect also designed the high school (1938).

### RS 26.03
### Russell County Courthouse
*1902–1903/1949. George Berlinghof*
*Fourth and Main Street*

A shaded block on the east side of the town's primary commercial street is the setting for this three-story limestone building. The tower was added in 1908. The building's ap-

## Hoxie

### SD 27.01
### Sheridan County Courthouse
*1917–1918. Thomas W. Williamson*
*925 Ninth Street*

pearance was substantially altered in 1949 when it was renovated and a steeply pitched roof removed. The smooth stone surfaces of the cornice and central tower contrast sharply with the rough stone of the walls. These elements and the tower's vertical glass-block strip windows reflect the aesthetic of a later time while also obscuring the building's original Romanesque Revival character. Nevertheless, the contrasts produce a beguiling composition.

The three-story buff-brick and limestone Neoclassical building occupies a full block near the central business district. It is the smallest of the architect's three Kansas courthouses of the late 1920s. Like the others, however, the building's assurance in both its proportion and detail reflects the architect's training under the Beaux-Arts system at the University of Pennsylvania.

### RS 26.04
### Nicholas Gernon House
*1872*
*818 West Kansas*

Constructed by a blacksmith, the Gernon house is the oldest stone home in the county. The two-story vernacular residence occupies a site in the central section of town amid a variety of building types. Now operated as a museum by the Russell County Historical Society, the exhibits are well presented and provide an effective view of late-nineteenth-century domestic life.

## Studley

### SD 28.01
### John Fenton Pratt Ranch*
*1880/1900*
*On U.S. 24 (one-half mile west of Studley)*

The residence, a symmetrical U-shaped one-story stone Victorian home, sits on a broad, open site on the Cottonwood Ranch. Pedimented bay windows and a spindled porch adorn an otherwise simple utilitarian structure. The site, which is based on the pattern of an old English sheep farm, is being developed as a living history museum by the Kansas State Historical Society.

# Goodland

### SH 29.01
## Sherman County Courthouse
*1931. Routledge & Hertz*
*East Ninth and Broadway*

The three-story buff-brick and stone courthouse occupies a portion of a large block, one street removed from the main commercial street. It demonstrates the pleasingly awkward exuberance of stylistic transition, from the Neoclassicism of the firm's five Kansas courthouses of the late 1920s to the then popular Art Deco style. The overall massing, composition, and proportions follow the firm's established pattern, but the ornament, on both the interior and exterior, is more experimental. The effort to resolve a symmetrical exterior with an asymmetrical interior results in the creation of some rather curious spaces, particularly around the stairs.

### SH 29.02
## Telephone Building
*1931*
*Tenth and Main Street*

Anchoring one of the town's most prominent intersections is this two-story brick and terracotta Art Deco building. The ornate, syncopated, geometric patterns in the color-

ful terracotta ornament demonstrate the expressive potential of the new nonhistorical style.

### SH 29.03
### Goodland City Library
*1912–1913. Barresson Brothers*
*120 West Twelfth Street*

The library, a one-and-one-half-story Neoclassical brick building, occupies a shaded lot near the center of town. It is typical in plan of the many smaller Carnegie-financed libraries throughout the state, notably those in Osborne (OB 21.02) and Stockton. It currently houses the Carnegie Arts Center.

# Smith Center

### SM 30.01
### First National Bank
*1930*
*Main and Court*

Facing a busy intersection on the town's main street, the two-story limestone Art Deco building demonstrates the evolution of this building type, both in style and composition, from what obtained in the 1880s. The ornament is less integral to the building structure, and less emphasis is placed on the expression of the entry. It was expanded in 1979.

### SM 30.02
### Bank Building
*ca. 1888*
*Main and Kansas*

Similar in both location and construction to the First National Bank in Mankato (JW

13.01), this brick and stone corner bank building features a more ambitious corner element. The walls give way to a circular bay set above a diagonal stone archway and topped by a conical roof. Unfortunately, it is less well preserved than its counterpart in the neighboring county.

**SM 30.03**
## Smith County Courthouse
*1918–1920. Thomas W. Williamson*
*Oak and Court*

This rectangular three-story Neoclassical limestone building is centered in a landscaped block. It is formal and symmetrical in character, featuring a continuous base and cornice separated by an uninterrupted row of embedded Ionic columns and corner piers. The equally dignified interior is enlivened by tile floors and wainscots.

# Colby

**TH 31.01**
## Thomas County Courthouse*
*1905–1906. Holland & Squires*
*300 North Court Street*

As is the case with many courthouses in the region, this three-story brick Richardsonian Romanesque building with stone trim is located on a block removed from the town's main commercial street. It is similar in form to the series of five nearly identical courthouses the architects designed in the first decade of the twentieth century but differs in appearance because all the others were built of stone.

**TH 31.02**
## Colby Community High School
*1935. Mann & Company*
*West Third and North Lincoln Street*

Long and asymmetrically balanced, this two-story Eclectic dark-brick building with a tile roof has a Mediterranean character. The imagery is carried through to the interior, particularly in the auditorium's beamed ceiling. It also has elements that are of more contemporary inspiration, such as the stone coping around the top of the entry tower. It was built as a federal WPA project.

### TH 31.03
### Pioneer Memorial Library
*1963. Richard C. Peters*
*West Fourth and North School Avenue*

The one-story tan-brick building is representative of the rather restrained aesthetic of the time. The building is simply organized with a glazed entry lobby separating the block of the adult section from that of the children's area. The windows are consolidated into a single full-height row of ten.

### TH 31.04
### Sacred Heart Church
*1950. Brinkman & Hagan*
*West Fifth and North French*

The church is a bold geometric Modern building of stone-trimmed brick occupying a corner site in a residential area. The symmetrical front facade features a large cross set in a stone panel above a tunnel-like entry portal. The section of the building with a tall central nave and two lower side aisles is clearly revealed in this elevation. A tall, flat-topped square bell tower, featuring a series of small windows at one corner, is set to one side of the rear of the structure.

### TH 31.05
### KXXX Radio Station
*ca. 1955*
*1065 Range Avenue*

This one-story Modern building is set well back from a busy highway. It is an ambitious structure for its type, containing a full soundstage for live recordings, and the glass cupola protruding from the flat roof incorporates a meteorological observation station. Its most significant features, however, are the giant concrete letters advertising the station's call letters, which support the roof of the covered entry.

### TH 31.06
### Cooper Barn (Prairie Museum of Art and History)
*1935*
*1905 South Franklin Avenue*

At 66-feet wide, 144-feet long, and 48-feet high, this gambrel-roofed wooden cattle barn is the largest in the state. It is part of a collection of buildings, including a replica of a sod house, a small country church, a one-room schoolhouse, and a 1930s farm-house, that illustrate life on the prairie. The complex also contains an interesting bermed concrete exhibition building by the California architect George Kuska, completed in the late 1980s.

# Ogallah

### TR 32.01
### Cedar Bluff Reservoir and Dam
*1949–1951. U.S. Bureau of Reclamation*
*On K 147 (twelve miles south of Ogallah)*

### TH 31.07
### Tastee Treat
*ca. 1985*
*Adjacent to the interchange between U.S. 83 and I 70*

The ice cream stand sits among a clutter of small structures at a major highway intersection fifteen miles southeast of Colby (and five miles north of Oakley in Logan County). The direct symbolism of this roadside stand, formed in the shape of a monumental ice cream cone, is at once humorous and effective in advertising its function. The illusion is carried even to the lifelike mannequins seated at a picnic table in front of the stand.

This dam on the Smoky Hill river is typical of the state's many river dams. They are impressive feats of engineering and provide some of the more dramatic views of the Kansas landscape. Cedar Bluff is the first of seven dams built by the U.S. Department of Reclamation through the mid-1970s, projects that were motivated primarily by concerns for water supply. The fifteen dams built by the Army Corps of Engineers, however, were undertakings motivated primarily by concerns for flood control. Lakes created by the dams also provide important recreational opportunities. The construction projects caused controversy among preservationists who lamented the loss of early settlements located in the flooded river valleys above the dams.

. . . . . . . . . . . . . . . . . . . . . . . . . . . . . . . . .

# Wakeeney

### TR 33.01
### Trego County Courthouse
*1888/1951/1988*
*George Ropes / Wilson & Company / Pierce-Shippers Murray Associates*
*Main Street and Warren Avenue*

The courthouse, a three-story limestone building occupying an open block in the center of town, provides an interesting example of the evolution of a building through time. When it was remodeled in 1951, its appearance was substantially altered; the roofs and tower, similar to those on the Linn County Courthouse (LN 16.01, Southeast Region), were removed. A 1988 remodeling is responsible for the replacement of a glass-block window above the entry with the present limestone-relief panel. An ongoing series of smaller remodelings have transformed the building's interior.

# Sharon Springs

**WA 34.01**
**Wallace County Courthouse**
*1914–1915. W. E. Hulse & Company*
*313 North Main Street*

The two-and-one-half-story Neoclassical building of limestone-trimmed buff brick occupies a block at the northern end of the business district. The structure is one of the four earlier of the eight remaining Kansas courthouses designed by the architect. Though slightly different programmatically, these four share common stylistic features, which include the frequent use of pedimented entries supported on pilasters with columns inset between them and a characteristic awkwardness in the proportion of the overly tall columns.

. . . . . . . . . . . . . . . . . . . . . . . . . . . . . . .

# Wallace

**WA 35.01**
**Pond Creek Stage Station***
*1865*
*On U.S. 40*

The station, a one-and-one-half-story rectangular board-and-batten gabled building, has been moved to a roadside park, the site of the Fort Wallace Memorial Museum. Fort

Wallace was established in 1865 to help protect settlers from Indian attack and was closed in 1881. A nearby cemetery is its only surviving remnant. The park also contains an early railroad station moved from Weskan.

**WA 35.02**
## Union Pacific Railroad Building
*1877–1878*

The simple two-story limestone building sits amid a shaded overgrown lot in the center of the nearly abandoned town of Wallace, a principal rail stop during the 1870s and 1880s. In addition to this structure, the railroad built shops, a roundhouse, and workers' housing. The town was the site of an early Harvey House restaurant and of Peter Robidoux's store, which reportedly was then the largest department store between Kansas City and Denver. After the closure of Fort Wallace, the railroad abandoned its roundhouse and shops, and the town began to decline.

# Southwest Region

West of the 100th meridian the High Plains dominate the landscape of south-western Kansas, much as they do in the Northwest Region. In both regions east of the meridian, elevations gradually drop and the terrain transforms into primarily hill country. Despite these shared characteristics, some important differences exist between the two areas. The Southwest Region has notably fewer surface-water features, but among them is the Arkansas River, which has been and still is a truly significant influence on development in southern Kansas. Over the years the breadth and flow of the river have diminished as people in both Colorado and Kansas diverted water to meet their needs. Even so, something of the river's earlier character can be read in the sand and gravel deposits found in the lowlands that spread south of it, sometimes for miles.

The Arkansas River rises in the mountains of Colorado and then passes through a good deal of Kansas before entering Oklahoma; from there it moves on through Arkansas to its junction with the Mississippi River. The Arkansas has always been a valued water resource for the people who chose to settle in those four states. In southwestern Kansas, where the river moves through eight of the region's twenty-eight counties, it provided a dependable lifeline and right-of-way for early travelers who had to cope with the hazards presented by a terrain once denominated as the Great American Desert, a place of limited and capricious rainfall, a region then bereft of trees except along the Arkansas.

When the survey party for the Santa Fe Trail began marking out a route through western Kansas, understandably they chose a path that closely paralleled the Arkansas River. Later, the surveyors for the Santa Fe Railroad placed the first right-of-way in the region generally along the line of the trail. The railroad reached the western border of Kansas in 1872, and locales proximate to the rail line were favored by settlers moving into western Kansas. Railroad service never became uniformly distributed throughout the region, however, a deficiency that along with other local factors limited the density and patterns of settlement, thus affecting the organization of the region's twenty-eight counties, which began in 1871 and finished in 1890 but with two-thirds organizing after 1880.

Population in the region now numbers 210,000, with slightly more than half located in just four (noncontiguous) counties—Barton, Ford, Finney, and Seward—

and then primarily in their county seats of Great Bend, Dodge City, Garden City, and Liberal. The first three towns are spaced along the Arkansas River; the fourth, Liberal, is near the state line with Oklahoma, about seventy miles due south of Garden City.

Three forts established by the army were the earliest non-Indian settlements in the region. They were founded to provide protection for the Santa Fe Trail and then for the railroad since conflicts with the Indians had become more serious and frequent as the tribes faced ever greater restrictions on their travel and traditional hunting practices. The army eventually prevailed, and Fort Zarah, the easternmost, which had been established in 1864, was dismantled in 1869. Two years later the lands were sold and the settlement of Great Bend was established near the site of the fort. The name for the community reflects its location on the sweeping bend that marks the most northern reach in Kansas of the Arkansas River.

Great Bend grew rapidly after the railroad arrived in 1872. Two years later the town assumed the role as the railhead for Texas cattle being driven north on the Chisholm Trail after a quarantine to protect the health of established herds of local cattle effectively terminated Wichita's brief involvement as a transfer point. In 1876 the quarantine line was moved west of Great Bend, and thereafter the city's economy had to rely on being a provider of services and as a regional distribution and flour-milling center. Augmentation of those resources came from the discovery of oil in the general vicinity, during the 1930s. Today, Great Bend has a population of 15,400; its broad, open grid of streets fills the area between the Arkansas River on the south and Walnut Creek on the north.

The oldest fort in the region, Larned, was located about thirty-five miles farther west on Pawnee Creek, a tributary of the Arkansas River. Established in 1859, the fort remained active until 1882 (PN 23.01). The town of Larned, the seat of Pawnee County, is some seven miles east of the fort and is on the Arkansas River where Pawnee Creek joins it.

Still farther west on the Arkansas River, Fort Dodge was established in 1864 near a favorite campground for wagon trains, about twenty-five miles east of the Cimarron Cutoff, an alternative route for the Santa Fe Trail. The first civilian settlement in its vicinity occurred in 1871 at a convenient ford over the river about five miles west of the fort (and thus beyond control of the military). A town was platted at the site a few months before the railroad arrived in 1872. By then the slaughter of the bison had reached new levels, and the shipping of buffalo hides became a major item of commerce for the railroad; literally hundreds of thousands of hides were shipped in the first year. By 1876 the herds were exterminated, and thereafter, until the supply was exhausted, the bleached bones were gathered for shipment east to be converted to fertilizer.

Dodge City's economy then became dependent in 1876 on its role as the railhead destination for the Texas cattle drives, an era that also proved comparatively short-lived. The last cattle drive into the city arrived in 1885, three years after the fort closed. By then, however, the reputation of Dodge City as a raucous cowtown was well established and soon would pass into the public's imagination as the quintessential wild western town with legendary lawmen striving to maintain order, an image that now has an apparently indestructible place in the popular history of the American West, a reputation that reaches far beyond the United States.

Today, Dodge City (population 21,100) is a major supply and trade center for a region whose economy is dependent on ranching and farming. Understandably, it has also capitalized on its history to become a tourist destination. To serve that role, the city re-created historic Front Street (FO 07.01), with replicas as well as some original nineteenth-century buildings moved to a site that occupies a low-lying area along the tracks of the Santa Fe Railroad near the city's Boot Hill Cemetery. The more modern downtown district occupies an area of several blocks in depth and about six blocks in length along the hillside that runs to the north. Recent developments have spread in all directions from the core but particularly to the north and west. The remaining stockyards lie to the east of the city.

Garden City (population 24,100) has a different reputation, one closely connected with the agricultural practices in the region, past and present. Founded in 1878 and incorporated in 1883, the city's development was first influenced by a major speculative land boom in the surrounding region during the late 1880s that encouraged the plowing up of the native buffalo grass in order to grow traditional crops, an effort soon doomed by the inevitable arrival of a period of prolonged drought. That experience demonstrated the need to be far more selective and prudent in the matter of farming in the area. One effort to solve the problem led to the construction of an extensive network of canals and ditches, dug to divert water from the Arkansas River. But in the mid-1930s another prolonged drought brought economic ruin to many farmers in Kansas. Today, the availability of electric motors and modern pumps allows water to be drawn from wells for irrigation purposes. The combination of new technologies and much improved farming techniques has enabled Garden City and the region it serves to prosper despite the setbacks encountered in earlier times. Garden City's principal commercial district stretches along Main Street, north from the Santa Fe Railroad tracks, to which the immediate street grid is oriented. Outside the core area the grid returns to a true north-south orientation that introduces a series of irregular intersections. Curving streets and cul-de-sacs in the recently developed northern parts of the city further complicate the layout.

Liberal (population 16,573) was founded in 1886, and its economy for many years depended on its role as the terminus for the Rock Island Railroad (sw 27.02). Liberal is also adjacent to the Hugoton natural gas field stretching out to the west that has become a nationally significant source of clean fuel, the demand for which is ever increasing, and for the extraction of helium (see sw 27.01). Consequently, the city has become a center for gas- and oil-related industries. Liberal—as well as Garden City—also has a sizable meat-packing industry, whose employees have contributed to the ethnic diversity of both cities. Liberal's older commercial district centers on Kansas Avenue, which runs through the city from north to south. Newer commercial development has taken place largely to the west, notably along Western Avenue.

Taken together, the several major cities and the twenty-eight counties of the Southwest Region represent an economy closely allied with agribusiness but not exclusively so. Furthermore, many parts of the region are noted for a history that significantly enhances our understanding not only of the development of Kansas but also of the semiarid West.

Although much of the region's most significant architecture will be found in the four cities described, other sites are important. The broader view reveals the architectural importance in the region of the county courthouse, where almost universally that structure will stand out as a county's most impressive and substantial building, suggesting both its practical value and the symbolic importance vested in it by its community. Yet we need also to look at lesser buildings in the region if we are to obtain proper insight into its diverse and sometimes colorful history as well as into its contemporary situation. The regional map and directory not only locate the counties, cities, and towns but also provide an outline for the sequence of the catalog entries for the region that speak to these concerns.

# SOUTHWEST REGION

Alpha-Numeric Directory

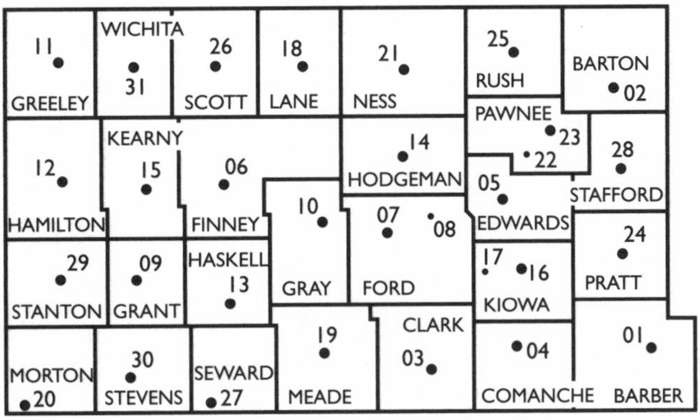

**BARBER (BA)**

01 Medicine Lodge†

**BARTON (BT)**

02 Great Bend†

**CLARK (CA)**

03 Ashland†

**COMANCHE (CM)**

04 Coldwater†

**EDWARDS (ED)**

05 Kinsley†

**FINNEY (FI)**

06 Garden City†

**FORD (FO)**

07 Dodge City†

08 Spearville

**GRANT (GT)**

09 Ulysses†

**GRAY (GY)**

10 Cimarron†

**GREELEY (GL)**

11 Tribune†

**HAMILTON (HM)**

12 Syracuse†

**HASKELL (HS)**

13 Sublette†

**HODGEMAN (HG)**

14 Jetmore†

**KEARNY (KE)**

15 Lakin†

**KIOWA (KW)**

16 Greensburg†

17 Mullinville

**LANE (LE)**

18 Dighton†

**MEADE (ME)**

19 Meade†

**MORTON (MT)**

20 Elkhart†

**NESS (NS)**

21 Ness City†

**PAWNEE (PN)**

22 Garfield

23 Larned†

**PRATT (PR)**

24 Pratt†

**RUSH (RH)**

25 LaCrosse†

**SCOTT (SC)**

26 Scott City†

**SEWARD (SW)**

27 Liberal†

**STAFFORD (SF)**

28 St. John†

**STANTON (ST)**

29 Johnson City†

**STEVENS (SV)**

30 Hugoton†

**WICHITA (WH)**

31 Leoti†

## Medicine Lodge

### BA 01.01
**Barber County Courthouse**
*1956. Brinkman & Hagan*
*South Walnut and East Washington*

This one-story Classical Modern stone building terminates a street vista. Despite its simple form and modest scale, the courthouse has an appropriate sense of monumentality. The framing of the deep-set windows not only provides shade for the openings but also gives the building a civic presence. The architects were Jerome W. Brinkman and J. Stanley Hagan; Brinkman was the son of the firm's founder, Henry Brinkman, who died in 1949.

### BA 01.02
**Carry Nation House***
*1882*
*Fowler and Oak Street*

The small vernacular one-story plastered masonry residence not only typifies the houses of the early settlers of the region but also is notable as the home of one of the nation's most outspoken proponents of Prohibition. Her crusade began in 1899 with the organization of a temperance rally outside a local saloon.

# Great Bend

### BT 02.01
## Barton County Courthouse
*1917–1918. W. E. Hulse & Company*
*Lafayette Park*

level, and office and meeting spaces occupy the upper floors.

### BT 02.03
## Crest Theater
*1945. Robert Boller & Dietz Lusk*
*1905 Lakin Street*

A monumental four-story stone Beaux-Arts building, the courthouse occupies a full block in the center of the business district. Classical ornament is freely applied; each of the sides of the building features a vestigial arcade of widely spaced Ionic columns. The entry originally was via exterior stairs leading to the second level, but these have been replaced with entries at the ground level. The interior is organized around a central lobby faced in book-matched marble. The building features a grand and graceful stair also faced in marble.

### BT 02.02
## Masonic Temple
*1928. Mann & Company*
*2015–2017 Lakin Street*

This three-story Eclectic limestone building features well-rendered abstract geometric carved ornament. The medallions across the cornice represent the different orders who meet in the building. It is also noteworthy for its effective zoning of uses. Storefront rental spaces create interest at the sidewalk

The glass-block and glazed-tile Moderne theater enlivens its downtown street. The facade is flush with the fronts of neighboring buildings on either side but curves back toward the center to create space around the entry. An ornate lighted marquee angles forward to cover the sidewalk and announce the current attraction. The streamlined motifs carry through into the 900-seat interior. The building has been recently renovated for live performances and is now owned by the city and operated by a local community theater group.

### BT 02.04
## E. J. Dodge House
*1873*
*On U.S. 281 (south of Great Bend)*

The Dodge house, a tiny one-and-one-half-story stone residence, is one of several buildings collected and moved to the site from around the county by the Barton County Historical Society. The building was originally located five miles northeast of Great Bend. Two other restored buildings on the site are St. Paul's Lutheran Church (1890), a simple Gothic wood structure moved from Albert, and the rather typical small Santa Fe Depot (1910) moved from Belpre.

# Ashland

### CA 03.01
## First National Bank*
*1887*
*Eighth and Main*

Many buildings similar to this two-story stone-trimmed brick Victorian corner bank building were erected about this time throughout the state. The exterior wall of this straightforward structure is enlivened by the direct expression of construction through the manipulation of the surface plane and by change of material.

### CA 03.02
## Clark County Courthouse
*ca. 1960. Thomas, Harris & Calvin*
*Tenth and Highland*

This two-story Modern limestone building occupies a sloping, open site along the town's main street. The courthouse consists of a largely unadorned block with large windows. A map of the county is etched in a panel adjacent to the main entry.

# Coldwater

## Kinsley

**CM 04.01**
**Comanche County Courthouse**
*1927–1928. Routledge & Hertz*
*201 South New York*

**ED 05.01**
**Edwards County Courthouse**
*1928–1929. Routledge & Hertz*
*West Third and Massachusetts*

A four-story Neoclassical brick building, the courthouse occupies an open site one block from the main commercial street. The stone ornament of this simple structure is concentrated about the main entry. The building remains in its original state.

One of five courthouses designed by the architects in the late 1920s, this three-story brick and stone Neoclassical building occupies a block in a residential district. These buildings follow a similar compositional formula: the ground floor usually is treated as a base and rendered in stone, and the next two floors are normally of brick with a two-story stone columns or pilasters, topped by a stone cornice. When a fourth floor is added, it is usually treated as an attic story, as with the Gray County Courthouse (GY 10.02). The formula is receptive to alterations to meet differing programmatic requirements.

**ED 05.02**
**Atchison Topeka and Santa Fe Railroad Station**
*1887. Perkins & Adams*
*On U.S. 56*

Now abandoned, the stone-trimmed brick station occupies an open site amid a rambling mixture of residential and commercial structures. It is a straightforward and handsome example of its building type.

Sturdy wooden brackets supported on stone
squinches and pilasters support a broad
overhang that rings the station. With the
exception of the removal of a small attic
story and a central capping tower, the building is relatively well preserved and provides
an alluring view of an earlier time.

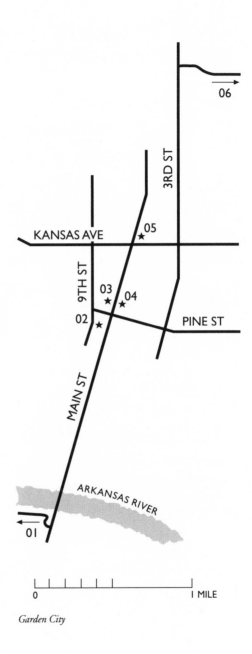

Garden City

# Garden City

carries through to the interior, particularly in the lobby.

### FI 06.01
## Hobson House

*1976. Gibson, Mancini, & Carmichael*
*Head south on U.S. 83 and take the first right*
*past the Arkansas River bridge. Sagebrush*
*Estates will be on the left; enter, take the first*
*right and then the first left.*

This semicircular one-story Modern house occupies a hilltop site amid an irregularly planned and sparsely settled subdivision on the arid bluffs south of the Arkansas River. The house seems well suited to its position, surrounded by the desertlike vegetation of the rugged and distinctive suburban development.

### FI 06.02
## Finney County Law Enforcement Center

*1981. Gibson, Mancini, & Carmichael*
*304 Ninth Street*

The center, a two-story Modern brick building, is part of a loose complex of governmental buildings in the central part of town. Nearby is the four-story limestone Neoclassical county courthouse, designed by Routledge and Hertz in 1928. The strong geometric massing, straightforward expression of function, and careful detailing of the understated Law Enforcement Center allow it to complement the earlier building. The blending of restraint and public presence

### FI 06.03
## Windsor Hotel*

*1886. Stevens & Thompson*
*421 North Main Street*

The bulk of this four-story brick Italianate structure continues to dominate the downtown district. The once opulent 125-room hotel was known as the Waldorf of the Prairies. The building is organized around a grand, three-story, central sky-lit atrium lobby at the second floor. The hotel's public facilities and special guest suites are located on this floor; the upper two floors consist of a double ring of private guest rooms. The lower level is given over to retail space, and the entry to the hotel is marked by a tower. The building is no longer occupied above the ground floor.

### FI 06.04
## Stevens Park Band Shell

*1931. A. C. Mitchell (designer)*
*Main Street between Pine and Spruce Street*

The concrete pavilion sits in the center of an open landscaped block at the heart of the business district. Fii.anced by contributions from the local business community, the band shell reflects the growing civic pride in the city. It is also representative of similar structures found across the state. The contrast between the vertically articulated corner towers and the intervening arch of this example is particularly striking. Public amenities during the time were often enhanced through the efforts of the WPA, as was the case with the bathhouse adjacent to the "world's largest" concrete free municipal swimming pool in nearby Finnup Park.

## FI 06.05
### First United Methodist Church
*1959. Howard Blanchard*
*Kansas Avenue and Main Street*

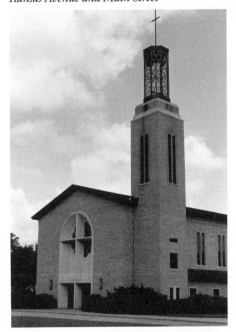

Located at the intersection of two of the city's most heavily traveled streets, the Modern brick church constitutes a significant landmark in the city. Both the exterior and interior draw upon the traditions of Scan-

dinavian Modernism, fusing concerns for geometric purity with an interest in traditional building patterns but paying careful attention to human needs. The horizontality of the principal building forms is complemented by the verticality of the bell tower added in 1961.

## FI 06.06
### Florence Wilson Elementary School
*1986. Gibson, Mancini, & Carmichael*
*Labrador and Pearly Jayne Boulevard*

This distinctive Modern school stretches across a broad, open site in the expanding suburbs on the northeastern edge of the city. The south-facing building is organized to make good use of natural sunlight, with solar collectors mounted on the front of the building and clerestory windows to bring daylight into the long parallel corridors. The building's form clearly reflects its ecological aspirations.

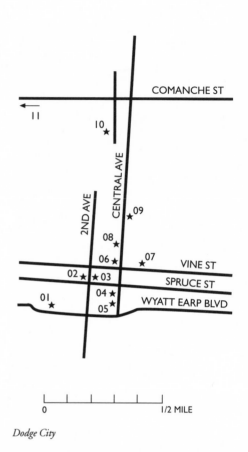

COMANCHE ST

11

10 ★

CENTRAL AVE

2ND AVE

09 ★

08 ★

06 ★    ★ 07    VINE ST

02 ★ ★ 03    SPRUCE ST

01 ★    04 ★    WYATT EARP BLVD
        05 ★

0                    1/2 MILE

*Dodge City*

# Dodge City

## FO 07.01
### Front Street Reconstruction
*1958*
*50 Wyatt Earp Boulevard*

The fenced row of one-story wooden commercial buildings is an accurate reproduction of a block of buildings along Front Street in 1876. At that time Dodge City was the terminal point of the Texas cattle drives and thus a recreational center for the cowboys who worked them. The buildings operate as a museum, and reenactments of nineteenth-century gunfights, along with variety shows, are featured.

## FO 07.02
### Carnegie Library*
*1907. Charles W. Squires*
*701 Second Avenue*

The library, a distinctive domed Eclectic structure of brick and wood, faces a busy intersection in the heart of the business district. The building clearly displays some of the architect's characteristic mannerisms: freedom of stylistic interpretation, preference for round-domed forms, and skill with complex massing. The building functioned as the city library until 1970; it now serves as the gallery and headquarters of the Dodge City Area Arts Council.

## FO 07.03
### St. Cornelius Episcopal Church
*1898. William B. Kimball*
*200 Spruce Street*

This gabled rectangular English Gothic church of rustic sandstone occupies a sloping downtown corner site. The stone used to construct the building was salvaged from an earlier building that had been demolished. It is the oldest church in continuous use in the city.

## FO 07.04
### Ford County Courthouse
*1912–1913. Ruel A. Curtis*
*Central and West Spruce Street*

Academically designed and monumental, this Neoclassical three-story building of limestone occupies a tight corner site. The equally formal interior is faced in white marble. An elevator has been added in the once-grand central lobby, and the courtroom has been remodeled.

## FO 07.05
### Lora Locke Hotel*
*1928. Ellis Charles & Company*
*Central and Gunsmoke Street*

This connected pair of five-story stone-trimmed brick Renaissance Revival Style buildings anchors a downtown block that also contains the Dodge Theater, completed the following year. The 115-room luxury hotel and the adjacent theater reflect the prosperity of Dodge City in the 1920s, which is also evident in the similarly styled six-story First National Bank Building at Second and Spruce Street, completed in 1930 and designed by Fred Organ.

## FO 07.06
### First Presbyterian Church
*1924–1925. Harry W. Jones*
*803 Central Avenue*

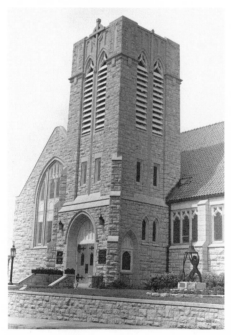

From its sloping corner site, the massive marble-trimmed limestone Gothic Revival church overlooks the downtown district. The dominant feature of the tile-roofed cross-gabled structure is a flat-roofed square entry tower.

## FO 07.07
### Mueller-Schmidt House*
*1879–1881. William Hessman (builder)*
*112 East Vine Street*

This limestone one-and-one-half-story Italianate home occupies a large shaded hillside lot. A stonemason and his sons, who emigrated from Germany, built the house using locally quarried stone. The original owner, John Mueller, was a bootmaker and cattle rancher who furnished the house with imported items. The building now functions as a museum operated by the Ford County Historical Society and provides a view of early life in the city.

## FO 07.08
### Sacred Heart Cathedral*
*1915–1916. Cram & Ferguson*
*903 Central Avenue*

The stucco Spanish Colonial Revival basilican church occupies a sloping corner site.

The cathedral's principal ornament consists of the sculptured limestone surround of the main entry. The building's style was made popular by the 1911–1915 designs for the Panama-California Exposition in San Diego by Bertram Goodhue, erstwhile partner of the cathedral's well-known architects. It is worth noting that the architect Ralph Adams Cram was an outspoken exponent of Gothic Revival styles.

## FO 07.09
### Central School
*1927. Mann & Company*
*1100 Central*

Collegiate Gothic in style, the two-story stone-trimmed brick school occupies a full block on a major street in a shaded residential neighborhood. The most interesting feature is the tower above the main entry, which is notable more for the geometric composition than for the historical accuracy of its ornament. Similar sensibilities are evident in the nearby First Baptist Church at

1310 Second Avenue, designed by the architects in 1930.

## FO 07.10
### Senior High School
*1927–1928. Mann & Company*
*1601 First Avenue*

This two-story Collegiate Gothic structure of stone-trimmed gray brick stretches out across a double block, anchored at one end by an auditorium and at the other by a gymnasium, each with separate entrances. The building exhibits well-established contemporary planning principles and stylistic guidelines. It also suggests the emergence of new traditions, as seen in the simplification and the sophisticated asymmetry of the entry tower, which reveal the architect's emerging Modernist sensibilities.

## FO 07.11
### Glen Mitchell House
*1968. Bruce Goff*
*1905 Burr Parkway*

Located in the northwestern part of the city, this unusual angular two-story wood-shingled house occupies a site in a fairly new subdivision. It is among the more restrained of the well-known architect's original and expressionistic works. Nevertheless, at the time of its construction it seemed startling to many in the city, and a local newspaper article referred to it as a Tibetan Castle.

## FO 07.12
### Immaculate Heart of Mary Catholic Church*

*1913. Preuss & Aimes with Emil Frei*
*Windthorst (twenty miles east of Dodge City on county road)*

The tower and spire of this stone-trimmed brick Eclectic building are visible for some distance across the fields surrounding the grouping of trees and houses that mark the Windthorst community, which clusters around the church. The interior possesses a restrained dignity in character with the exterior. The church and the settlement are typical of others across the state established by religiously oriented immigrant groups, in this case by a group of German Catholics who had originally settled near Cincinnati.

. . . . . . . . . . . . . . . . . . . . . . . . . . . . . . . . . .

# Spearville

## FO 08.01
### St. John the Baptist Church

*1917*
*Main Street and Davis Avenue*

Sitting at an oblique angle to the line of sight, the red-brick Romanesque Revival Catholic church effectively terminates the view down the town's main street. The interior is equally dramatic; pilasters support a low arched vault that unites the single volume. The adjacent rectory, built in 1928, was designed by Henry Brinkman of Emporia.

# Ulysses

## GT 09.01
### Grant County Courthouse
*1929–1930. Smith & English*
*East Grant and South Glen*

This four-story tan-brick building with Art Deco terracotta ornament shares a full-block site, dominated by a grove of mature trees, with a library and police headquarters on either side. A central split stair leads to a remodeled upper-level courtroom.

## GT 09.02
### Crocker Theater
*1948*
*Main Street & Kansas Avenue*

The marquee of this Moderne brick theater boldly marks the northern end of the town's main commercial street. It is a well-preserved example of the pragmatic but optimistic commercial architecture of the postwar era.

## GT 09.03
### Mary Queen of the Peace Church
*1963. George L. Pitcher & Company*
*North Colorado Street and West Wheat Avenue*

Situated on an open suburban site, the Modern church consists of a surrounding

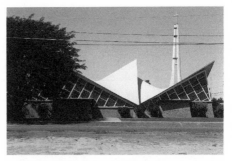

canted concrete base, three hyperbolic paraboloid wood roof structures, and continuous stained-glass windows between. The light entering the church is kaleidoscopic, but the effect of the combined construction is serene and contemplative.

# Cimarron

### GY 10.01
### Cimarron Hotel*
*1886. John Opp*
*203 North Main*

The hotel, a three-story Second Empire brick building, sits adjacent to the town's wide central street. It was built to accommodate a rapid influx of population and still continues to operate as a hotel.

### GY 10.02
### Gray County Courthouse
*1927. Routledge & Hertz*
*Main and Avenue B*

The four-story stone-trimmed brick Neoclassical building is illustrative of the larger among the architects' several contemporary courthouses in the region. As with other early courthouses, requirements for handicapped accessibility have necessitated the addition of elevators; here they have been appended to the side of the building.

# Tribune

### GL 11.01
### (Old) Greeley County Courthouse
*1890. W. T. Heaps*
*Second and Harper*

The old courthouse, a two-story rustic limestone structure, sits adjacent to the new red-brick Modern courthouse, designed by Kiene & Bradley in 1975, in a residential area one block from the town's main street. The building now houses the Horace Greeley Museum. Despite its new function, the older structure remains largely unchanged, and the collection is accommodated within existing spaces.

### GL 11.02
### Greeley County Library
*1968. George Pritchard*
*Broadway and Harper*

The low-pitched roof supported on laminated wood beams and the sloping stone walls of this Modern building give it a rustic, lodgelike feeling. The stone walls enclose a planter on one side and a small courtyard on the other. The interior is spacious and open.

## Syracuse

**GL 11.03**

### Airplane Hangar (Tribune Airport)
*On KS 27, one-half mile south of U.S. 96*

The semivaulted metal hangar is one of many similar structures that line an unpaved landing strip. The building's simple and elegant form clearly expresses its use; the wide and tall front portion accommodates a plane's wings, and a projecting smaller vaulted element houses the tail section. The airport serves crop-dusting operations.

**HM 12.01**

### Hamilton County Courthouse
*1937. Overend & Boucher*
*East C and North Main*

This two-story stripped Neoclassical building of buff brick and limestone occupies a portion of a block on the northern end of the town's main commercial street. The interior has a similarly austere Federal Deco feeling. The entry faces a once-open clerk's area, and a flanking stair on one side leads to the upper-level courtroom at the building's rear. The structure has been more extensively modified than the similar Kearny County Courthouse (KE 15.01).

**HM 12.02**

### Syracuse City Hall and Jail
*1983. Gibson, Mancini, & Carmichael*
*East C and North Main*

The simple Modern one-story building effectively completes a civic center, which includes the older county courthouse and a civic auditorium, located as the terminus of the one- and two-story commercial buildings lining the town's main street. Although stylistically dissimilar, it is sensitive spatially to its context.

**HM 12.03**
## Northrup Theater
*1932*
*116 North Main*

The shape of the colorful terracotta-trimmed blond-brick theater reveals the building's main interior volume. It was built to accommodate stage productions; a movie screen was added later. Interior renovations of 1948 were designed by J. M. Lort and included large wall paintings by Muriel Ellis. The theater is now operated by the chamber of commerce.

## HASKELL COUNTY

# Sublette

**HS 13.01**
## Haskell County Courthouse
*1976–1977. Gibson, Mancini, & Carmichael*
*300 Inman Street*

This one-story tan building of precast ribbed concrete panels occupies a shaded block on the town's main street. It is the antithesis of the typical monumental courthouse. The L-shaped structure wraps around a memorial courtyard and nearly disappears within the grove of surrounding trees.

**HS 13.02**
## Roland Jacquart House
*1965. Bruce Goff*
*Inman Street and Edelle Avenue*

Organized around an interior courtyard, the rock and wood-shingle house occupies a flat suburban site at the southern end of the main street. The site also contains a small studio building in the rear and an assortment of assembled rocks and sculptures. The boulders as well as the rock used in the house reflect the owner's love of stone. The sculptures were designed by the architect and were given to the owner as a token of their continuing friendship.

## HS 13.03
### Vince Mancini House
*1983. Gibson, Mancini, & Carmichael*
*Go north of Sublette on U.S. 83, west on U.S. 150 for four miles, and then north two miles*

This flat-roofed two-story geometric wood International Style home sits amid a vast agricultural landscape. A wide ring of trees around the house echoes the sweep of the many surrounding irrigation machines. The house reflects the 1970s resurgence of interest in the 1920s work of the French architect Le Corbusier, as embodied in the work of a group of architects known as the New York Five.

# Jetmore

## HG 14.01
### First National Bank
*1889*
*North Main Street*

The county courthouse sits opposite this simply adorned two-story stone corner building. Although less detailed than many, it follows the pattern of other corner bank buildings in smaller towns across the state.

## HG 14.02
### T. S. Haun House*
*1879*
*North Main Street*

This rectangular two-story gable-roofed vernacular stone building is located across the street from the county courthouse and next to the First National Bank. It was built the year the town was founded and now houses a museum. The house is visible in the photograph of the bank (HG 14.01), and together they provide an interesting contrast of scale.

## HG 14.03
### Hodgeman County Courthouse
*1929–1930. Routledge & Hertz*
*Main Street*

The four-story Neoclassical brick and stone building occupies a block along the town's

primary commercial street. It is similar to and follows the pattern established in the Edwards County Courthouse (ED 05.01) but begins to show the stylistic transitions evident in the Sherman County Courthouse (SH 19.01, Northwest Region), both by the same architects.

# Lakin

### KE 15.01
### Kearny County Courthouse
*1939. Overend & Boucher*
*304 Main Street*

The courthouse, a simplified tan-brick and limestone Neoclassical building, has received additions of a library and a law enforcement center to the sides and a senior center to the rear. It was built as a WPA relief project. The interior layout of the courthouse is nearly identical to its counterpart in Hamilton County (HM 12.01).

### KE 15.02
### White House (Kearny County Historical Museum)
*1876*
*Buffalo Street and Waterman Avenue*

The stuccoed two-story L-shaped house shares its site with an 1893 schoolhouse and the 1876 depot, which were also moved to the location. It is laudable that these buildings have been preserved; however, their close proximity makes it difficult to visualize their original context.

# Greensburg

### KW 16.01
### Kiowa County Courthouse
*1913–1914. W. E. Hulse*
*South Oak and East Florida*

Occupying a public square, this three-story Neoclassical brick and limestone building is one block removed from the town's main street. Renovations and additions have introduced a seriously discordant note, such as the glass block placed in the window openings. The resulting effect has reduced significantly the original stylistic coherence of a major building, thereby providing proof through example that established historic preservation standards should be followed in making necessary changes to a building to avoid diminishing its architectural importance.

### KW 16.02
### Greensburg Well*
*1887*
*315 South Sycamore Street*

This 32-foot-diameter, 109-foot-deep well is architecture in the broadest sense of the word; it is an adaptation of the environment to accommodate human needs. It is the world's largest hand-dug well, created by a crew of twelve to fifteen men from the

Santa Fe Railroad, working for three years. It is open for public viewing.

### KW 16.03
### Miller-Yohn Barns
*1928 and 1985*
*On U.S. 183 (1.5 miles west and 6.5 miles north of Greensburg)*

These two barns represent the changes in agricultural outbuildings through the twentieth century. The earlier wooden barn was built on site through the collective effort of the family in accordance with traditional plans. The advent of large farm equipment made it obsolete since the machinery could not fit between the pairs of supporting columns. The newer metal barn was prefabricated in sections and assembled on site by a firm from Hutchinson that specialized in the building type. Although the newer building lacks the earlier one's character and singularity, its large unencumbered spans easily accommodate modern equipment.

. . . . . . . . . . . . . . . . . . . . . . . . . . . . . . . .

# Mullinville

### KW 17.01
### Sherer Barn
*1916. Patrick Campbell (builder)*
*Main Street (one-half mile north)*

The elegant three-towered gambrel-roofed horse barn is one of four nearly identical barns in the Mullinville vicinity. The first

was built for John Sherer, near U.S. 54 east of Mullinville. This barn is one of the three he built for his sons.

### KW 17.02
### Fromme-Birney Barn*
*1912. Patrick Campbell (builder)*
*South of Mullinville (on Main go four miles south past the turn in the road, then take the first road to the right for two miles)*

This round-domed wooden barn is in an isolated field along a lonely gravel road. It is an extremely well-preserved example of its type and is now used primarily for storage. Like the barns he built for Sherer, this building is a testament to Campbell's vision and skills.

# Dighton

## Meade

### LE 18.01
### Lane County Courthouse
*1930. Mann & Company*
*East Pearl and South Lane Street*

### ME 19.01
### Meade County Courthouse
*1928. Fred Hopper*
*West Belle Meade and North Fowler Street*

Built of yellow-brick and limestone, this four-story Classical Art Deco structure occupies a corner lot. Although different in plan, the building shares details with the Stafford County Courthouse of the previous year (SF 28.01). The building is entered at a half-level, with offices on each adjacent level and the courtroom on a level above. The interior features Art Deco appointments; the light fixtures are of particular interest.

The Neoclassical brick building occupies a half block near the center of town. The courthouse is cleverly and convincingly composed; although it appears to be two stories in height, it contains four levels of offices. Its most dominant feature is an arcade of well-scaled two-story Doric columns. An elevator is currently being added to the north side of the building, but otherwise it remains substantially unaltered.

### ME 19.02
### Southwestern Bell Telephone Company Building
*1934. Glen H. Thomas*
*North Springlake and West Bell Meade Street*

The one-story brick building nestles into a small tree-shaded lot and features an Art Deco–inspired door surround of stone with terracotta buffalo heads on flanking pilasters. These elements and terracotta panels above the windows are reminiscent of the decorative work on the Wichita High School (North) (SG 24.26, Southcentral Region). The front of the building is now leased, but the rear continues to house telephone switching equipment.

MORTON COUNTY

# Elkhart

**MT 20.01**
## First State Bank
*1960. Robert E. Cobb*
*432 Morton*

A clever adaptation of a standard prefabricated metal building, this one-story Modern bank occupies a prominent site in the center of the commercial district. When built, it was featured in the national advertisements of the building fabricator, the Butler Manufacturing Company. Its notable features include colorful decorated columns at the drive-through window and an interior fountain and waterfall.

**MT 20.02**
## Elkhart Co-op Grain Elevators
*ca. 1950–1960*
*Kansas and Border Avenue*

Concrete grain elevators of this sort can be found along the railroad tracks that pass through most western Kansas towns. As in many cases, these elevators and related out-buildings were built over time, and the juxtaposition of various utilitarian forms creates interesting patterns. Forms such as these were an inspiration to the pioneer Modern French architect, Le Corbusier.

## Ness City

**NS 21.01**
### Ness County Bank*
*1889–1890. J. C. Holland and C. B. Hopkins*
*Main and Pennsylvania*

The four-story limestone Romanesque Revival corner bank building towers over other structures in the modest, largely one-story commercial district. It reflects the optimism of the original owners in regard to the commercial prospects of the town. The building is a product of James C. Holland's first partnership. The architect, a native of Lima, Ohio, came to Kansas in 1885 after studying at Cornell University. He served as state architect (1895–1897) and as architect for the Santa Fe Railroad (1897–1898). He also practiced independently and from 1903 to 1910 with partner Frank C. Squires and his sons. Holland died in 1919.

# Garfield

### PN 22.01
### Peterson Barn
*1904. Charles A. Peterson (builder)*
*North Pawnee Street*

Representative of many similar structures, this rectangular clapboard barn with a shingled gable roof sits at the eastern edge of town. It was built by a farmer and a friend who were amateur carpenters. The building has begun to show wear, and the wood siding on one side has been replaced with metal. Buildings of this type require continuing maintenance.

. . . . . . . . . . . . . . . . . . . . . . . . . . . . . . . . .

# Larned

### PN 23.01
### Fort Larned Barracks Buildings*
*1866–1868*
*On K 156 (six miles west of Larned)*

The long one-story colonnaded stone buildings front one side of a 400-foot-square parade ground. The other sides are formed by seven structures, including storage and shop buildings and officers' quarters. The buildings were constructed with locally quarried sandstone and timbers imported from Michigan, replacing the fort's original adobe structures built in 1860. The post was established to provide protection to travelers on the Santa Fe Trail. The coming of the railroads made the trail and also the fort obsolete; in 1884 the site was sold. The federal government acquired it again in 1964, and the National Park Service operates the site as a National Historic Landmark. The information center is housed in one of the barracks buildings.

### PN 23.02
### Lustron House
*1949. Morris H. Beckman*
*West Eighth and Martin Avenue*

The prefabricated metal-panel home is one of a number of similar residences in town (e.g., across the street at 721 Martin and at 823 Starks Boulevard) and is representative of such compact and economical two-bedroom houses across the state. The components were manufactured and sold through the short-lived Lustron Corporation, an organization established in an effort to use the technology developed in World War II defense industries to solve the nation's postwar housing shortage.

# Pratt

## PR 24.01
### Pratt County Courthouse
*1909–1910/1923*
*George P. Washburn / Mann & Company*
*300 South Ninnescah*

This three-story Eclectic brick building sits on an open block to the east of the downtown. The original courthouse burned and was rebuilt in 1923 without the earlier architect's typical roof forms, which apparently were destroyed in the fire. The proportions of the building as reconstructed appear somewhat awkward.

## PR 24.02
### Liberty Middle School
*1983*
*Gossen & Livingston with Griffith & Bonham*
*Fourth and Iuka*

The school, a boldly geometric Modern brick building, is located near the central business district. The architects make the most of a constrained site by wrapping the building forms around the track and playing fields.

## PR 24.03
### S. P. Gebhart House*
*1907–1910*
*Henry Newton Duckworth (builder)*
*105 North Iuka*

The square two-story wood frame Colonial Revival house, with a tiled hipped roof, occupies much of its modest lot. Although it is representative of many similar sturdy foursquare houses built at the time across the state, it is distinguished by the pretension of its ornament and the variety of texture of its siding.

## LaCrosse

**RH 25.01**

**Stone Fence Post**

*U.S. 183 (one mile south of LaCrosse)*

Limestone fence posts were used in the late nineteenth and early twentieth centuries in a central portion of Kansas, where an easily workable supply of limestone is found in an area between ten and seventy miles wide, following a line from Belleville in Republic County southwest to Dodge City in Ford County. Fence posts of this distinctive nature became a common feature in the landscape because of the relative scarcity of trees and the availability of the easily quarried stone. This limestone corner fence post with its diagonal stone bracing is typical.

**RH 25.02**

**Rush County Courthouse***

*1888–1889. L. L. Levering*

*715 Elm Street*

The two-and-one-half-story Romanesque Revival building of stone-trimmed brick occupies a full block near the central commercial area. The removal of the pitched roof above the square tower has altered the balance of the building's massing; the interior has also been remodeled.

# Scott City

### SC 26.01
### El Quartelejo Remains
### (Lake Scott State Park)*
*1650. Taos Indians*
*Off K 95 loop from U.S. 83 (twelve miles north of Scott City)*

The exposed rubble foundations are the only remains of the pueblo built by a band of Taos Indians from what is now New Mexico. The site, which lies in an oasislike valley among a series of steep sandstone hills, was occupied for only about twenty years before the Indians abandoned it and returned to their home territory. The site is now a National Historic Landmark. Lake Scott State Park also contains several early stone buildings, including a one-room school and a settler's cabin as well as several structures built in the 1930s by the Civilian Conservation Corps.

### SC 26.02
### Scott County Courthouse
*1924. Mann & Company*
*Fourth and Court Street*

The four-story Neoclassical red-brick building, occupying a block near the central business district, features a porch consisting of four double-height Ionic columns support-

ing a stone entablature with a central medallion. A comparison between this building and the architects' Lane County Courthouse of five years later (LE 18.01) demonstrates the evolution of architectural tastes through the late 1920s.

### SC 26.03
### Scott Community High School
*1930. Mann & Company*
*Seventh and Main Street*

The two-story brick Art Deco building occupies an open block on the town's wide central street. The school consists of a long symmetrical classroom wing with an entry centered on the front and a gymnasium protruding from the rear. Terracotta ornament of the type used to accent the pilasters and to decorate the area above the front door was popular at the time.

# Liberal

### SW 27.01
## Mighty Samson of the Cimarron
*1940*
*Adjacent to U.S. 54 (twelve miles northeast of Liberal)*

The size of this steel box-girder railroad bridge over the Cimarron River and its valley is impressive even in its ponderous setting; it is the largest bridge of its type. The large onion-shaped objects visible in the valley beneath the bridge are helium storage tanks.

### SW 27.02
## (Old) Rock Island Depot✦
*1910*
*1 East Railroad Street*

Standing isolated near the center of town, this curvilinear-gabled brick and stucco Mission Style building is one of only a few depots of this style to be found in the state. Its strong simple geometry is impressive, despite its current state of disrepair. The complex originally included a restaurant-hotel building that has been removed.

### SW 27.03
## Landmark Center
*1929. Ellis Charles*
*Third and Kansas*

The four-story brick Art Deco terracotta-trimmed building sits at the heart of the town's business district. It was erected as the Warren Hotel; the lobby and retail spaces were on the lower floor, and the upper floors consisted of a U-shaped band of hotel rooms. The building has been renovated for use as offices on the ground floor and luxury condominiums on the upper floors. Concurrently with the construction of this building, the architect also designed the Blakemore House at Seventh and Sherman.

### SW 27.04
## Memorial Library
*1987. David Thompson*
*Sixth and Kansas*

The one-story stone and stucco building is set back to form a public space containing a small version of the Statue of Liberty facing the town's main street. A giant-sized replica of a book placed on the front of the library proclaims the building's function.

The structure is organized along a barrel-vaulted skylight.

### SW 27.05
## Seward County Community College
*ca. 1975. Shaefer & Associates*
*Sixteenth and Kansas*

busy street and is flanked by playgrounds and parking lots. Playful elements such as the arched notched wall, inset tile panel, and glazed vestibule at the main entry add interest to the vast and repetitive brick elements.

The college's tan-brick Modern buildings and their surrounding parking lots occupy a large open site. Each of the buildings is distinctive, reflecting the mix of interior functions that can include classrooms, offices, laboratories, studios, and a gymnasium. The composition is united by common materials and details as well as by crisp geometric massing. The spaces between the buildings, including a central courtyard, are reserved for pedestrians.

### SW 27.06
## Liberal High School
*1982. Woodson Star*
*Second and Western Street*

Cleanly detailed, this Modern school of brick, glass, and tile stretches back from the

# St. John

## Johnson City

### SF 28.01
### Stafford County Courthouse
*1928–1929. Mann & Company*
*209 North Broadway*

### ST 29.01
### Stanton County Courthouse
*1925–1926. Smith & English*
*North Main Street and Logan Avenue*

Opposite a park, this three-story brick and limestone Eclectic Modern courthouse occupies a prominent corner site at the center of town. The building marks a point of transition where historical imagery is being abandoned in favor of more abstract expression. Remnants of classically inspired frontispieces are inserted at the corner entry and on the two side elevations. The triangular plan of the building, organized around the stair hall at the diagonal corner entry, is unique among Kansas courthouses.

The two-and-one-half-story Neoclassical building of red brick and limestone faces the town's main commercial street. The glazed addition to the south side of the courthouse houses a ramp that allows wheelchair access to the lower level. Substantial additional remodeling was undertaken in connection with the installation of an elevator.

### ST 29.02
### First Methodist Church
*1950/1993. Buck/Art Woodman*
*West Lincoln and South Nipp Street*

The church, a simplified Gothic Revival Style of brick and stone, occupies a site near the center of town. A more contemporaneously styled recent addition at the rear of the building accommodates a square fellowship hall with a pyramidal skylit ceiling, and a new lobby entry area unites the two portions of the building.

# Hugoton

### SV 30.01
### Stevens County Courthouse
*1952/1990*
*Mann & Company/David O. Thompson & Associates*
*East Sixth and South Monroe*

This Modern concrete building with red-marble trim occupies a site one block east of the center of town. The recent addition, made of concrete that closely matches the original material, allows for wheelchair accessibility and provides an auditorium. The geometric form of the addition complements that of the original structure. The building's interior features the extensive use of marble.

### SV 30.02
### Oil Derrick (Stevens County Gas and Historical Museum)
*1927–1930*
*905 South Adams*

Like several other structures from around the county, the early oil derrick and drilling machinery have been relocated to a block near the edge of town. Other historic buildings on the site include two late-nineteenth-century one-room school buildings, the first county jail (1887), a frame house of the same

# Leoti

**WH 31.01**
## Wichita County Courthouse
*1916–1917. W. E. Hulse & Company*
*206 South Fourth Street*

date, St. Anthony's chapel (1905), and the 1913 Atchison Topeka and Santa Fe Railroad station. The derrick was assembled from several that were constructed soon after the oil strike of 1927.

The two-and-one-half-story building of stone-trimmed red brick is centered in a block near the middle of town. The plan cleverly recognizes the asymmetry of the site yet maintains the formality of the east-facing classical facade. The interior stair occupies the northern portion of the building where a half-level entry faces a mid-block street; the courtroom occupies the southern portion on the upper floor.

**SV 30.03**
## Rural District no. 3 High School
*1931. W. E. Hulse & Company*
*West Eleventh and South Van Buren*

**WH 31.02**
## St. Anthony Church
*1965. Calvin H. Bowden & Associates*
*Fourth and Olive Street*

The tan brick and limestone building sits amid a sprawling complex of a more recent school building along U.S. 56; it is on axis with the secondary street. The tile roof and tower form of the symmetrical building create a feeling of Mission Style, but the details reflect other traditions, including the Gothic.

A strongly geometric Modern building of stone, brick, and tile, the church occupies a flat site at the southern end of the town's major cross street. The roof structure, supported on massive laminated wood beams that extend to the ground outside the building, is organized so that the ridgeline is along the diagonal of the essentially square form. A tile mural depicts St. Anthony.

# SELECTED BIBLIOGRAPHY

The bibliography derives from the many sources consulted in the preparation of *Guide to Kansas Architecture* and is intended to aid readers seeking additional background information on the issues and items covered in it. For ease of use we have separated the listing into three categories: Local Kansas References (providing more information about a specific city or area of the state); General Kansas References (providing additional background on the historical or physical circumstances of Kansas); and General Architectural References (providing a context for a broader understanding of particular architectural developments in the state). Most of the sources listed are accessible through local libraries or through interlibrary loan services.

Additional information is available through the Kansas State Historical Society. The Historic Preservation Office, for example, keeps copies of the nomination forms for properties listed in the State and National Registers of Historic Places; the Archives Department keeps a newspaper clipping file on architecture. Additional information on particular locales often can be found through city or county libraries or local historical societies, who often keep and catalog area newspapers. Promotional literature circulated by chambers of commerce or individual tourist sites is another source of information.

## LOCAL KANSAS REFERENCES

Barker, Deborah. *George Washburn's Ottawa*. Ottawa: Ottawa Community Arts Council, 1989.

Bigham, Harriet, ed. *Kansas City Kansas Architecture: A Gift to the Future*. Kansas City: Kansas Board of Education, 1988.

Bird, Roy. *Topeka: An Illustrated History of the Kansas Capitol*. Topeka: Baranski Publishing Company, 1985.

*Celebrate Wichita Century Old Architecture: Proudfoot and Bird*. Wichita: Wichita Section of the Kansas Society of Architects, 1987.

Coburn, Carol K. *Life at Four Corners: Religion, Gender, and Education in a German-Lutheran Community, 1868–1945*. Lawrence: University Press of Kansas, 1992.

Davis, Gordon A., and Julianne McCarthy. *Wichita Architecture, 1874–1947*. Wichita: Wichita Public Schools, 1979.

*Douglas County Historic Building Survey—A Photo Sampler*. Lawrence: American Revolution Bicentennial Administration and Douglas County Bicentennial Commission, 1976.

Ehrlich, George. *Kansas City, Missouri: An Architectural History, 1826–1990*. Columbia: University of Missouri Press, 1992.

Fischer, Emil C. *Kansas State University: A Walk through the Campus*. Manhattan: Kansas State University Foundation, 1975.

Glaab, Charles N. *Kansas City and the Railroads: Community Policy in the Growth of a Regional Metropolis*. Lawrence: University Press of Kansas, 1993.

*History of Overland Park.* Overland Park: City of Overland Park, Kans., Community Development Department, Comprehensive Planning Division, 1979.

Jaderborg, Elizabeth. "Swedish Architectural Influence in the Kansas Smoky Valley Community," *Swedish Pioneer Historical Quarterly* 32, no. 1 (1981): 62–79.

Jones, Carolyn. *The First One Hundred Years: A History of the City of Manhattan, Kansas, 1855–1955.* Manhattan, Kans.: Official Booklet of the Manhattan Centennial, 1955.

Litteer, Loren K. *Baldwin City's Historic Sites.* Baldwin, Kans.: Champion Publishing, 1987.

Longstreth, Richard. "From Farm to Campus: Planning Politics, and the Agricultural College Idea in Kansas." *Winterthur Portfolio* 20, nos. 2–3 (1985): 147–79.

——. "J. C. Nichols, the Country Club Plaza, and Notions of Modernity." *Harvard Architecture Review* 5 (1986): 120–35.

McClellan, Charlotte, and John W. Ripley. *Potwin Place: Its History and Traditions.* Topeka: Shawnee County Historical Society, 1984.

Miller, Glenn W., and Jimmy M. Skaggs. *Metropolitan Wichita: Past, Present, and Future.* Lawrence: University Press of Kansas, 1978.

Miner, Craig. *West of Wichita: Settling the High Plains of Kansas.* Lawrence: University Press of Kansas, 1986.

——. *Wichita, Magic City.* Wichita: Sedgwick County Historical Museum Association, 1988.

Muilenburg, Grace, and Ada Swineford. *Land of the Post Rock.* Lawrence: University Press of Kansas, 1975.

*Nineteenth Century Houses in Lawrence, Kansas.* Lawrence: University of Kansas Museum of Art, 1968.

Olivia, Leo E. *Stockton Heritage in Wood Stone and Brick.* Ellsworth, Kans.: Ellsworth Printing Company, 1985.

*On the Hill: A Photographic History of the University of Kansas.* Lawrence: University Press of Kansas, 1983.

Peltzer, Theodore F. *Atchison, Kansas: A Photographic Study of Nineteenth Century Architecture.* Atchison, Kans.: Atchison Art Association, 1976.

*Promised Land on the Solomon: Black Settlement at Nicodemus, Kansas.* Washington, D.C.: U.S. Government Printing Office, n.d.

*Remembrances in Wood Brick and Stone: Examples from the Architectural Heritage of Shawnee County.* Topeka: Topeka–Shawnee County Metropolitan Planning Commission, 1974.

*Roots: The Historic and Architectural Heritage of Kansas City, Kansas.* Kansas City: City of Kansas City, Kans., 1976.

Shortridge, James R. *Kaw Valley Landscapes: A Traveler's Guide to Northeastern Kansas.* Lawrence: University Press of Kansas, 1988.

Waltner, Rachel. *Brick and Mortar: A History of Newton, Kansas.* Newton, Kans.: Mennonite Library and Archives, 1984.

Wenzl, Timothy F. *Dodge City Landmarks.* Spearville, Kans.: *Spearville News,* 1980.

GENERAL KANSAS REFERENCES

Ashbury, Robert F. "Kansas Architecture: A Survey of Development from the Pre-Territorial Period to the Present." Master's thesis, University of Kansas, 1961.

Baughman, Robert W. *Kansas in Maps.*

Topeka: Kansas State Historical Society, 1961.

Buchanan, Rex, ed. *Kansas Geology: An Introduction to Landscapes, Rocks, Minerals, and Fossils.* Lawrence: University Press of Kansas, 1984.

Buchanan, Rex C., and James R. McCauley. *Roadside Kansas: A Traveler's Guide to Its Geology and Landmarks.* Lawrence: University Press of Kansas, 1987.

Cawthon, Richard J. *Kansas Preservation 6,* no. 2–7, no. 3 (January/February 1984–March/April 1985). Kansas State Historical Society. Series on Kansas Architecture.

Collins, Joseph T., ed. *Natural Kansas.* Lawrence: University Press of Kansas, 1985.

Davis, Kenneth S. *Kansas: A History.* New York: W. W. Norton and Company, 1976.

De Zurko, E. R. "Early Kansas Churches." *Kansas State College Bulletin* 33, no. 5 (April 1949).

Ernst, Sandra. "Reflections on Regional Architecture: A Conversation with the Eidsons." *Kansas Quarterly* 6, no. 2 (1974): 15–23.

Fischer, Emil C. "A Study in Types: Rural Churches of the Plains." *Kansas Quarterly* 6, no. 2 (1974): 39–53.

Fitzgerald, Daniel C. *Ghost Towns of Kansas.* Lawrence: University Press of Kansas, 1988.

Glenn, Andrea, ed. *Kansas in Color.* Lawrence: University Press of Kansas, 1982.

Hall, Charles L. "The Kansas Courthouses of George P. Washburn." *Journal of the West* 17, no. 1 (1978): 74–81.

———. "People and Places of the Past: An Architectural Study of Some Kansas Buildings." *Kansas Quarterly* 6, no. 2 (1974): 71–94.

Haywood, C. Robert. *Victorian West: Class and Culture in Kansas Cattle Towns.* Lawrence: University Press of Kansas, 1991.

Heintzleman, J. Cranston. "A Century of Kansas Architecture." *Kansas Magazine* (1957): 63–64.

———. "The Kansas Courthouses of George P. Washburn." *Journal of the West* 17, no. 1 (1978): 74–81.

*Historic Preservation in Kansas: Black Historic Sites: A Beginning Point.* Topeka: Kansas State Historical Society, n.d.

Longstreth, Richard. "Richardsonian Architecture in Kansas." In *The Spirit of H. H. Richardson on the Midland Prairies: Regional Transformations of an Architectual Style,* edited by P. C. Larson. Ames: Iowa State University Press, 1988. pp. 67–85.

Miner, H. Craig, and William Unrau. *The End of Indian Kansas: A Study in Cultural Revolution, 1854–1871.* Lawrence: University Press of Kansas, 1978.

O'Brien, Patricia J. *Archaeology in Kansas.* Lawrence: University Press of Kansas, 1984.

Painter, Nell Irwin. *Exodusters: Black Migration to Kansas after the Reconstruction.* New York: Knopf, 1976; Lawrence: University Press of Kansas, 1986.

Peterson, John M. *John Haskell, Pioneer Kansas Architect.* Lawrence: Douglas County Historical Society, 1984.

Richmond, Robert W. *Kansas: A Pictorial History.* Lawrence: University Press of Kansas, 1992.

Shirmer, Sherry Lamb, and Theodore A. Wilson. *Milestones: A History of the Kansas Highway Commission and*

*Department of Transportation.* Topeka: n.p., 1986.

Shortridge, James R. *The Middle West: Its Meaning in American Culture.* Lawrence: University Press of Kansas, 1989.

———. *Peopling the Plains: Who Settled Where in Frontier Kansas.* Lawrence: University Press of Kansas, 1995.

———. "Vernacular Regions in Kansas." *American Studies* 21, no. 1 (Spring 1980): 73–94.

Socolofsky, Homer E., and Huber Self. *Historical Atlas of Kansas.* Norman: University of Oklahoma Press, 1972.

*Sod House Days: Letters from a Kansas Homesteader, 1877–78.* New York: Columbia University Press, 1937; Lawrence: University Press of Kansas.

Von Achen, J. Kurt. "Lives and Works of Early Kansas Architects." Master's thesis, University of Kansas, 1966.

Wilson, D. Ray. *Kansas Historical Tour Guide.* Carpentersville, Ill.: Crossroads Communications, 1987.

Winkler, Suzanne. *The Smithsonian Guide to Historic America: The Plains States.* New York: Stewart, Tabori and Chang, 1990.

Wortman, Julie A., and David P. Johnson. *Legacies: Kansas' Older County Courthouses.* Topeka: Kansas State Historical Society, 1981.

*The WPA Guide to 1930s Kansas.* Ca. 1939. Reprint. Lawrence: University Press of Kansas, 1984.

GENERAL ARCHITECTURAL REFERENCES

Blumenson, John J. G. *Identifying American Architecture: A Pictorial Guide to Styles and Terms, 1600–1945.* Nashville, Tenn.: American Association for State and Local History, 1977.

Hitchcock, Henry-Russell. *Architecture: Nineteenth and Twentieth Centuries.* Harmondsworth, Middlesex, UK: Penguin Books, 1958.

Longstreth, Richard. *Main Street: A Guide to American Commercial Architecture.* Washington, D.C.: Preservation Press, 1987.

McAlester, Virginia, and Lee McAlester. *A Field Guide to American Houses.* New York: Alfred A. Knopf, 1989.

Maddex, Diane, ed. *Master Builders: Guide to Famous American Architects.* Washington, D.C.: Preservation Press, 1985.

Noble, Allen G. *Wood Brick and Stone: North American Settlement Landscape.* Amherst: University of Massachusetts Press, 1984.

Peterson, Fred W. *Homes in the Heartland: Balloon Frame Farmhouses of the Upper Midwest, 1850–1920.* Lawrence: University Press of Kansas, 1992.

Roth, Leland M. *A Concise History of American Architecture.* New York: Harper and Row, 1979.

Whiffen, Marcus. *American Architecture Since 1780: A Guide to the Styles.* Cambridge: MIT Press, 1969.

Note: **Boldface** page references indicate the beginning of relevant catalog sections.

Museums, *continued*
      239 (*see* SG 24.04), 247 (SG 24.31),
      253 (*see* SG 24.47), 269 (*see* EW 08.02),
      276 (*see* LG 16.01). *See also* Historic dis-
      tricts, groupings of buildings
   interpretive, 37 (*see* JO 01.01, JO 02.01),
      42 (*see* JO 09.01), 80 (*see* DP 03.01),
      98 (*see* JF 13.01), 141 (*see* CK 06.01),
      178 (GE 05.04), 184 (*see* MR 11.05),
      196 (*see* RL 21.17), 202 (*see* WS 26.01),
      224 (*see* MN 13.01), 225 (*see* MN 15.02),
      255 (*see* SG 24.57), 267 (*see* EL 05.04),
      284 (*see* RS 26.04 & SD 28.01),
      288 (*see* TH 31.06), 308 (*see* FO 07.07),
      312 (*see* GL 11.01), 322 (*see* PN 23.01),
      329 (SV 30.02)
   house, 61 (*see* WY 14.26), 102 (*see* LV 17.07),
      153 (*see* LN 17.02), 156 (*see* MG 20.05),
      196 (*see* RL 21.16)

Nemaha County, **185**
Neosho County, **158**
Ness City, **321**
Ness County, **321**
Newton, 204, **219**
Nichols, J. C., Company, 31, 37 (*see* JO 02.03),
      40–41 (*see* JO 08.01 & .04),
      63 (*see* WY 04.31)
Nicodemus, 14, **272**
Norton, **278**
Norton County, **278**

Oakley, **275**
Oberlin, **265**
Office buildings. *See* Commercial and office
      buildings
Ogallah, **289**
Oil derrick, 329 (SV 30.02)
Olathe, 19, 30, 32, **42**
Opera houses. *See* Theater and auditorium
      buildings
Osage City, **114**
Osage County, **114**
Osawatomie, **112**
Osborne, **279**
Osborne County, **279**
Oskaloosa, **98**

Oswego, **151**
Ottawa, 8, 65, 68, 69, **94**
Ottawa County, **188**
Overland Park, 19, 31 32, **43**
Oxford, **256**

Paola, **112** (*see* MI 21.02)
Parks and related buildings, 71, 114 (OS 22.02),
      245 (SG 24.25), 246 (SG 24.30),
      304 (FI 06.04)
Parsons, 130, **151**
Pawnee County, **322**
Peabody, **227**
Phillips County, **280**
Phillipsburg, **280**
Piedmont, **149**
Pittsburg, 129, **143**
Pleasanton, **153**
Post offices, 76 (AT 01.08), 169 (CY 01.03)
Pottawatomie County, **189**
Power plants, 142 (CF 07.01), 189 (PT 17.01)
Prairie Village, 16, 19, 31, **48**
Pratt, **323**
Pratt County, **323**
Prescott, **154**
Prisons. *See* Law enforcement and detention
      facilities

Quindaro, 29–30

Railroads, 4, 11–12, 14, 15, 68, 259, 293–296,
      326 (*see* SW 27.01)
   buildings, 44 (JO 10.03), 82 (DG 06.02),
      91 (DG 08.24), 103 (LV 17.12),
      104 (LV 17.14), 115 (OS 23.02),
      125 (SN 26.26), 158 (NO 22.01),
      220 (HV 11.03), 240 (SG 24.09 & .10),
      291 (WA 35.02), 301 (ED 05.02),
      326 (SW 27.02)
Rawlins County, **281**
Religious structures, 40 (JO 07.01),
      44 (JO 10.05), 49 (JO 11.04), 51 (JO 12.02),
      60 (WY 14.20 to .22), 61 (WY14.24),
      74 (AT 01.01 &.02), 75 (AT 01.04),
      78 (AT 01.14 & .15), 80 (DP 03.03),
      89 (DG 08.16), 94 (FR 10.03 & .04),
      100 (LV 17.01 & .02), 103 (LV 17.13),